Christian
Ministries
and the Law

Also by H. Wayne House

The Christian and American Law

Israel: The Land and the People
(general editor)

Living Wisely in a Foolish World
(with Kenneth M. Durham)

Christian Ministries
and the Law

What Church
and Para-Church Leaders
Should Know

H. WAYNE HOUSE
REVISED EDITION

PUBLICATIONS

Grand Rapids, MI 49501

Christian Ministries and the Law: What Church and Para-Church Leaders Should Know

© 1992, 1999 by H. Wayne House
Second edition

Published in 1999 by Kregel Publications, a division of Kregel, Inc., P.O. Box 2607, Grand Rapids, MI 49501. Kregel Publications provides trusted, biblical publications for Christian growth and service. Your comments and suggestions are valued.

For more information about Kregel Publications, visit our web site at: www.kregel.com

Cover design: Frank Gutbrod
Coverphoto: Photodisc

The author and publisher are not engaged in rendering legal advice, and this book is not intended to replace the counsel of a professional. If legal assistance is required by the reader, please seek the services of an attorney in your area.

ISBN 0-8254-2882-3

Printed in the United States of America

1 2 3 4 5 / 03 02 01 00 99

To

John Eidsmoe and **Edwin Youngs**

teachers and friends

and to the students of
Simon Greenleaf University School of Law

List of Contributors

Jeffrey A. Aman (M.A., Dallas Theological Seminary; J.D., University of Florida), a practicing attorney in Tampa, Florida. He is also adjunct professor of theology at Tampa Bay Theological Seminary.

Michele Bachmann (J.D., O.W. Coburn School of Law; L.L.M., College of William and Mary), a tax litigation attorney currently practicing federal tax law in Minnesota.

Charles R. Chesnutt (J.D., Louisiana State University; Th.M., Dallas Theological Seminary), a specialist in the areas of consumer and business bankruptcy law, certified by the Texas Board of Legal Specialization.

Alan P. Dye (J.D., Florida School of Law; L.L.M. [Taxation], New York University), a partner with the Washington, D.C., law firm of Webster, Chamberlain, and Bean.

Brad N. Gahm (J.D., Southern Methodist University School of Law), an attorney and lobbyist in Austin, Texas. He is a former Deputy Secretary of State for the State of Texas.

V. William Moritz (J.D., O.W. Coburn School of Law), a practicing attorney in Colorado Springs, Colorado. His legal concentration is in the areas of tax exempt organizations and estate and business planning.

Karl F. Pansler (J.D., O.W. Coburn School of Law), a licensed civil trial attorney practicing in Bartow, Florida.

Contents

Part 4
Counseling Church Members
Regarding the Law

Preface

This book is intended primarily for pastors, Christian school administrators, and other church leaders in local churches or para-church organizations, though certainly laypersons may gain much value in reading it. Some of the matters presented in this book are handled in more detail or in more technical terms in Richard R. Hammar's *Pastor, Church & Law.* My book is not intended to be a substitution for Hammar's work or any similar work. Through *Christian Ministries and the Law,* church leaders may gain some perspective in dealing with current legal problems facing the church today and thus avoid many legal minefields, as well as acquire general familiarity with the relationship between the church and the law. The law in America is constantly in flux, so that the matters on the law discussed in this book will not always be up-to-date. In view of this, there is no substitution for consultation with competent legal counsel when a legal matter arises.

A word of explanation should be given as to how this book was written. Several of the chapters are written (to varying degrees) in cooperation with recognized experts in particular areas of law, while others were written solely by me. Chapters in which I share the authorship have the additional author mentioned at the bottom of the first page of the chapter.

Acknowledgments

I wish to thank the following persons:

Jim Eriksen for his assistance in reading through the book and his constant support to me as a friend

My law professors at O. W. Coburn School of Law for the excellent teaching and guidance they provided when I was a law student

Brant Bailey for reading chapters 12 and 13 on taxation to check for any errors

Greg Trull for his assistance on chapter 10

Ken Sande for helping me by reading chapter 8 on reconciliation

John Ketchum and Michael Holmes for their assistance with the second printing

And finally, **each of the numerous friends and attorneys** who worked with me on this project

Part 1

The American Legal System

1

A Biblical View of Law and Government

In America today, we citizens constantly face issues that involve federal, state, and local law, as well as those that involve the operation of the governmental authorities at each of these three levels. How do we Christians, citizens of heaven, relate to our earthly citizenship? What guidance does the Bible offer in terms of the Christian's relationship to and view of law and government? What is the purpose of law and government? Should we always obey them?

This chapter will articulate a normative approach to law and government as a basis for the discussion and evaluation of the actual state of the law today with regard to the specific issues discussed in the remainder of the book.

Introduction

There has hardly been a more important time in the history of the United States for Christians to be aware of the nature and function of law and government. Law is the skeletal structure of society, and Christians must work within that structure every day. Jesus said that we are not to be of the world, that is, we are not to adopt its values and ideology. He continues, however, by saying that we are in the world, surrounded by it and interacting with it. The problem is that many Christians in that contact are not having an impact on the world; rather, they are merely bombarded by its values and often succumb to its pressures. To interact with and have an impact on the society in which we live, it is important that we develop a biblical view of the purpose of law and government.

The Nature and Function of Law

The Meaning of Law

Law primarily relates to order based upon a standard. It may be divided, usually, into three different categories: the law of God revealed in nature, the law of God revealed in Scripture, and the implementation or enactment of the law by statute or ordinance.[1]

The word *law* generally refers to a standard of conduct to which individuals are held. The Greek word *nomos*, translated "law" in the New Testament, carries the idea of what is distributed, or a custom. A major sense of the word as it is developed in the New Testament also reflects the Hebrew word *torah*, or instruction. Instruction, then, which is distributed (or taught) to people is the resultant meaning.

The Source of Law

The source of law is ultimately God. One should not think it odd that law is of divine origin. Rushdoony is correct when he avers that "law in every culture is religious in origin," and the "source of law in any culture is the god of that culture." Much of the discussion today about pluralism in society reflects the movement from one orthodoxy to another, for when law fundamentally changes in a society, in reality there is a change of religion; the separation of law and ethics is a myth. In any given society, either the laws will reflect the character of God as reflected in nature or in the Scriptures, or they are, to use the words of Jesus, "the traditions of men which pervert the law of God."

The Reason for Law

Why has God given us law? First, he is a God of order. The creation is to follow naturally from the Creator. The intrusion of sin has distorted that ideal so that man is not as willing to obey the will of God. Second, since creation is to reflect the character of its Creator, God has privileged us to magnify his character through obedience to his will. Third, obeying the law of God will result in benefits to humanity. As the psalmist said long ago, it is he who has made us, not we ourselves. He knows the ways in which our lives will be more enriching to ourselves and others; he knows what will bring devastation and how we may avoid it.

Ascertaining the Proper Laws

How may one know what laws truly reflect the character of God? God has not left us without clarity on this issue. Throughout Scripture we have witness to the thinking of God on interpersonal relationships. The law should not be thought to be synonymous with the Mosaic codes, which are one manifestation of the law for a specific purpose in the nation of Israel. Rather, from the creation through the writings of the apostle John we see ways in which God attempts to direct the lives of his creatures through specific and general revelation. And for the Christian there is also the leading of the Holy Spirit. When we Christians observe laws that promote freedom and liberty while at the same time do not advocate debasing practices contrary to nature, these laws reflect the dignity of our being in God's image. Laws that curb the excesses of our sinful natures properly recognize the fallen condition of man.

The various teachings and examples on rights and wrongs in the Old and New Testaments come from eternal principles that may be implemented according to the contexts of given cultures. One might hear of the absolute laws of God. Certainly the moral character of God is unchanging, but the specific laws may vary. Should one view the taking of the shewbread by David and his friends as a crime or sin in violation of the command not to steal? Rather than see these commandments as eternal verities, it would be better to view them as expressing eternal principles. Note the following positive principles that flow naturally out of the apodictic law of the Ten Commandments:

Commandment 1	Sanctity of the special claims of God on his people
Commandment 2	Sanctity of the incomparability of God
Commandment 3	Sanctity of the character of God
Commandment 4	Sanctity of the worship of God
Commandment 5	Sanctity of parents as the reflection of God

Commandment 6	Sanctity of human life
Commandment 7	Sanctity of marriage as the reflection of God
Commandments 8 & 10	Sanctity of private property or sole stewardship over God's creation
Commandment 9	Sanctity of the person's character from defamation

The way in which these eternal moral principles may be expressed in a given society can be observed in the casuistic law of the book of the covenant in Exodus 21–23. In our society, the desire to preserve the sanctity of life may be applied in legal form from constitutional principles of rights to statutory laws against murder, descending down to traffic ordinances.

The Law of God in a Pagan Society

Though as Christians we may follow God's law in our personal lives, and even in our interaction with society, how far do we proceed in trying to make his will be done in a pluralistic society? Is it possible to establish God's law in a secular society? This really underlies the question as to whether we should legislate our perspective of morality. But is this a proper question? Since all law is built upon a religious foundation,[2] a morality is already being legislated; a religious worldview guides the direction of all governments and cultures. The correct question to pose is, *Whose* morality is being legislated? We should not attempt to establish a tit-for-tat legislation with ancient Israel, for many of their laws had meaning and purpose within the more limited scope that God had for them. But we Christians should seek to establish laws in our country that coincide with the moral law of God. Christians have as much right as anyone to exert their influence on the direction of the state.

When some claim that Christians should not attempt to have their moral laws upheld in society because it violates separation of church and state, they really mean something else. They really mean that Christians and certain areas of Christian morality are not welcome in politics and government.

The approach to lessen Christian influence may be illustrated from the attempts of The People for the American Way. Norman Lear and his disciples sought to confuse the issues by saying the American way is to let everyone have his own view of morality, unfettered in expression under the law. Some people like scrambled eggs, some hardboiled. Some people like football, some baseball. Some like heterosexual sex, some homosexual sex. This is the American way. The attempt of Lear to classify preference for eggs and sports with moral decisions on sex and abortion is not dissimilar to the confusion Douglas postulated in his debates with Lincoln in 1858. Douglas said he considered slavery wrong but preferred to leave it to the states to decide for themselves. Lincoln replied: "When Judge Douglas says that whoever, or whatever community, wants slaves, they have a right to have them, he is perfectly logical if there is nothing wrong in the institution; but if you admit that it is wrong, he cannot logically say that anybody has a right to do a wrong."[3]

So even in a society where people differ on many subjects, a consensus may be found on certain moral topics, and legislation on these areas is appropriate. Even in Israel, and later in the Roman Empire with the triumph of Christianity, not all accepted the law of God. A lack of total consensus should not distract us. Since someone's morality is going to be law, and since Christian morality preserves society, benefits individuals, and glorifies God, Christians should seek to have a public morality based upon Judeo-Christian moral standards.

We cannot *not* legislate morality. It is inevitable. Hadley Arkes says that the difficulty with discussing the imposition of morals is society's identification of them with religious belief or subjective judgments. He characterizes the inconsistency of today's society with the Vietnam protestors. They wanted the United States to pull out of the Vietnam war, not because of bad management but because they considered it immoral. Some of those same students, however, did not want the government to be involved in issues such as drugs or abortion since, they said, morals was not the business of the government but personal taste or private belief.[4]

When speaking of legislating morality we must distinguish between attempting to establish a public morality and trying to save people by the law. The latter would be futile. People cannot be saved by law. However, the former is appropriate. All laws reflect a morality. Laws against murder are moral laws, as are laws against theft or perjury. Even traffic laws are designed to prevent injury or loss of life and may be considered as moral. So then, people may differ on which moral laws to legislate, but all agree to legislate morality.

Today, legislators are instituting many new laws built upon a new religion. The biblical foundations for American law have gradually been eroded away. Unfortunately the new laws are offering salvation—salvation by government—based on the religion of humanism. In contrast, the biblical faith recognizes man is to be restrained by law but not saved by law. Christians cannot sit on the fence in this struggle for morality. Dante poignantly wrote: "The hottest places in hell are reserved for those who, in a time of crisis, maintain neutrality. When bad men combine, the good *must* associate." It is necessary for us Christians to take a stand on the moral issues of our day. Our and our children's futures depend on it.

Changing the Law

How does one go about making a change in the law? In our society law is expressed basically in the courts and in the legislature; the executive power carries out the laws. Obviously we cannot simply walk into a court or legislature to demand change. We must operate within the "rules of the game," conscience notwithstanding, and change them based on the revelation of God and under the guidance of the Holy Spirit. Changes that we would like to see enacted may come more slowly than we would desire, but changes *can* be made. We should strive to establish laws that preserve the jurisdictions God has established, such as the local governments, the home, and the church; we should work for equity in societal relationships, giving preference to neither the high nor low; we should quickly punish crime; we should require that vows or contracts be maintained; we should take away controls imposed by government that tend to inhibit individuals from using their own initiative in solving problems in society, to exercise the dominion that God intended for men and women (Gen. 1:26, 27). Most of all, we must practice righteousness ourselves.

2

The Origins
of Anglo-American Law

The Categories
of Law and Their Application

Where did we get the law that guides us today? What is the difference between statutory and case law? Is one type more binding or powerful than another?

This chapter presents a brief historical sketch of the origins of Anglo-American law, going back to the common law of England and Blackstone's Commentaries on the Law of England. *The influence of Blackstone and other English jurists on the American founding fathers is briefly described. (N.B. We will not argue here for a "Christian America" to which we should return today. Our purpose is to show the significant contribution of English jurisprudence to the legal and political thought involved in the formation of the American nation.)*

Law in Eighteenth-Century America

Modern law has greatly departed from the intentions of the founders of our nation. The men who wrote the Declaration of Independence and the

Constitution shared a view of man, nature, and law that produced a legal system unrivaled in the world. They structured checks and balances in government both horizontally and vertically. This was necessary, because the hearts of men are inclined to do evil and seek to gain unlimited power over others. They believed that nature was a reliable guide to God's intentions for man, so that it was self-evident that God the Creator had made all having equal right to life, liberty, and the pursuit of happiness. Moreover, they believed that law was not merely the feeble attempts of men to ensure order and justice in society but that it was built upon a higher law of God and properly reflected the natural order of the universe.

These ideas of our founding fathers did not originate with them. They reflect a thinking that came from England primarily, and specifically the works of Sir William Blackstone. At the time of the American War of Independence, Blackstone's commentaries on law had sold more copies in the colonies than they had in England. The drafters of our Constitution, as well as Jefferson and his advisers who wrote the Declaration, represent Blackstone's thinking on law and government.

Law in England

The perspective of law in England was influenced not only by Blackstone but earlier by the jurist-theologian Saint Thomas Aquinas. The history of this dates to the conquest of England in A.D. 1066 by William the Conquerer. After the Norman Conquest, England quickly became Christianized by Catholic missionaries. An antagonism existed originally between the common law courts and the church courts established by the pope. The pope declared the common law as pagan and required the church courts to follow the church law. Even with this division, both courts borrowed from the thinking of St. Thomas. He believed that God had communicated to each person's soul through nature, a divine impartation of truth about God found in Romans 1 and 2.

St. Thomas Aquinas (A.D. 1225–1274)

Aquinas developed his theory of law on four categories: eternal law—identical to the divine reason that governs the universe; natural law—

consisting of what goodness man has, his instincts, and the personal manifestations of man's God-consciousness; divine law—revealed in Scripture; human law—the ordinances of society.

These perspectives of law were adopted in the courts of England and became ingrained into the common law. In the aftermath of the struggles between the kings and the popes and the corollary struggle between the common law courts and the ecclesiastical courts, the views of Aquinas remained firm.

When Blackstone wrote his works, Aquinas' theory of law was still prevalent, as Amos says:

> By the time Blackstone compiled his Commentaries in the 1760s, some of the terminology from Catholic jurisprudence had changed in England, but the span of four centuries had made only nominal differences in the approach to law between Blackstone and Aquinas. They differed only on their explanation of the importance of reason in the process of jurisprudence.[1]

Sir William Blackstone (A.D. 1723–1780)

Blackstone likewise divided law into four categories: the law of nature—the order of creation as the will of God; law of Scripture—a revelation from God serving as a remedy to man's inability to perceive properly the law of nature; natural law—man's distorted interpretation and application of the law of nature; human law—the practical implementation of the law of nature as understood by men. This was the essence of common law.

Blackstone and Aquinas are often seen in disagreement because of a misunderstanding of their different uses of the word *reason*. Aquinas, as stated before, saw reason as the communication of God to the soul of man whereby he could understand certain truth of God. On the other hand, Blackstone used reason in speaking of man's mental processes or thinking.

This concept is central to Blackstone's view of the judiciary and its role. Since man's mind was affected by the fall, "[n]o matter how hard a judge might try to think correctly, he would sooner or later make mistakes because of his fallen condition that affected his ability to reason clearly." Thus, judicial opinions were not to have strong import, because they were subject to error and would periodically need revision.[2]

Let us look briefly at Blackstone's categories of law again.

The law of nature referred to the ordering by God of his creation. Before the fall everything in nature was in harmony and followed the will of God. With the fall came disorder; and with the will of man often being discordant with God's will, there appears to be lack of design.

The revealed law of Scripture is the second form of law. By his Word God has sought to remedy man's failure to understand the law of nature. Even with this, man cannot understand perfectly.

Then, there is the natural law. Whereas natural law was regularly used by Aquinas and others for understanding God's work in nature, Blackstone distinguished between the "law of nature" and "natural law." Though "natural law" referred to nature, to Blackstone the term took on a specialized meaning different from Aquinas and his contemporaries. The natural law is man's imperfect understanding of the law of nature given by God. Finally, there is human law, or specific ordinances enacted by men. Persons look at what God has said in his moral law and his laws in nature and then enact ordinances and statutes to reflect God's law in nature and Scripture. This human statement of God's law makes up the bulk of common law, the ordinances of a civil nature legislated and implemented in society. Scholars who discuss the natural law arguments today widely vary on what is meant by natural law. The framers of the Constitution, as well as Justice Clarence Thomas, seem to understand that God has created certain rights in the nature of humanity that should be followed. Following the Declaration of Independence statement of inalienable rights of life, liberty, and pursuit of happiness, the framers and Thomas would appear to believe that we should be able to agree on certain basics about who we are as creatures of God and what our responsibilities and rights are in this world. However, other natural law theorists would reject this perspective and believe that what is natural for us does not relate to God's creation but the nature of our humanity, even an evolved humanity. Truth is found in the society in which we live, not some deity.

The natural law is man's imperfect understanding of the law of nature. Finally, there is human law. This law makes up the bulk of common law, the ordinances of a civil nature legislated and implemented in society.

The judge had the responsibility of perceiving the laws of nature and applying principles of this law in view of the particular circumstances of people. Amos says:

> The judge had the duty to compare his own perception of the law of nature with the entire historical legal record that preceded him. He had eternal principles and compared his own perception of legal principles with the perception of all others. The judge was obligated to undertake and complete exhaustive legal research. This was the first part of his judicial task; [if] he acted arbitrarily, without first discovering the principle in point, he failed as a judge.[3]

Post-Blackstonian Era

Since the time of Blackstone the courts have adopted a positivistic view of law based upon evolutionary process, a doctrinaire position of randomness and change. The biological view popularized by Darwin soon became a worldview by the generalizing and application of the theory to all disciplines of human knowledge by Herbert Spencer. It affected the law, specifically, through the efforts of Christopher Langdell at Harvard Law School and Oliver Wendell Holmes. It was their view that no eternal principles dwell outside man's experience to guide man; the judges view their sense of public good or public policy as being ultimate, and this varies from generation to generation. The balanced approach of the writing of the Constitution has been superceded by frustrated jurists and lawmakers who, in the words of William Buckley in his foreword to Robert Cord's book on separation of church and state, appear to be disappointed that the American Revolution was not the French Revolution and the ideas of the founding fathers not those of the Enlightenment.

What Buckley is saying is that many are disturbed that the rationalistic and anti-theistic basis of the French Revolution was greatly different from the ideas of those who fought for independence in the colonies. The faith of the founding fathers of this nation was in the God who is revealed in Christ. Many of the leaders of the war were Protestant clergy, theologians, and devoutly evangelical men, such as Samuel Adams and Patrick Henry.

Whereas the law of God (Scripture) and the law of nature (God's revelation in nature) were considered by Blackstone and the framers of our legal documents as being the proper source for human law, a change from this thinking began toward the end of the nineteenth century with the rise of the legal positivism mentioned above. Before this time, the view was that the judges were to interpret the laws passed by the legislatures. When Holmes and others applied an evolutionary perspective that law is in flux in society and is not founded on some absolute principles, judges began to make the laws. With this has come the usurpation by the court of functions of the other branches of government as well as the other jurisdictions God created in society. Jurisdictions that God has established—the state, the family, the church, and finally the individual—have been trampled on by the state, especially the courts, so that little has been untouched by their designs of social engineering. The proper function of the state will be discussed in the section on authority.

The Law of the Spirit

In addition to the laws that Aquinas and Blackstone set forth, the Christian recognizes another, the law of the Spirit. God has revealed his will not only through nature and Scripture but also in his daily contact with his children. The Word of God contains passages that indicate the law of God has been written on the hearts of believers (Rom. 2:16; Jer. 31:33; 2 Cor. 3:3, 6). Though this law is not in contradiction to the written law of God or contrary to the laws of nature, the law of the Spirit helps us to apply the principles of the will of God in a personal way in our lives and in interactions with others. Our minds are to be renewed (Rom. 12:1, 2) and we are to walk in the Spirit (Rom. 8:2). By so doing we will not walk contrary to the law of God but will go far beyond what the mere letter of the law requires.

The development of law by Aquinas, Blackstone, and others must be commended. If they are followed properly, our society may once again reflect true justice and liberty. If Christians will manifest the law of the Spirit in interpersonal relations, in the courtrooms, and in the legislatures, a revival could occur that would bring a greater hope for the future of our country than we can presently envision.

3

An Introduction to the American Legal System

The legal system in the United States is divided into three categories: federal law, state law, and private law. An understanding of these three groups and how they interrelate will help the Christian leader and layman alike to work with the law for promoting Christian justice and mercy in our society.

Before launching into a consideration of the law and its impact upon the pastor and church, it is imperative that the reader have a firm understanding of the American legal system. With so many laws already in force, to which more are added every day, it is easy to lose sight of the structural hierarchy that exists in our system of law. What happens, for example, when a state legislature passes a law that is in conflict with another one, a provision of that state's constitution, for example? Which law prevails? Similarly, why is it that courts sometimes refuse to enforce a provision of a private contract to which two parties agreed to bind themselves?

Our system may be broadly divided into three categories: federal law, state law, and private law (also known as the law of contract). Within the federal and state categories are further classification and subordination, which may be characterized as constitutional law, statutory law, and case law. Each of these categories and subcategories will be considered in turn.

This chapter was written by Jeffrey A. Aman.

Federal Law

The supreme law of our country, the standard by which all laws are ultimately judged, is, of course, the Constitution of the United States of America. This document was hammered out at the Philadelphia Convention during the summer of 1787. In attendance at the convention were fifty-five representatives from twelve of the thirteen states (Rhode Island did not participate). These men sought to establish a founding document that would be superior to the Articles of Confederation, which had failed because of its weak central government. The result was a document that is truly a work of political genius, unmatched in history for its characteristic system of checks and balances and its ability to continue to speak authoritatively in a rapidly changing society.

In the first three articles of the Constitution, three branches of the federal government were established: the legislative (Congress, subdivided into the House of Representatives and the Senate); the executive (the president and vice president); and the judiciary (the Supreme Court of the United States, and "such inferior courts as the Congress may from time to time ordain and establish," which now include the federal district courts, bankruptcy courts, tax courts, and federal courts of appeal). Although the president has certain limited lawmaking functions, such as the power to make treaties with foreign nations and to veto congressional legislation, the primary federal lawmaking authority is reposed in Congress. The Supreme Court and its inferior courts are given the authority to apply the judicial power to certain cases, most of which are those that arise "under this Constitution, the laws of the United States, and treaties made, or which shall be made, under their authority" (Art. III, Sec. 2). This means that the federal courts, and ultimately the Supreme Court, has the authority to test all federal legislation by the standards of the U.S. Constitution and its amendments. In subsequent cases, the Supreme Court has held that the Fourteenth Amendment functions so as to hold the states similarly accountable to the dictates of the federal Constitution and its amendments.

In the federal scheme, then, are generally three kinds of law: the U.S. Constitution, including its amendments; federal legislation, as enacted by Congress; and federal court case law, the most significant of which is the corpus of decisions made by the Supreme Court. Indeed, the latter is of ultimate significance since the Constitution is, in practice, what the Supreme Court says it is.[1]

State Law

From the inception of the nation in 1776, each state has had its own constitution. The three-branch system of a bicameral legislature, executive, and judiciary is followed in all states except one. As on the federal level, each state's constitution serves as the primary document of government, with all other areas flowing from it and being subordinate to it. One area of law in the state which is not present on the federal level is local law, namely, the ordinances of local governing bodies such as municipalities and counties.

At the state level the bulk of all legal disputes are litigated. These would begin at the trial court level, and would then follow a hierarchy of appellate courts up to the state supreme court. In most cases, the decision of the state supreme court is final, with no further recourse available in federal court. This is because state courts generally apply state law, with which federal courts ordinarily do not concern themselves. The exception to this would be in a case where a "federal question" is involved, such as the freedom of speech or press, free exercise of religion, etc. As a practical matter, however, most of these kinds of cases are brought to federal court from inception.

What is the relationship between federal law and state law? As stated previously, the U.S. Constitution is supreme over all the laws of the nation; thus, even though states are left with considerable freedom in areas to which the federal constitution does not speak, all state laws, including state constitutions, are subject to scrutiny under the U.S. Constitution. When a state legislature passes a law, therefore, it is subject to constitutional challenge under the state's constitution as well as the federal constitution.

One significant difference between state and federal law is that the former has a vast body of law referred to as common law. As indicated in chapter 2, all of our laws derive historically from the common law of England. These laws are developed on a case-by-case basis as lawsuits are brought and decisions are rendered by the courts. The ruling principle here is that of *stare decisis* (from the Latin "to abide by, or adhere to, decided cases"), which means that, given similar facts, courts will generally follow the rule of law that was followed in previous cases. Although this body of law is similar from state to state, each state has its own precedents, which are binding in disputes brought in that state's courts.

Although there is a body of federal common law, most federal litigation relates to either federal constitutional issues or federal legislation. Moreover, in the case of *Erie R. Co. v. Tompkins*,[2] the U.S. Supreme Court significantly curtailed the application of federal common law when it ruled that the federal courts are to apply state law except in those cases governed by the U.S. Constitution and congressional legislation. Thus, unless the state dispute implicates some element of federal law, a decision rendered in the state courts is ultimately made in the highest court of a given state.

A significant similarity between federal and state law is in the review function of the courts. The state supreme court has the ultimate power to construe the state constitution and test any challenged action or legislation against that document. Further, state legislatures have the power to enact legislation which is binding throughout the state, and this legislation can operate to change the common law of the state where the legislature chooses to do so. In such an instance, the courts would follow the new legislation in a given case rather than the case law existing prior to its enactment.

On the state level, then, there are basically four types of law: the state constitution, along with its amendments; statutes, enacted by the state legislature; common law, i.e., the corpus of precedents established by state courts (which, as we have seen, is more significant than federal common law); and local law, enacted by the governing bodies of local units of government such as municipalities and counties. Within a given state, the state constitution is the final authority, but all state law is ultimately subject to the limitations imposed on it by the U.S. Constitution. It should be noted here that the federal constitution generally protects states from being preempted by congressional legislation, although there are exceptions to this rule, such as where state laws adversely affect interstate commerce.

Private Law

The final area of law for consideration is private law, or the law of contracts. Whenever two or more entities enter into an agreement, they are bound by that agreement—the document they sign is "the law" as it relates to the subject matter of the relationship into which they desire to enter. It would seem at first that this area of law would be rather simple, especially where the agreement is in writing and both parties signed. Should not such agreements always be upheld, regardless of the circumstances? If so, then why is there so much litigation between parties to contracts?

The reason is that there is an entire body of law devoted to the interpretation and application of contracts. Although parties usually try to create a document which is clear and unequivocal, it is nearly impossible to foresee all the circumstances that might later transpire which the parties did not consider. What happens, for example, when Bob Jones hires Jim Smith to paint his fence, and a hurricane comes along and wipes it out? Is Smith entitled to his money, even though he did not perform any work? Or, to use a more timely example, what happens when Bob Jones hires Betty Brown to be impregnated using his sperm and carry a child through birth for him, because he and his wife are not able to conceive? Should the courts enforce such a contract when Betty decides that she wants to keep the child?

This question brings in a firmly established principle of contract law, namely, that courts will not enforce contracts that are manifestly against public policy. Thus, courts would not enforce a contract for the services of a prostitute, or to sell a slave, for example. On the basis of the common law, such contracts are simply void, and there is no judicial redress available as to them.

The law of contracts consists of many such common law rules and exceptions which must be adhered to in order to have an enforceable contract. In view of the many problems that can arise, even in what appears to be the most simple agreement, pastors should retain the services of good lawyers to counsel them with regard to the contractual aspects of their churches (more on this in chapter 14).

Conclusion

In this chapter, we have seen the general framework of laws in our nation today. These may be summarized thus:

Federal	State	Private
U.S. Constitution	State constitutions	Law of contracts
Acts of Congress	State statutes	
Federal court case law	State court case law	
	Local ordinances	

4

Church and State in America

The nature of the relationship of the church to the state has been an issue ever since the inception of the church in Jerusalem nearly 2000 years ago. In that history, the spectrum has ranged from virtual identification of church and state to radical separation. In America's history, the relationship of church and state may be said to have come from near the identification pole to the radical separation pole today. The closer some governmental institutions (e.g., the U.S. Supreme Court) have moved toward the latter pole, however, the more volatile this issue has become in recent years. It is crucial that thinking Christians have an informed understanding of the proper relationship of church and state. Although it is not the purpose of this book to solve this important issue, it is hoped that it will stimulate further thought and research in the area.

In one of his best known phrases, the early church father Tertullian posed the question, What has Athens to do with Jerusalem? Today we might contemporize Tertullian's inquiry with the question, What has the modern church to do with the state? Or, What has evangelicalism to do with Washington, D.C.? This is one of the most pressing issues of our time, for the implications are significant and multitudinous. One need only consider some of the most divisive political issues currently being debated in courts and legislative bodies across the land to appreciate the significance of this issue: abortion, homosexual rights, prayer in public

33

schools, and the political ramifications of the AIDS virus. What is the role of the church in these issues? What is the role of the church in other areas such as military strategy, foreign policy, economic policy, and domestic social programs?

A complete answer to these questions is obviously beyond the scope of this chapter. However, it is important that those in Christian ministry have a basic understanding of how the church and para-church ministries are to be politically involved. Our lack of knowledge and conviction would undoubtedly cause us to sit idly by while the state, in its various forms, led predominantly by non-Christians, proceeds with an agenda which is neither informed by nor interested in a perspective that judges all political decisions in the crucible of moral clarity and universal truth.

Our purpose, then, is to provide a biblical approach toward the church's relationship with the state in America today. Keeping one eye on the exigencies of the current state of affairs, we will seek to forge out reasoned, biblical responses to current political issues. The analysis involves first a brief summary of the views held by several Christian traditions historically. Next, we will survey the current debate within evangelicalism with regard to this issue. Finally, we will suggest an approach that is both biblical and designed to achieve the maximum impact on the world (specifically, the state) for the cause of Christ.

Christian Views on Church and State Relationships

The various major traditions throughout church history have held to differing views on the church's relationship to the state. It is instructive to consider how each would be structured to work in today's political climate in the U.S.

Roman Catholicism

Catholic theologians have generally recognized a difference between the church and the state—the two kingdoms, to use Luther's terminology—but have usually viewed the church as the greater of the two. The reasoning for the church as greater than the state largely rests on the perspective of Augustine. He argued for the superiority of the church since it is eternal and the state temporal, and because the church must answer to God for the conduct of the state.

Roman Catholic View

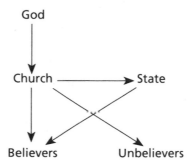

Lutheranism

Luther viewed the state as being responsible to restrain evil. Christians belong to both kingdoms, the church and the state, and have responsibilities to each. Luther believed that Christians relate to the first kingdom, the church, by faith, and to the second kingdom, the state, by reason.

Luther, unlike Calvin, did not believe that Christians have the right to use the state to promote Christianity. Christians who are in government should use Christian principles in government only inasmuch as the principles can also be justified by reason. Even a prudent but evil ruler is to be preferred to an imprudent but virtuous ruler, since the latter may bring ruin to the state while the former at least may resist evil.

Lutheran View

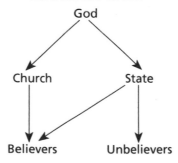

Calvinism

Calvin believed that the state's authority comes directly from God and not through the church, the Roman Catholic position. The Christian is a citizen of both kingdoms, being under the authority of both the state and the church. The state's authority, however, is limited to the areas of authority given to it by God. If the state steps beyond its authority, its acts are without legitimacy and are lawless, to which authority believers owe no duty and should resist. The church is to affect the world by its Christian principles and may properly use the vehicle of the state to accomplish this purpose.

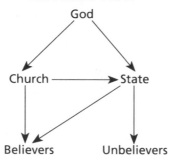

Calvinist View

Anabaptism

Many of the Anabaptists (and some of their descendants) believed that the state was part of the evil world system ruled by Satan, and thus Christians were to do all possible to remove themselves from it and its

Anabaptist View

God   Satan

Church   State

Believers   Unbelievers

affairs. Thus Christians were not to vote, hold public office, serve in the armed forces, or be involved in government in any other way. Christians, generally, were to obey the state, but the state had no real authority over Christians, nor did the church have any authority over unbelievers.

The Current Debate within Evangelicalism

Variations on the historical views summarized above continue to be asserted by evangelical thinkers today. In recent years, a plethora of books has been published dealing with the issue of church and state.[1] Some writers call for a return to the "Christian America" of our forefathers,[2] while others question the thesis that there ever was a "Christian America" to which we may return.[3] Still others, primarily of the postmillennial persuasion, believe that, regardless of what may have taken place in the past, Christians today must take over government and install a theonomic reign on the earth,[4] that is, one in which all the God-given laws in the Bible, even the Mosaic laws, are practiced in society.

The primary issue which should be addressed is whether there is a biblical mandate for the church to engage in political debate.[5] Related questions would include what areas the church should speak to and in what manner various political issues ought to be addressed. One modern example of the latter question would be that of abortion. Many Christians believe that the church should speak out and protest this widespread taking of innocent life. Organizations have been formed to lobby legislators, disseminate information, and picket abortion clinics. Some have a conviction that this particular issue is of such a magnitude that political protest in the form of civil disobedience is called for.[6] Still others, who claim to act for the church, believe that they have been called to use violence to oppose abortion, and have bombed abortion clinics in recent years.

Unfortunately, the questions are not simple. Moreover, because the stakes are currently very high on political issues like abortion, euthanasia, and homosexuality, it is important that the church speak with a clear voice rather than engage in intramural debates that diminish its potential impact on such issues. Certainly, Jesus' primary concern was not the prevailing political institutions of his day. On the other hand, the witness of Scripture does not lead us to conclude that God would have us sit idly by and not oppose legislation that promotes, rather than prohibits, sin.

A Call for a Biblical Approach to the Problem

From a biblical standpoint, one cannot ignore the fact that often the authors of Scripture were not primarily concerned with political issues and problems. Indeed, Jesus came not to transform the prevailing political authority, but "to seek and to save" lost men and women (Luke 19:10). Similarly, although Paul suffered greatly at the hands of government officials throughout his ministry, he "resolved to know nothing while I was with you except Jesus Christ and him crucified" (1 Cor. 2:2). It is clear, then, that whatever may be the church's response to political issues, its primary focus must always be the fulfillment of the Great Commission, as stated by our Lord in Matthew 28:18–20.

Part of the solution to the problem, however, lies within the fulfillment of the Great Commission itself. Jesus mandates that we teach disciples to obey everything he has commanded (Matt 28:20). The first challenge of the church in confronting political issues, then, is that its disciples be obedient to the teachings of Christ. This would necessarily include, as examples, an appreciation for the value of life, so that believers would not be having abortions themselves, and a recognition of homosexuality as sin, so that believers would not be engaged in that lifestyle. In short, as in the case of the individual believer seeking to have an impact on the lives of unbelievers with whom he or she comes into contact, the church as a whole must stand as a testimony of purity to the watching world so that we, as a body, earn the respect, if not the admiration, of the political leadership. Unfortunately, however, in many instances the church has lost its "saltiness" by conformity to the world; therefore its salt "is no longer good for anything, except to be thrown out and trampled by men" (Matt. 5:13).

Beyond its function as "salt" and "light," though, is there anything further that the church should be doing in response to the political issues of our day? First, at a minimum, Christians, as concerned, responsible citizens, should *voice opposition* to unjust or immoral actions on the part of government. They can use all lawful forms of opposition and protest, such as the utilization of the freedoms of speech and assembly

enjoyed in our country, to write letters, sign petitions, form political lob-
bies, picket, run for political office, etc., in short, to aggressively engage
in the many lawful forms of protest available to us under applicable federal and state law. Biblical support for this function is found in the Old
Testament prophets, who regularly denounced the social injustices of
their day on the authority of "thus sayeth the Lord."

Second, the church should *provide solutions* as a demonstration of its
true concern for the problems that exist, as opposed to simply arguing
against the status quo. An excellent example of this is the emergence of
Christian ministries (both within the church and through para-church
organizations) to unwed mothers, who but for those ministries might have
aborted their babies. Similarly, there are increasing numbers of ministries
to homosexuals, resulting in many individuals being led into a saving
knowledge of Jesus Christ, and changing their lifestyle into one that
brings glory to God. Practical concern such as this is mandated by the
biblical principle of demonstrating our faith by our deeds (James 1:27;
2:14–17), as well as by Paul's exhortation that we "do good to *all people*,
especially to those who belong to the family of believers" (Gal. 6:10).

Third, we must never forget the biblical injunction to *pray* "for kings
and all those in authority, that we may live peaceful and quiet lives in all
godliness and holiness" (1 Tim. 2:2). The implication of this passage,
deduced from the following verse, is that we should pray for our political institutions so that there is an environment in which the gospel can be
freely propagated and people will "be saved and . . . come to a knowledge of the truth" (1 Tim. 2:4). Although it is error to rely *exclusively* on
prayer, often the temptation is to "meet fire with fire," become angry,[7]
and engage in a flurry of activity unsupported by a great deal of prayer.
This especially happens in our society, where we all have been imbued
with a greater sense of the prevailing pragmatism than we often realize.
It is still true that "the prayer of a righteous man is powerful and effective" (James 5:16).

Fourth, there may arise some instances in which it is appropriate for
Christians to *engage in civil disobedience* in response to certain actions by
the state. From a biblical viewpoint, however, those situations are narrowly defined. It must be remembered that the general principle is that
Christians are to "submit . . . to the governing authorities" (Rom. 13:1ff.).

Biblically, there are only two limitations on the general principle of
submission to government. The first is where *the Christian is commanded*

to do something God does not permit. In the first chapter of Exodus, the king of Egypt, in an effort to stunt the population growth of the nation of Israel, instructed the Hebrew midwives to murder all male sons as they were born to Israelite women. They refused to obey: "The midwives, however, feared God and did not do what the king of Egypt told them to do; they let the boys live" (Exod. 1:17). The text goes on to note that their civil disobedience was approved by God (1:20, 21).

The Book of Daniel contains two more clear examples of this first limitation. In Daniel 1:5–20, Daniel and his three friends were given food and wine to eat from the table of the king of Babylon. Because this food was contrary to Daniel's Hebrew dietary laws, he "resolved not to defile himself" with it (1:8). In Daniel 3:1–30, Shadrach, Meshach, and Abednego refused to follow the decree of the Babylonian king to fall down and worship the image of gold. The result in both cases, as with the Hebrew midwives, was that God approved of their civil disobedience; indeed, civil disobedience in all three instances brought glory to him.

The second limitation on the general principle is where *the Christian is prevented from doing something God has commanded.* Again, the Book of Daniel provides an excellent example. The "administrators and satraps" in Babylon feared Daniel, because the king planned to promote him. They could find no basis for bringing a charge against him under existing law, so they had the king pass a law whereby anyone who was found praying to any god or man would be thrown into the lions' den (Dan. 6:6–9). What was Daniel's response? "Now when Daniel learned that the decree had been published, he went home to his upstairs room where the windows opened toward Jerusalem. Three times a day he got down on his knees and prayed, giving thanks to his God, just as he had done before" (6:10). Daniel openly (and apparently hurriedly) violated the new law. After God delivered Daniel from the lions' den, King Darius issued a subsequent decree "that in every part of my kingdom people must fear and reverence the God of Daniel" (6:26). Once again, God clearly indicated his approval of civil disobedience.

We find the classic New Testament example of this second limitation when Peter and John were brought before the Sanhedrin and commanded "not to speak or teach at all in the name of Jesus" (Acts 4:18). They responded with the familiar statement, "Judge for yourselves whether it is right in God's sight to obey you rather than God. For we cannot help speaking about what we have seen and heard" (4:19, 20). They openly defied the governing authorities when they were told not to do something God had commanded them to do, namely, preach the gospel of Jesus Christ.

A major problem today concerns the question of rescue at abortion centers. Those who are against rescue argue that the kinds of civil disobedience allowed for Christians must be determined by the specific examples one finds in the Bible, such as those acts done by Daniel, the Hebrew children, and Peter and John in the temple. Civil disobedience in those cases were refusals to stop actions of praying or witnessing or the refusal to worship other gods. Christian civil disobedience, then, requires that the Christian must be directly commanded by government to do or not do an act required by God. There is presently no law which *requires* anyone to have an abortion, nor is abortion presently illegal. Existing case law simply prohibits states from passing laws which totally prevent a woman from having an abortion. Thus, while the woman and the other people involved in the abortion process will have to give an account before God for what they have done, there is (they argue) no biblical mandate for Christians to break the law to prevent abortions from occurring. The solution is, rather, to actively engage ourselves in exerting influence to change existing law, provide education and alternatives for mothers who are considering abortions, and to pray. Those who advocate rescue argue that one should not only follow the specific kinds of civil disobedience described in Scripture but also use those as principles along the lines of the two rules for disobedience described in the previous two paragraphs. These Christians believe that abortion is murder and that Christians have a duty of love, a command of God, to love their little brothers and sisters by the act of stopping them from being killed. The state, through the law against trespass, is seeking to prohibit them from doing what God has commanded, namely, to help the weak unborn children and oftentimes exploited women. They believe that God has commanded them to hinder abortions, even if the law of trespass is transgressed, because of the biblical teaching found in the Golden Rule, the Royal Law (James 2:8 "You shall love your neighbor as yourself") and the Good Samaritan ethic.

Consider another example: prayer in public schools. According to the example of Daniel, civil disobedience is justified *if* individuals are commanded not to pray to God. There is no biblical principle, however, which would give a teacher the right to require all students to pray to the teacher's God in a public school. Christians should not want that either, because in fighting for that right they assume that the teacher is a Christian. But if a Christian has that right, then so will the Hindu or secular humanist teacher down the hall in the next classroom, whose prayer they would not want their children to have to follow.

We may expect that in our society the issue of the relationship between church and state will grow in intensity. A great deal of thought has already gone into the subject, and many excellent books and articles have been written by evangelical Christians; but the task of relating the truths of Scripture to the world is one that must be pursued vigorously for significant results to be achieved. Whatever the issue, though, and however complex it may seem, we must never forget to seek answers primarily from Scripture, and only secondarily from reason and rhetoric. It is always a humble yet firm commitment to God's revealed Word that provides meaningful solutions in any area of endeavor and which results in the God of the Word being glorified.

5

A Look at the First Amendment

*This chapter surveys the meaning of the First Amendment of
the United States Constitution, especially in its provisions
regarding the establishment and free exercise of religion.
Included will be a survey of the major Supreme Court decisions
and trends in the areas of establishment and free exercise.*

American society makes much of *rights* and minimizes *responsibilities*. At the same time, many Christians have neglected their *constitutional* rights. The recent national resurgence of a distinctively Christian voice encourages us to plead these civil rights in our courts. We cannot allow ourselves to be intimidated into silence.

This chapter briefly surveys those rights in the United States Constitution that are of special interest to Christians. As our courts become battlefields, we must arm ourselves with the weapons provided by our founding fathers.

The First Amendment: An Introduction

When our Constitution was drafted, special provision was made for particular freedoms. These were later embodied in the first ten amendments, commonly called the Bill of Rights. Even these are not exhaustive of our rights, as the Ninth[1] and Tenth[2] Amendments show. Our federal government received its powers by delegation from the several states. What was left undelegated is reserved to the state governments or the people. This concept of delegated powers is markedly different from one which allows the federal government to do anything not prohibited by the Constitution. Those who support an excessively powerful central government can be termed *statists*, because they believe that the state is supreme. We are fortunate that our founding fathers' vision was "we the people," not "I the state" (*state* here meaning national or central government).

Motivated by their concern for religious and political liberty, the founding fathers created the First Amendment:

> Congress shall make no law respecting an establishment of religion, or prohibiting the free exercise thereof; or abridging the freedom of speech, or of the press; or the right of the people peaceably to assemble, and to petition the government for a redress of grievances.[3]

These forty-five words provide the meat for our discussion.

It is hard to see, at first glance, how this amendment could be used against local school boards or state agencies. But through the Fourteenth Amendment's due process clause,[4] nearly all the guarantees of the Bill of Rights have been "incorporated" to apply to the states. All of the liberties protected by the First Amendment—the religion clause,[5] free speech,[6] free press,[7] assembly,[8] and petition[9]—now equally apply to the states. When a federal or state policy violates the due process clauses of the Fifth or Fourteenth Amendments, the right that allegedly has been violated determines the court's "standard of review." The highest standard of "strict scrutiny" is used when "fundamental or preferred freedoms"[10] are being litigated. When a government policy seems to restrict a fundamental right under this standard, the state must prove its interest is "compelling" and that it is achieved by the "least restrictive means."[11] All of the civil rights which follow are protected by this highest judicial standard of review. In addition to First Amendment problems, we will touch upon the rights to privacy and other rights.

The Religion Clauses

The establishment clause and the "absolute separation of church and state" interpretation it has received have sometimes caused Christians to view it with consternation.[12] Nevertheless, since 1970 the Burger Court's modified interpretation of this clause has helped to protect the church from government interference.

For a statute or policy to pass constitutional muster, it must pass all parts of a three-pronged test. The government action must (1) have a secular purpose; (2) have a principle or primary effect which neither advances nor inhibits religion; and (3) avoid excessive government entanglement with religion.[13] In developing the excessive entanglement test, Chief Justice Burger greatly helped Christian churches and organizations to resist intrusions by the state.

Three cases should be mentioned here. The first is *Walz v. Tax Commission*,[14] a controversy over New York's property tax exemption for religious institutions. The Supreme Court upheld the exemption after reviewing the law's legislative history and purpose, saying it did not violate the establishment clause. The court declared it better to allow the exemption than to risk excessive entanglement through taxation. In both *Walz* and *Lemon v. Kurtzman*[15] (a similar case), the Supreme Court said that programs or policies which require state surveillance or supervision cannot be tolerated. The church thus enlisted excessive entanglement as a weapon of attack as well as defense.

In the second case, *St. Martin's Evangelical Lutheran Church v. South Dakota*,[16] President Carter's Secretary of Labor tried to force all religious schools to participate in the unemployment tax program. The Supreme Court overruled the secretary to avoid excessive entanglement. *St. Martin's* reaffirmed exemption for church-owned-and-operated schools, while a later case[17] did the same for church-controlled schools. The fate of parent-run Christian schools is still in the courts, with the trend, fortunately, toward exemption.

The third case, *NLRB v. Catholic Bishop*,[18] dealt with an attempt by the National Labor Relations Board to regulate a church school's employment practices. The Supreme Court barred the NLRB's action, stating that it presented too many First Amendment problems, especially with excessive entanglement. This case was unique in that the court implied that entanglement might be considered in a free exercise claim.

These cases show that the establishment clause is a double-edged sword that must be drawn against statist efforts to intrude on religious liberties.

The free exercise clause protects not only religious beliefs but actions as well. Only the most compelling state interest will supercede the free exercise of religion,[19] for it is considered a fundamental freedom.

A landmark case in the area of free exercise is *Wisconsin v. Yoder*,[20] where the State of Wisconsin sued the Yoder family for violating compulsory school attendance laws. The Yoders, who were Amish, sent their children to public schools only through the eighth grade. Thereafter they placed them in unaccredited Amish vocational schools that used unlicensed Amish teachers.

The Supreme Court applied its standard three-part test to judge the free exercise claims. First, did the Yoders have sincerely held religious beliefs that were significantly burdened by the state's policy? Second, was the state's interest so paramount as to override and burden the religious beliefs of the defendants? Third, did the state, in achieving its legitimate purposes, use the least intrusive means so that freedom was not burdened beyond necessity?

The state's interest in education includes fostering a healthy citizenry that does not become a "ward of the state." The court held that the Yoder's beliefs were sincerely held and that the state's interests were met by the Amish schools. The compulsory attendance requirements were constitutional in general, but unconstitutional as applied to the Yoders, because the requirements violated their religious beliefs.

Courts on Neutrality

Courts usually do not strike down a law that is superficially neutral, but rather provide a constitutional exemption to the law and prevent its enforcement against the complaining parties. This religious argument for exemption is being alleged in many courts by unaccredited Christian and home schools that reject not only public education but the state's jurisdiction over education as well.[21]

The ability of a court to judge a person's religious beliefs was refined in *Thomas v. Review Board*.[22] A court cannot inquire into the reasonableness of someone's beliefs.[23] Neither can it penalize an inarticulate person who is "struggling" with a position different from others in his church or religious sect. The Court said:

> Intrafaith differences . . . are not uncommon among followers of a particular creed, and the judicial process is singularly ill-equipped to resolve such differences in relation to the religion clauses . . . and the guarantee of the free exercise is not limited to beliefs which are shared by all the members of a religious sect. . . . Courts are not arbiters of scriptural interpretation.[24]

If you object to public education on religious grounds but belong to a denomination where most members do not, that is no bar to your first amendment claim; all you need is sincerely held religious beliefs.

Limitations on Freedom of Religion

Some have argued that we should enjoy absolute freedom of religion with no state intrusions. Let us examine this position briefly.

The first question we must answer concerns governmental jurisdiction. God ordained certain institutions with definite spheres of authority. These are the family, the church, and the government. Civil government is limited in its authority.

What if the ancient cult of Baal reappeared in modern America, complete with its practice of sacrificing children to the god of pleasure? (By the way, that may not be so far-fetched. It has been suggested that abortion is a modern version of this abomination.)

On what grounds can or should the state intervene to stop the practice? This is an issue of jurisdiction—God has given the state authority to protect and defend human life (see Gen. 9:6; the Mosaic criminal code of Exod. 20–23, Rom. 13; 1 Peter 2:13, 14). It *must* step in.

Erosion of Religious Freedom and Legal Strategy

We have enormous religious freedom here in America, but the past few decades have shown we need to guard it jealously in and out of the courts. It is unfortunate that some lower courts seem disinterested in protecting the religious rights guaranteed by the Constitution. To overcome this apathy (or even opposition), one tactic that has produced favorable court rulings is to combine a free exercise claim with another fundamental freedom, such as freedom of speech, freedoms of association and assembly, and freedom of petition.[25]

Free speech is one of this nation's most cherished guarantees. Most of us take for granted our freedom to share the gospel, display bumper stickers, criticize the government, or air our own views without threat of government retaliation or suppression. The daily newspaper confirms that this freedom is the world's exception rather than the rule. This right is essential to us as Christians, for speech is the primary way we carry out the Great Commission of Matthew 28:20.

The freedom of speech[26] clause guarantees not only pure speech but also actions that demonstrate the speech. Because the rights of free speech, freedom of association, assembly, and petition are often intertwined in practice, the courts have used the term *freedom of expression* to encompass all of them. The extent of this expression is clarified by the concept of public forum.

As citizens we may use public forums to discuss public issues. Sidewalks, soapboxes, streets, and public parks can all be forums. The state may reasonably regulate these gatherings (through issuing permits for public parks, for example). Regulation may not discriminate on the basis of the speech's content, nor may it discriminate against unpopular groups. To deny a permit to anyone because an official dislikes their doctrine is unconstitutional.[27] Christians can equally claim this protection.

One view of free speech is that it is absolute, though some forms of speech are outside the clause's protection. Professor John Eidsmoe, a skilled constitutional lawyer, has listed *nine categories* he believes are outside the First Amendment's control and are, therefore, open to state regulation:

Defamation

Obscenity (offensive to the community)

Commercial speech (limited perfection)

Restricted environs (prison or military base)

Speech outside a First Amendment forum

Speech which presents a clear and present danger to public order
    ("fighting words")

Clear and present danger to national security (military secrets)

Clear and present danger to public safety (yelling "fire" in a crowded theater)

Speech that advocates violating law[28]

Another view sees free speech as a *relative* right to be balanced against the rights of society. Society's rights prevail in the previously listed categories. In explaining the concept of a First Amendment forum, Eidsmoe writes:

If a place or facility is a First Amendment forum, then freedom of speech applies and may not be restricted without a compelling state interest. If it is not a First Amendment forum, then the right does not apply and speech is a privilege which may be regulated according to reasonable purposes of the state.[29]

Following this guideline, the court held that a city-owned bus service is not a first amendment forum. Political advertising on buses could be denied.[30]

Between these two extremes is the "limited First Amendment forum." When the state opens a forum to free speech rights, speech cannot be abridged because of its content. The landmark case of *Widmar v. Vincent*[31] illustrates.

The University of Missouri regularly made its facilities available to registered student groups. One group was Cornerstone, which met regularly for Bible study, prayer, and worship. When university policy changed to preclude religious groups from using the facilities (based on alleged "separation of church and state" problems), Cornerstone sued.

The plaintiffs alleged in federal court that the university had violated their constitutional rights of free exercise of religion, freedom of speech, and freedom of association. The United States Supreme Court ultimately declared the university policy unconstitutional, because it violated the free speech and associational rights of the students. Once the university had opened its facilities, it could not bar groups because of their beliefs. The courts held that religious speech, including worship, was protected by the free speech clause. The ruling did not decide the free exercise claim.

This "equal access" rationale has recently been applied in a high school setting to allow a Christian club to meet.[32]

Freedoms of Association and Assembly

Intimately connected with free speech are the freedoms of association and assembly. While assembly is explicit in the first amendment, association has been implied by the courts as part of the umbrella term *freedom of expression*.[33] Parades, marches, and other forms of peaceable assembly are included under the umbrella.

Christians have this right in common with all Americans. They may associate to advocate their religious views on crucial issues, regardless of their political (or nonpolitical) viewpoints.[34]

Freedom to Petition

This right to petition the government for grievances is the last component of freedom of expression. It permits peaceful marches and parades; the right to sue the government in court; and the right to lobby and influence the government in its decisions or policies.[35] The court has held that this right is not limited solely to religious or political activity, but is applicable to any field, including business or other economic activity.[36]

Freedom of the Press

"The Liberty of the press is indeed essential to the nature of a free state; but this consists in laying no previous restraints upon publications, and not in freedom from censure for criminal matter when published." This quotation is from Sir William Blackstone,[37] the noted English jurist of the seventeenth century. Our nation's founders knew Blackstone's work intimately, and they intended to prohibit arbitrary government censorship in this nation by following Blackstone's counsel through enacting the free press clause. For the government to censure prior to publication, it must meet an extremely high burden—usually of grave national security matters.[38]

All publications, whether dealing with politics, religion, or anything else, are protected by this constitutional guarantee. Things that we normally do not think of as press, such as handbills, leaflets, or gospel tracts, are covered by this freedom. In a case involving the publication and distribution of religious literature, the Supreme Court said, "The 'press' in its historical connotation comprehends every sort of publication which affords a vehicle of information and opinion."[39] This protection does not as liberally extend to commercial handbills. This constitutional right of free press applies to the individual mom and pop basement printers as well as to ABC or X and Z Publishing House.

The Fourteenth Amendment: Due Process and Equal Protection

We limit our discussion of the Fourteenth Amendment's due process clause to the "liberty" guarantee, because it provides some significant rights to Christians. For a right to be considered within the liberty promise, it "must be so related to the traditions and conscience of our people as to be fundamental . . . and implicit in the concept of ordered liberty."[40]

The liberty clause protects (among other things): (1) parental control in child rearing, and (2) decisions about the child's education."[41] These decisions show a historical recognition of a right to private decision making regarding family matters as inherent in the concept of liberty,"[42] said one expert. Both situations have recently been cited with approval and are regarded as fundamental rights. Today they would probably be considered under the category "right to privacy" and within the liberty guarantee. Combine these rights with a free exercise claim, and the result was the favorable ruling in *Wisconsin v. Yoder*.[43]

Other rights guaranteed all citizens include the right to vote and to participate in the electoral process. One recent case (although more properly falling under the free exercise clause) is *McDanel v. Paty*.[44] The Supreme Court in 1977 struck down a Tennessee statute that prohibited clergymen from running for public office. Although the court reasoned that the law violated the clergyman's freedom to practice his religion by forcing him to give up another right (running for office), it could well have used an equal protection analysis.

The equal protection clause of the Fourteenth Amendment provides: "Nor shall any state . . . deny to any person within its jurisdiction the equal protection of the laws." This clause became a favorite of the Warren Court for invalidating state-sponsored segregation, but it is also a valuable tool for Christians who claim the government or its agents discriminate against them. The equal protection clause does not prohibit all discrimination, only that which lacks a rational basis. When this protection is combined with other fundamental First Amendment rights, it presents a much stronger case and stiffer standards of review for the courts.

Non-Constitutional Remedies

Two remedies deserving brief mention are the protections provided by state constitutions and a federal statute called The Civil Rights Act of 1871. When suing in state court, it is best to cite state constitutional protections as well as federal ones. Most state constitutions have provisions protecting first amendment liberties, although phrasing differs from state to state.

The Civil Rights Act of 1871, 42 U.S.C. 1980, provides in part:

> Every person who, under color of any statute, ordinance, regulation, custom, or usage, of any State or Territory, subjects, or causes to be subjected, any citizen of the United States or other person within the jurisdiction thereof to the deprivation of any rights, privileges or immunities secured by the Constitution and laws, shall be liable to the party injured in an action at law, suit in equity, or other proper proceeding for redress.[45]

In analyzing this statute, Eidsmoe writes:

> The practical meaning of this statute is that when one's civil rights are violated, be the violation racial, political, or otherwise, by someone acting under cover of state law (such as a school board member, zoning official, etc.), the injured person has the right to sue in federal court. . . . This includes the right to sue the offending officials for monetary damages, both in their official capacities and in their own persons, and at times can include attorney fees. The courts have held that the plaintiff in such a suit need not have exhausted his state and local judicial remedies, but he must have exhausted his state and local administrative remedies. That is, before suing in federal court, he must go through whatever administra-

tive hearing the local officals provide; but he is not required to sue in state court before federal court.[46]

This statute is another powerful weapon in our arsenal to combat any creeping statism in our nation.

Conclusion

Our founding fathers provided us all the freedoms necessary to fulfill the Great Commission and to be the salt of the earth. We must regain our savor if we are to help our nation and resist attempts to keep us in the shaker through legal intimidation. Let us use our legal and constitutional rights to keep the salt pouring and the leaven spreading.

Part 2

Counseling, Church Discipline, and Conflict Resolution

6

The Minister as Counselor

What is the role of the pastor or other Christian worker when he or she is involved in counseling? Is the Christian counselor held to the same standards as a professional counselor such as a psychiatrist or psychologist? How have the courts dealt with these issues? Does the law protect the privacy of the minister's office as much as it does the professional counselor's? What are the chances of his being sued for counseling malpractice? What steps can he take to avoid such a lawsuit?

This chapter will provide some guidance from the current state of the law for those Christians who regularly counsel but who do not consider that ministry to be their focus.

As one can easily discern by following the daily news, our society is increasingly prone towards litigation. It seems that, more and more, when something "bad" happens to someone, that person or others close to him (in some cases encouraged by opportunistic lawyers) want to see the "wrong" redressed in court by suing some allegedly responsible party and recovering monetary damages. Various factors no doubt are to blame for this phenomenon, and it is not our purpose here to explore them.

What is significant for our purposes, however, is that this litigious attitude has insinuated its way into the domain of pastoral counseling, with potentially devastating results to the pastor and local church ministry. Only in the past several years have insurance companies begun to

This chapter was written by Jeffrey A. Aman.

offer policies covering clergy malpractice, much like the policies that have long been in existence for the other professions such as medicine and law. Should clergy malpractice ever become a recognized cause of action, churches would have to make similar provision for potential claims. As a practical matter, doctors and lawyers are able to charge their clients enough to cover the cost of obtaining malpractice insurance, whereas the average church would find this very difficult, if not impossible. The result could be less and less pastoral counseling. This would be devastating, for relatively few professional counselors and psychiatrists use a biblical, spiritual element in their work, although this is the type of counseling most people need.

This chapter introduces the current state of the law regarding clergy malpractice, primarily through a close look at one important California case. It then suggests how the pastor or other church staff personnel involved in counseling can best proceed so as to lessen the risk of having legal problems arise.

The first true clergy malpractice claim was brought fairly recently in California in the case of *Nally v. Grace Community Church of the Valley*.[1] Walter and Maria Nally, parents of deceased Kenneth Nally, filed a complaint[2] in a state court of California against Grace Community Church of the Valley and several individuals, including the senior pastor of the church, John MacArthur, Jr. Kenneth Nally was a young man who had attended Grace Community Church, where church counselors gave him spiritual counseling. Tragically, despite the care and concern demonstrated toward Mr. Nally by the church staff, he took his own life.

In their action for the wrongful death[3] of their son, the plaintiffs alleged three theories of law in support of their claim for damages: (1) the church negligently failed to refer their son to a licensed psychologist or psychiatrist when he had suicidal tendencies; (2) the church was negligent in the training and hiring of its counselors, who were not available when Kenneth needed them; and (3) the defendants intentionally inflicted emotional distress upon the deceased; i.e., their influence actually exacerbated Kenneth's condition through talk about sin that deepened his depression and guilt feelings and thereby they acted with reckless disregard for Kenneth's health, safety, and wellbeing.

In short, the parents of the deceased sought to recover damages for the alleged harm that resulted from the church's attempts to help Kenneth. This is the kind of situation to which pastors and Christian counselors need to be very attentive. The counseling in Kenneth's case was not unusual, and the evidence showed that it was "biblical counseling," the sort that is commonly found in seminary and Christian counseling curricula. Thus, the result of this case portends a dramatic chilling effect on Christian counseling ministries.

At the trial level, the judge granted a summary judgment in favor of the defendants. This was a very favorable ruling for the church and its representatives because of the nature of a summary judgment. In a summary judgment ruling, the court takes all of the plaintiffs' allegations of fact as being true and then decides that, as a matter of law, the plaintiffs could not prevail. In other words, the court said that even if the plaintiffs were correct in claiming that the church did not refer Kenneth to a psychologist or psychiatrist, and that as a result he took his life, the law of California does not recognize this conduct as the type for which someone can recover damages. An analogy might be where you ask a friend who is an accountant for some tax advice, and he gives you well-intentioned, correct advice. You misinterpret that advice, fill out your own tax return, make several mistakes, and later end up owing a substantial sum of money to Uncle Sam. Now, you have relied on the accountant's advice to your injury; why would you not be able to recover that money from him? Because he did not owe you a *duty* of care. There are several elements to a legal action for personal harm (called a tort in legal terminology), but in this case a legal action does not exist, because there was no duty owed to you by this gratuitous advice.

The four elements of a tort or action for personal injury are: (1) a *duty* owed to the one harmed; (2) a *breach* of that duty, (3) which *causes* (4) *damages* to the person of another. Take, for example, the doctor who performs surgery and leaves a scalpel in his patient's chest cavity. Clearly the doctor, in undertaking to operate on the patient, has a duty to exercise the standard skill of his profession. Here he breaches that duty by leaving a scalpel inside the patient. Thus, the doctor would be responsible for the complications or damages caused by the scalpel's presence, including sums for pain and suffering.

The basis for the trial court's decision in the *Nally* case was that the church and its representatives did not have a *duty* with regard to the defendant's actions that allegedly resulted in his suicide. There was no duty because of the First Amendment's protection of the defendant's free exer-

cise of religion. Thus the plaintiffs lost at the trial level, but they appealed
to the Second District Court of Appeal of California (*Nally I*).
In *Nally I* the court of appeal stated the issue and its decision as follows:

> We are thus confronted with the question *whether a clergyman or church
> should be immune from liability for intentional infliction of emotional
> distress caused by the nature or content of counseling simply because
> the counseling may have a spiritual aspect. . . .* We hold that, while defen-
> dants' religious beliefs are absolutely protected by the First Amendment,
> the free exercise clause of the First Amendment does not license inten-
> tional infliction of emotional distress in the name of religion and cannot
> shield defendants from liability for wrongful death for a suicide caused by
> such conduct.[4]

Thus, on appeal, the trial court's ruling of summary judgment was
reversed, and the case went back for jury trial, which began on April
22, 1985, amidst considerable press coverage. At the conclusion of the
plaintiffs' case (which lasted three weeks) the defendants entered a
motion to dismiss the case on similar grounds as their previous motion
for summary judgment. After vigorous argument, the trial court granted
the motion. This meant that the plaintiffs had not presented sufficient
evidence from which the jury could award damages to the plaintiffs.
Once again, the plaintiffs appealed to the Second District Court of Appeal
of California (*Nally II*).

With a trial record containing evidence to work with on the second appeal,
the appellate court rendered a more thorough opinion than its first and again
the result was unfavorable to the defendant church and its workers.

On the question of negligence, the court stated that, just as with psychiatrists, a minister who undertakes to counsel a suicidal individual has
a duty to prevent the suicide, whether that involves "proper training" of
its counselors or the duty to refer the individual to a "professional," i.e.,
a psychiatrist or psychologist. Similarly, with regard to the count for
intentional infliction of emotional distress, it was held that a church
counselor is not immune from liability for such conduct because of the
free exercise provision of the First Amendment.

Attorneys for the defendants argued that there is no duty owed by a
church for the conduct of its counselors, because such religious counseling is absolutely protected by the free exercise clause. The argument
is that what these counselors were engaged in was *spiritual counseling*,

which obviously involves religious beliefs, protected by the First Amendment. For example, a Christian counselor who holds the conviction that it would not be right for him to refer one of his counselees to a secular psychiatrist or psychologist is free to hold that conviction without fear of being sued for failure to refer. Thus, a court should not be permitted to step in and say that he has the *duty* to do something that goes against the free exercise of his religion.

The rationale for this argument is that when it is held that there is such a duty, the next step is to determine whether that duty has been breached, and that determination necessarily involves a decision on the part of the fact finder (typically a jury) as to the truth or error of the counseling decision. Courts have long held that the legal process will not make such decisions in the area of religious beliefs. Sam Ericsson, formerly executive director of the Christian Legal Society and one of the attorneys for the defendants, argued from the important Supreme Court case of *United States v. Ballard*.[5]

Writing for the majority, Justice Douglas stated that the First Amendment forbids the courts to examine the truth or verity of religious representations:

> The First Amendment has a dual aspect. It not only "forestalls compulsion by law of the acceptance of any creed or the practice of any form of worship" but also "safeguards the free exercise of the chosen form of religion. . . . Thus the Amendment embraces two concepts—freedom to believe and freedom to act. The first is absolute but, in the nature of things, the second cannot be." Freedom of thought, which includes freedom of religious belief, is basic in a society of free men. . . . It embraces the right to maintain theories of life and of death and of the hereafter which are rank heresy to followers of orthodox faiths. Heresy trials are foreign to our Constitution. Men may believe what they cannot prove. They may not be put to the proof of their religious doctrines or beliefs. Religious experiences which are as real as life to some may be incomprehensible to others. Yet the fact that they may be beyond the ken of mortals does not mean that they can be made suspect before the law. Many take their gospel from the New Testament. But it would hardly be supposed that they could be tried before a jury charged with the duty of determining whether those teachings contained false representations. The miracles of the New Testament, the Divinity of Christ, life after death, the power of prayer are deep in the religious convictions of many. If one could be sent

to jail because a jury in a hostile environment found those teachings to be false, little indeed would be left of religious freedom. The Fathers of the Constitution were not unaware of the varied and extreme views of religious sects, of the violence of disagreement among them, and of the lack of any one religious creed on which all men would agree. They fashioned a charter of government which envisaged the widest possible toleration of conflicting views. Man's relation to his God was made no concern of the state. He was granted the right to worship as he pleased and to answer to no man for the verity of his religious views. The religious views espoused by the respondents might seem incredible, if not preposterous, to most people. But if those doctrines are subject to trial before a jury charged with finding their truth or falsity, then the same can be done with the religious beliefs of any sect. When the triers of fact undertake that task, they enter a forbidden domain. The First Amendment does not select any one group or any one type of religion for preferred treatment. It puts them all in that position.[6]

The analysis by Justice Douglas would apply with equal force to clergyman malpractice cases. The fact that *Ballard* involved criminal fraud, rather than a civil action, should make no difference. In either case, the First Amendment protects the communication of beliefs that cannot be proved and that "might seem incredible, if not preposterous, to most people." Thus, under *Ballard*, the only issue for the secular courts would be a determination of whether the asserted religious belief was sincerely held.

Unfortunately, this argument was not persuasive to the appellate court in the *Nally* case. It ruled that the First Amendment does not operate to protect the "spiritual counseling" of a suicidal individual, and maintained that there is a duty on the counselor in spite of his sincerely held religious beliefs. A significant part of its rationale was that although these counselors may *believe* whatever they wish, when they undertake the *activity* of counseling seriously disturbed individuals, the free exercise of their religion is not absolute.[7]

The court in *Nally II* again reversed the trial court's ruling and remanded the case to the trial court to consider additional evidence consistent with the appellate court's ruling. However, rather than allowing the case to again return to the trial court, the defendants chose to appeal the *Nally II* decision to the Supreme Court of California (*Nally III*). The issues on appeal in Nally III were stated by the court as follows:

(i) [W]hether we should impose a duty on defendants and other "nonthera-
pist counselors" (i.e., persons other than licensed psychotherapists), who
counsel others concerning their emotional and spiritual problems, to refer
persons to licensed mental health professionals once suicide becomes a
foreseeable risk, and (ii) whether the evidence presented at trial supports the
plaintiffs' cause of action for wrongful death based upon defendants'
alleged "intentional infliction of emotional distress" on [Kenneth] Nally.[8]

Fortunately, the Supreme Court of California reversed the appellate
court's ruling in *Nally II,* thus concluding the litigation in favor of the
defendant church and its staff. The plaintiffs appealed the ruling of the
Supreme Court of California to the United States Supreme Court, but
the Supreme Court declined to consider the case.

Although the Supreme Court of California's opinion in *Nally III* could
have gone further in supporting the position of the defendants, and thus
provide more certainty to those faced with similar problems, the result
still serves to protect the province of biblical counseling in general.

In particular, the Supreme Court of California rejected the appellate
court's "imposition of a broad 'duty to refer' on defendants and non-
therapist counselors in general."[9] A significant reason for its conclusion
was that "the secular state is not equipped to ascertain the competence of
counseling when performed by those affiliated with religious organizations."[10] Thus, the kind of argument asserted by Sam Ericsson from the
Ballard case, summarized above and rejected by the *Nally II* court, was
accepted by the Supreme Court of California in *Nally III.* The court summarized its holding as follows:

[W]e conclude that plaintiffs have not met the threshold requirements for
imposing on defendants a duty to prevent suicide. Plaintiffs failed to persuade us that the duty to prevent suicide (heretofore imposed only on
psychiatrists and hospitals while caring for a suicidal patient) or the general professional duty of care (heretofore imposed only on psychiatrists
when treating a mentally disturbed patient) should be extended to a non-
therapist counselor who offers counseling to a potentially suicidal on secular or spiritual matters.

In the present case, the Court of Appeal erroneously created a broad
duty to refer, and to hold defendants potentially accountable for Nally's
death based upon their counseling activities would place blame unrea-
sonably and contravene existing public policy. Accordingly, we conclude

the trial court correctly granted defendants' nonsuit motion as to the "clergyman malpractice" or negligence causes of action. . . The suicide of a young man in the prime of his life is a profound tragedy. After considering plaintiffs' arguments and evidence, however, we hold that defendants had no duty to Nally on which to base liability for his unfortunate death.[11]

Notwithstanding the favorable result in the *Nally* case, Christians who counsel regularly, but who do not hold themselves out as professional counselors or therapists, should exercise caution when dealing with counselees who appear to have serious psychological problems. Although the *Nally* case would no doubt be persuasive in other jurisdictions, it has binding authority only in the State of California. Thus, courts in other states, when confronted with similar facts, could take a position that is less favorable to biblical counselors.

First, any ministry which incorporates counseling as a significant part of its activities should strongly consider consulting a local attorney who can provide guidance with respect to the particular nature of the counseling involved. The attorney should elicit facts regarding the type of counseling involved, and then analyze the counseling activities within the framework of state law as to potential liability and how to avoid it.

Second, the ministry may consider purchasing professional negligence insurance for counseling activities, as well as coverage for other activities of the church which may be related to counseling. Such policies have become increasingly available since the notoriety of the *Nally* case.

Third, several seminaries now offer continuing education courses or workshops which deal with the potential liability associated with ministry activities in more detail, including clergy malpractice issues. Attendees are afforded the opportunity to interact with fellow counselors and deal with specific issues in light of current law.

Fourth, the counselor should consult sources which address specific issues in more detail, such as confidentiality, the right to privacy, and church discipline.[12]

In conclusion, the area of biblical counseling can, unfortunately, become a mine field in our litigious times. Anyone who regularly counsels should be prepared for the risks involved, and most important, should not hesitate to refer severely troubled individuals to professional therapists. In all circumstances, nonprofessional counselors should take reasonable measures to protect against expensive and time-consuming litigation, while at the same time maintaining high standards of biblical and spiritual counseling.

7

Church Discipline
and the Right of Privacy

Should a church decide to engage in church discipline, what legal consequences may follow? In what kinds of cases have people disciplined by a local church been successful in bringing a lawsuit against the church? At what point is one's right of privacy violated in this context? What can and should the church do in light of these possibilities?

What constitutional basis does a court have to interfere in intrachurch disputes? Does the state have a compelling interest to involve itself in establishing church practice even when it is of theological determination?

This chapter will survey the current state of the law regarding church discipline and attempt to provide guidance as to how the church should make policy in the area of church discipline.

Today we live in an unrestrained, unruly, unashamed, and undisciplined world. Even in the church, members defiantly break biblically based rules of conduct. If the church tries to discipline a disobedient member, he is often unrepentant and outraged. Instead of crying out for forgiveness, he may cry out, "See you in court."

Church discipline is a potential litigation nightmare for churches, pastors, church officers, and other church leaders. Historically, American

This chapter was written by Karl F. Pansler.

65

civil courts had little to do with cases involving the church. Times change, and American civil courts today are not hesitant to invoke jurisdiction in church-related controversies. In the past decade, American civil courts, including the U.S. Supreme Court, have carried jurisdiction of the courts one step further by hearing and ruling on religious doctrine.

From a practical standpoint disgruntled church members and other individuals have sued churches since the advent of insurance. Many churches now have insurance covering claims for personal injury/ liability and clergy malpractice. In any type of dispute, aggressive lawyers will spend the time and the money necessary to "hit" the insurance funds. Churches and the clergy are not exempt from the litigation game. Litigation involving churches is increasing mainly because the First Amendment to the U.S. Constitution is becoming less respected by the American civil courts.

Litigation for those who bring lawsuits—plaintiffs—and especially for those who defend lawsuits—defendants—is a very emotional and financially expensive experience. Many times there is no clear winner. Playing the litigation game is much more emotional when a disgruntled parishioner and his former church are involved. With the number of civil suits against churches on the dramatic increase, church pastors, officers, and leaders must be cautious when they discipline church members to avoid subjecting the church, themselves, and quite possibly their religious doctrine from being put on trial.

Under the most recent judicial decisions of American civil courts, a religious body may be sued over the decisions made by the religious leaders regarding doctrinal discipline of a member of a religion. The First Amendment has been so misinterpreted and misapplied by American civil court justices, that the intent of the founding fathers to keep church and state separate institutions is no longer the result of the First Amendment's application to a given case. To fully understand how recent judicial decisions have eroded the right of religion to be free from state involvement, it is necessary to briefly review the history of the First Amendment, the First Amendment as written, and the First Amendment as applied by the courts.

The theory of separation of church and state as set forth in the First Amendment to the U.S. Constitution is one of the most distinctive concepts ever contributed to the institution of political ideas. In 1791, when the First Amendment was adopted, no other country had provided so carefully to prevent the entanglement of state power with the institution of religion. From its adoption, the First Amendment has required that the government "be a neutral (element) in its relation with religious believers and non-believers."[1] The First Amendment prohibits the state from taking action that favors or disfavors a religion. Since the time of the First Amendment's ratification, American courts have struggled to apply the theory embodied in the First Amendment to church-related controversies that invoke its application.

The First Amendment to the Constitution provides in part that, "Congress shall make no law respecting an establishment of religion, or prohibiting the free exercise thereof."[2] The search for religious tolerance by early American religious dissenters played a basic part in the formation and adoption of the First Amendment. The American people framed the First Amendment clause because centuries of religious oppression and persecution in Europe had proved the utter hopelessness of attempting to proffer religious opinions by the terror of human laws. The idea of the founding fathers embodied in this guarantee was that church and state be kept separate so that the legislative powers of the government could reach actions only and not opinions. The clause, it has been said, was intended to erect a wall of separation between church and state.[3] Two clauses of the First Amendment deal with religion. The first clause is referred to as the establishment clause; the second is the free exercise clause. The Supreme Court has held that both of these clauses are applicable to the states by the due process clause of the Fourteenth Amendment. The free exercise clause was first held applicable to the states in the case of *Cantwell v. Connecticut*,[4] and the establishment clause was held applicable to the states in the case of *Everson v. Board of Education*.[5] These two clauses express two distinct constraints on the federal and states' involvement in religion—one prohibits religious establishments; the other guarantees the individual's or group's free exercise of religion.

The U.S. Supreme Court, in numerous decisions in the past, has made it clear that there will be times when state entanglement with religion is necessary. The state, without violating the First Amendment guarantee of religious liberty, has the power to prevent and punish when clear and present danger appears.[6] The U.S. Supreme Court has recognized certain necessary and permissible contacts that the state may have with religion.[7] Supreme Court Justice Burger has stated: "Fire inspections, building and zoning regulations, and states' requirements in compulsory school attendance laws are examples of necessary and permissible contacts."[8] The U.S. Supreme Court has recognized in the past that the state cannot excessively entangle itself with the organization, authority, responsibility, and doctrines of a religion.[9]

In recent years, the U.S. Supreme Court has decided cases involving the constitutionality of school prayer,[10] Bible reading in the public schools,[11] tax exemption for church property,[12] Sunday closing laws,[13] and tuition tax credits for parents who send their children to private schools.[14] In deciding these kinds of cases the Court has tended to misconstrue the intent of the founding fathers in adopting the First Amendment that the federal government stay out of religion. By this is meant that government is not to be hostile against religious practices by the people either in the private, public, or government sectors. In prohibiting prayer or Bible reading the Court is showing hostility, not neutrality. The reason given by the Court is that such practices violate the establishment clause. However, the establishment clause in no way was intended to prohibit religious expressions in public or by the government. The establishment clause prohibits Congress, the lawmaking branch of the government, from preferring one religious denomination or organization above another. As long as government allows or encourages religious expression without prejudice, silent or public moments of prayer or reading from religious literature is permitted under the first amendment. In the private sector, moreover, government should only be involved when its actions are tangential to religious expression or practice, such as zoning and building inspections, or issues solely of a secular nature. As stated by one of the more enlightened Supreme Court jurists, Justice Jackson, before the First Amendment judicial erosion began:

> If there is any fixed star in our constitutional constellation, it is that no official, high or petty, can prescribe what shall be orthodox in . . . religion, or other matters of opinion or for citizens to confess by word or act their faith therein.[15]

Has the Supreme Court in its more recent decisions caused a First Amendment nova in the United States' constitutional constellation?[16] Although the Supreme Court's assault upon the First Amendment has for the most part been implicit, lower American civil courts, relying on recent U.S. Supreme Court opinions, have definitely answered the above question affirmatively. One such case that indicated a First Amendment nova and further contributed to the undermining of the First Amendment protection of religious rights was the Oklahoma court's adjudication of the case *Guinn v. The Church of Christ of Collinsville*.[17] In this case, the Oklahoma civil courts invoked jurisdiction in a religious dispute, which under the First Amendment and earlier U.S. Supreme Court decisions should have been left to the church's ecclesiastical authorities. The question raised in *Guinn* was where a church's right to discipline a member ends and the member's right to privacy begins.

The plaintiff, Marian Guinn, became a member of the Collinsville Church of Christ in 1974. While a member, she became familiar with and adopted the beliefs of the Church of Christ, including, most importantly, the organization of the church, the authority and responsibility of its elders and members, the use of church discipline, and the belief that adultery and fornication are wrong. In 1979, the church elders became aware of a rumor circulating around Collinsville that Guinn was committing fornication. The elders privately discussed this matter with Guinn, and she informed them that the rumor was unfounded. The elders believed Guinn. Later the rumor was verified by various circumstances and by the admission of the individual with whom Guinn had been committing fornication. The church elders had a second private meeting with Guinn in 1981. She admitted committing fornication but said she had ended the relationship. Despite what Guinn told the elders, she continued to see the man.

In a September 21, 1981 letter to Guinn, the church elders informed her that if she continued to commit fornication, they would have no alternative but to "tell it to the church" and "withdraw fellowship" from Guinn. On September 25, 1981, Guinn delivered a letter to a church elder in which she expressed her desire to withdraw her membership from the church. On October 4, 1981, the church elders informed the congregation of the Collinsville Church of Christ that Guinn was being disfellowshipped for committing the sin of fornication. Four neighboring Churches of Christ were also informed of Guinn's scriptural violations.

Guinn filed a suit in Tulsa County District Court alleging invasion of privacy and outrage resulting in emotional anguish. The case was tried in Tulsa County District Court, resulting in a jury verdict against the Collinsville Church of Christ and its elders awarding Guinn $205,000 in actual damages and $185,000 in punitive damages. The trial court then added $44,737 in prejudgment interest against the church.[18]

The Collinsville church appealed the case to the Oklahoma Supreme Court. On January 17, 1989, the case was reversed and remanded back to the lower court to be retried.[19] The Oklahoma Supreme Court determined that Guinn should not have been allowed to recover for the disciplinary actions of the church elders that occurred prior to her withdrawal from the church. However, she could recover for the postwithdrawal acts of the elders, which had been proven to be tortious, though, in my opinion, this was decided wrongly since this was a religious duty as viewed by the elders. Had they, however, informed the general public this would have been tortious. The Court should not have exercised jurisdiction and fined the Collinsville church for its religious practices, including those after Guinn attempted to withdraw membership.

The lower court's invocation of jurisdiction in *Guinn* violated the First Amendment, for the excessive entanglement test was clearly disregarded. The Church of Christ doctrine holds to a literal interpretation of the Bible that serves as the Church's sole source of moral, religious, and ethical guidance upon which its disciplinary procedures are founded. Guinn admitted to the church elders that she had committed fornication, and as a member of the Church of Christ, she became subject to the disciplinary procedures set out by the Bible (Matt. 18:15–17; 1 Cor. 5:13; 1 Cor. 6:9, 10). These Scriptures, theologically and procedurally, clearly authorized the action taken by the church and the elders when they withdrew fellowship from Guinn. The elders carried out the scripturally mandated disciplinary procedure against Guinn in three stages. The entire process lasted more than one year.

The Oklahoma civil court, by invoking jurisdiction into this church controversy, granted itself the power and authority to determine whether the Church of Christ's doctrine regarding membership and disciplinary procedure was, in fact, religious. The Oklahoma court's decision to adjudicate this case gave the state the right, power, and authority to judge the Scriptures relied on by the Church of Christ in disciplining Guinn. It ultimately gave the state, through its judicial branch, the power to decide whether the Collinsville Church of Christ's doctrinal belief was false or wrong. Such power and authority allowed the State of Oklahoma to deny the Church of Christ the freedom to doctrinally discipline its members. The effect of the *Guinn* decision is that the Church of Christ cannot legally discipline its members according to the Scriptures. The Oklahoma courts' invocation of jurisdiction in this case and their written opinions regarding their judicial findings constitute a grant upon the State of Oklahoma of the supreme right to prescribe what shall be orthodox in the Church of Christ religion.

What about the First Amendment? Surely the Oklahoma Supreme Court is not comprised of jurists who would draft an opinion in flagrant disregard of the First Amendment of the U.S. Constitution. These jurists must have been perceptive enough to recognize the most fundamental issue involved in this case dealing with the First Amendment. As a matter of fact, the Oklahoma Supreme Court saw the First Amendment issue clearly and even stated the issue in the appeal, as follows: "The dispositive first impression question presented is whether a state forensic inquiry into an alleged tortious act by a religious body against its former member is an unconstitutional usurpation of the church's prerogatives by a secular court and hence, prohibited by the First Amendment."[20] The court answered this question in the negative, concluding that the First Amendment did not bar its jurisdiction to hear this case.

> While this dispute involved a religiously-founded disciplinary matter, it was not the sort of private ecclesiastical controversy which the court has deemed immune from judicial scrutiny.* * *Because the controversy in the instant case is concerned with the allegedly tortious nature of the religiously-motivated acts and not with their orthodoxy vis-a-vis established church doctrine, the justification for judicial abstention is not existent and the theory does not apply.*
>
> The dispute between parishioners and the elders is clearly not immune from secular judicature and was properly before the trial court[21] (citations omitted; emphasis added).

The court in no more than one sentence to explain or justify its reasoning, determined that the Church of Christ's biblically based policy for discipline was subject to the state's interpretation as to whether the Church of Christ's methods and procedures for discipline of a member may be legally exercised by the Church of Christ religion.

The court further found that jurisdiction was proper in the *Guinn* case because the procedure followed by the elders could constitute a threat to the public safety, peace, or order that justified the court's compelling interest of providing citizens with a means of enforcing their rights under the law. In other words, the Oklahoma Supreme Court found that the biblical doctrinal procedure followed by the Church of Christ can constitute, and did in fact constitute in the *Guinn* case, a threat to the rights of individuals, and if followed can present a clear and convincing danger to society.

After paying lip service to the First Amendment issue, the Oklahoma Supreme Court in its written opinion in the *Guinn* matter proceeded to address the right of privacy issue. It reasoned that once Guinn withdrew her membership from the Church of Christ, she withdrew her consent to participate in a spiritual relationship in which she had agreed to submit to ecclesiastical supervision. Thus, the court found that disciplinary actions taken by the elders against Guinn after her withdrawal from membership were outside the purview of the First Amendment and were an invasion on her right of privacy.

The right of privacy has been defined as the right of the individual to be left alone, to live a life of seclusion or to be free from unwanted publicity.[22] Invasion of privacy actions generally recompense individuals for emotional injuries. Most states recognize invasion of privacy actions by case law; however, some states do so by statutes. The right of privacy is designed to protect those individuals with affairs over which the community has no legitimate concern from being dragged into an undesirable and undesired publicity, and to protect all persons from having matters made public against their will, which they may properly prefer to keep private.[23]

The right of privacy may be waived by the individual or by anyone authorized by him, and this waiver may be expressed or implied.[24] A person may be estopped from claiming the right of privacy if he or she engages in conduct that contradicts the assertion of privacy.[25] A person may waive or lose the right of privacy by becoming a public figure or personage, and the existence of a waiver carries with it the right to an invasion of privacy only to such an extent as may be legitimately necessary and proper in dealing with the matter which brought about the waiver or to the extent warranted by the circumstances which brought about the waiver.[26]

In the United States, no one is compelled to ally himself, or to remain identified, with any religious organization, but when he does join a church and becomes a member of that ecclesiastical body, he voluntarily surrenders his individual freedom to that extent.[27] As a general rule, the rights and obligations of members of a religious society are governed by the laws of that society.[28] Every person entering into a religious society impliedly, if not expressly, covenants to conform to its rules and to submit to its authority and discipline.[29] Who are members of a religious society must be determined by reference to the rules, constitution, or bylaws of the society, and by reference to the statutes governing such bodies.[30] The agreement of the parties determines the requirements of membership in a religious society.[31] This includes financial support in some form where the religious society requires it, generally a profession of faith, adherence to the doctrines of the church, and a submission to its government.[32] In *Watson v. Jones*, U.S. Supreme Court Justice Miller stated:

> The law knows no heresy, and is committed to the support of no dogma, the establishment of no sect. . . . All who unite themselves to such a body [the general church] do so with an implied consent to [its] government, and are bound to submit to it. But it would be a vain consent and would lead to the total subversion of religious bodies, if anyone aggrieved by one of their decisions could appeal to the secular court and have them reversed. It is of the essence of these religious unions, and of the right to establish tribunals for the decisions of questions arising among themselves, that those decisions should be binding in all cases of ecclesiastical cognizance, subject only to such appeals as the organism itself provides for.[33]

The Church of Christ holds as the laws of their religious society the entire Old and New Testaments and contended at trial that the relationship between Guinn and the church was to be determined by reference to the Scriptures. Scriptural provisions relied upon by the church clearly supported the proposition that the actions taken and the procedures used by the Collinsville church and its elders were an expression of their right to free exercise of religion in withdrawing fellowship from Guinn. Furthermore, the Collinsville Church of Christ congregation, as well as the other local Church of Christ's congregations, had a right to know the reasons why one of their fellow members was being disfellowshipped. Had the general public been informed of Guinn's sin, a cause of action alleging invasion of privacy may have very well been founded.[34] However, such was not the case.

The Oklahoma Supreme Court found that once Guinn communicated her withdrawal from the church body, then the church could not withdraw congregational fellowship from Guinn despite the fact that the church considered such actions to be scripturally based. The court stated:

> Upon her withdrawal, parishioner urges, the church was precluded from sanctioning her as if she were a current member. By continuing to discipline her as though she were a practicing Church of Christ member, the elders are alleged to have invaded her privacy and caused her emotional distress.[35]

In defense of their actions, the elders claimed that the Church of Christ has no doctrinal provision for withdrawal of a membership. According to their beliefs, a member remains a part of the congregation for life. Like those who are born into a family, they may leave but they can never really sever the familial bond. The court's determination that Guinn effectively withdrew her membership, and thus her consent to submit to church doctrine would, according to the elders, be a constitutionally impermissible state usurpation of religious discipline accomplished through judicial interference.

The Oklahoma Supreme Court went on to state:

> Just as freedom to worship is protected by the First Amendment, so also is the liberty to recede from one's religious allegiance. * * * The First Amendment clearly safeguards the freedom to worship as well as the freedom not to worship. * * * Here, it is the Collinsville Church of Christ that, by denying parishioner's right to disassociate herself from a particular form of religious belief, is threatening to curtail her freedom to worship according to her choice. Unless parishioner waived the constitutional right to withdraw her initial consent to be bound by the Church of Christ discipline and its governing elders, her right was a constitutionally protected right.[36]

The Oklahoma Supreme Court never addressed the issue regarding the church's First Amendment constitutional right to hold as its doctrinal creed that a member of the Church of Christ remains a part of the congregation for life and is subject to the Church's disciplinary procedures for withdrawal despite a church member's attempt to withdraw from the church body. In the Guinn case, the court relied upon Guinn's argument that the process of indoctrination into the Church of Christ did not teach her that the body considers membership to be an insoluble bond. Guinn contended that she was unaware that becoming a member of the Collinsville church meant voluntarily relinquishing her civil right to disassociate herself from the body. The court accepted Guinn's plea of ignorance of the church doctrine and found that once she removed herself from the Church of Christ congregation roll, she had withdrawn her membership and the church could do nothing about it. The fact that Guinn had voluntarily joined the church and was a member was undisputed at trial. Guinn had met the requirements so as to become a member of the Church of Christ by confessing Jesus Christ as her Savior and by agreeing to follow the guidelines and rules for Christian conduct as prescribed by the Bible. In becoming a member, she agreed to adhere to the doctrines of the Church of Christ and submit to the government of the church. Apparently, however, Guinn accepted the benefits of becoming a Church of Christ member even though she was ignorant, by her own admission later at trial, of its doctrine. The court determined that Guinn's right to be informed of the religious doctrine was a more compelling interest than the church's right to religious freedom.

By becoming a member of the Church of Christ, Guinn gave the church a legitimate interest in her character. The Church of Christ, obviously relying on the teachings of the Bible, believes that sexual relations outside of marriage are wrong. When Guinn became a member of the church, she agreed to obey the church's rules and to submit to its scripturally based authority and discipline. By becoming a member of the Collinsville Church of Christ, Guinn relinquished a part of her right to privacy to the extent that her conduct was unbecoming of a church member. The circumstances were such that the church's reputation, and the reputation of the individual members, would have been damaged greatly had the elders not acted. By becoming a member of the Church of Christ, Guinn implicitly waived a part of her right to privacy regarding her moral character.

The decision in the Guinn case concerning the right of privacy issue hinged on Guinn's lack of knowledge of the Church of Christ's doctrine that the religion considers membership to be a lifetime commitment. The indication in the Oklahoma Supreme Court's opinion is that had she been made aware of this doctrinal tenet, she would have relinquished her civil right to disassociate herself from the Church of Christ membership. According to the court's opinion, the elders never contested Guinn's claim that she was not taught the church's prohibition against withdrawal of membership. Therefore, the court determined that Guinn's testimony must be taken as true.

One cannot help but wonder what the outcome on the right of privacy issue in the Guinn case would have been had the church conducted some type of educational classes for new members. What if a document had been signed by Guinn stating that she had been taught the basic tenets of the Church of Christ doctrine, had understood its doctrinal beliefs, and submitted to its beliefs and discipline? Unfortunately for the Church of Christ in Collinsville, Oklahoma, none of these evidentiary factors were present in its case. Had these factors been present, the case may have been decided in the church's favor.

Churches, pastors, and church leaders can avoid becoming participants in the litigation game by following some very basic steps and guidelines. By no means is the following meant to be an all-inclusive list of things to do and things not to do. The Oklahoma courts may have very well dismissed Guinn's claim for violation of right of privacy had the Collinsville Church of Christ implemented the following basic steps and guidelines.

1. *Consult an attorney.* The pastor or church leader whose legal standing is ever in doubt should always consult someone who knows the law, preferably a practicing attorney. Be sure that the attorney is provided with all relevant documents such as bylaws, doctrinal creeds, and any documents outlining disciplinary procedures. Any message to be communicated orally or in writing to a member who is subject to discipline should be thoroughly reviewed first by an attorney. Only after the message has been reviewed from a legal standpoint should it be communicated to the disciplined parishioner.

2. *Be consistent.* Consistency is the most important factor in disciplining members of a religious body. If A has committed the same sin as B, then the discipline for A and B should be the same. If it is not, one can expect A to complain of inconsistency, arbitrariness, and unfairness, and these are the types of allegations that will usually support a lawsuit.

3. *The bylaws of the church and its religious tenets should be clear and understandable to the average member.* The documents by which the church is governed, including procedures for disciplining a member, should be clear and understandable so that the disciplined member cannot later plead ignorance. The documents should communicate the basic

beliefs and doctrinal tenets of the religion and the basic lifestyle and practices expected of the members.

4. *Signed documents.* All documents by which the church is governed, including disciplinary procedures, bylaws, doctrinal statements, etc., should be in writing and given to the members. Additionally, new members should sign a statement that they have been taught the basic doctrinal creeds of the religion, and that they are fully understood by them. The written signed statement should also confirm that they have fully discussed all questions with church officers and that they submit to the authority of the church.

5. *Membership classes.* As part of the membership procedure, require classes or seminars that teach the soon-to-be member the doctrines and tenets of the religion. If the religion is based upon the Bible, reading of the entire Old and New Testament should be mandatory. The new member should also sign a statement that he has read the entire Old and New Testament and has discussed any questions with the pastor of the church or some other designated church officer.

6. *The tenets and doctrines as expressed by the church should be practiced by the church members.* This prevents an argument that the church's lack of enforcement of a particular tenet was an implied waiver of some kind. This would also avoid any argument about acquiescence.

7. *Church tribunals, mediation, and binding arbitration.* If consistent with the doctrines of the religion, adopt a procedure that allows for disputes to be settled only in the church through binding mediation or arbitration. Explain to new members why it is important that the church handle the disputes of members within the church and not before a secular tribunal. Have new members sign a written document that in any disputes they will agree to binding arbitration in lieu of a lawsuit. Be sure in the written documents signed by the new member is an explanation of how mediators and arbitrators will be picked, how many, and from what type of organization.

8. *Be up front and honest.* Never compromise your position by attempting to cover up a mistake. If a mistake is made, correct it. Always be candid with church members who may be potential plaintiffs against the church, and if a mistake is made, explain what happened. Of course, do not expose yourself or the church to a lawsuit by admitting to a mistake you have not made. Attempt to soothe the church member in situations where either a mistake was actually made or where the church

thinks a mistake was made. Remember, "A soft answer turneth away wrath."

The church is trying desperately to maintain moral and spiritual law and order in an undisciplined world. People are tearing down the wall of separation of church and state and the courts are providing the tools to do it. However, the erosion of the First Amendment freedoms by American civil courts will stop if pastors and other leaders take precautions.[37]

8

Reconciling Disputes among Christians

How should a church handle a situation in which two of its members, or one of its members and another Christian, are contemplating or are involved in litigation? What is the role of the church in such a dispute?

This chapter will examine a couple of key New Testament texts that deal with this issue and propose some models for applying those biblical principles today. Suggestions will be made for establishing a viable conflict-resolution service through the local church.

America has become the most litigious society on the face of the earth. Though certainly there are times when parties must go to court to settle disputes, these should be rare in the case of Christians against Christians, as will be argued in the chapter on lawsuits. This chapter is concerned with avoiding lawsuits, with Christians seeking a noncourt means of reconciling their differences. The believer may seek persons who are leaders in the church to settle some disputes. In more technical legal matters they may seek help from Christian lawyers who may either arbitrate or mediate regarding the claims against one another.

Christian Conciliation

Conflicts between Christians are not rare in today's society. Often believers find themselves at opposite ends of the legal spectrum as a result of their interaction in the business affairs of society, or due to remediable-at-law wrongs done to them. For example, Joe leased a building to Fred for his gardening business. Fred was never able to generate the kind of work or income he had hoped for, so he fell behind in lease payments. Joe was patient for a couple of months and accepted Fred's promises that he would soon get caught up on the rent. When the third month went by without any rent being paid, however, Joe finally notified Fred that he was in default on the lease and asked him to vacate the building. Fred's relative, a lawyer, described various delaying tactics Fred could use to stay in possession of the building a few months longer. These tactics angered Joe, who finally filed a wrongful detainer action to force Fred from the building. At that point, communication between the two men broke down completely. They were dealing with each other only through their lawyers. As they waited for their trial date, both Fred and Joe took every opportunity to speak critically of each other in front of other people. The only time they restrained their slander was when they went to worship in their different churches on Sunday.

Such disputes between Christians hurt all parties concerned and often belie our Christian testimonies before the world. A thoughtful Christian response to a legal dispute must consider an option known as Christian conciliation.

Beginning in 1980, the Christian Legal Society challenged the Christian attorneys in various communities to assist in providing a viable alternative to the civil court system. These leaders were inspired to pursue such an alternative because of Paul's statement in 1 Corinthians 6:1–6:

> If any of you has a dispute with another, dare he take it before the ungodly for judgment instead of before the saints? Do you not know that the saints will judge the world? . . . are you not competent to judge trivial cases? Do you not know that we will judge angels? How much more the things of this life! Therefore, if you have disputes about such matters, appoint as judges even men of little account in the church! I say this to shame you. Is

it possible that there is nobody among you wise enough to judge a dispute between believers? But instead, one brother goes to law against another— and this in front of unbelievers!

Paul's primary reasons for this admonition were twofold. First, it was an embarrassing witness for the Christian community to exchange disparaging characterizations and accusations before unbelievers in a public forum. Second, Paul knew that the adversarial civil court system encourages the type of behavior that nurtures spirits of contentiousness, resentment, unforgiveness, and bitterness, which are the exact opposites of the fruits of the Spirit: love, joy, peace, patience, kindness, goodness, fidelity, gentleness, and self-control.

The same concerns with the civil system apply today. The adversarial process still encourages the depersonalization and destruction of an opponent. Often trials conclude with both parties feeling even more angry at each other, the judges and attorneys, and the system as a whole.

Today, however, addressing the problem is much more complicated. It was comparatively easy for the Christian community to resolve their disputes internally when there was only one Christian church in a given city and all the Christians in that location knew each other. It is a different story today, when the Christian community consists of numerous denominations meeting in a myriad of locations, the vast majority of whose members will never meet on this side of heaven.

The leaders of the Christian Legal Society took on the challenge, because despite the complicity of the modern Christian community it is still an embarrassment and defeat when fellow Christians resolve their disputes through the civil courts. The result of a decade of their efforts has been a network of about thirty Christian Conciliation Services, which provides a viable interdenominational alternative for Christians to resolve their disputes within the Christian community through a process that integrates the values of the Christian faith. Each of the local ministries is autonomous and establishes policies by the local personnel, so their programs may vary. Nevertheless, the following is an accurate generic description of these programs.

What Is Christian Conciliation?

Christian conciliation consists of simultaneously applying the following instructions found in Micah 6:8 (NIV): "And what does the LORD require of you? To act justly and to love mercy and to walk humbly with your God."

I emphasize applying these goals simultaneously, because often Christians in conflict apply them sequentially. For example, in the lease dispute described earlier, Joe prayed that the Lord would solve the problem when it first arose. When the problem continued, Joe was merciful in providing opportunity for Fred to pay the overdue amounts. When the problem persisted, however, Joe became angry and frustrated and concluded that he had been merciful long enough and now it was time for justice. The approach to justice at this stage is often clothed in anger or frustration and is rarely gentle.

In contrast, the principle behind Christian conciliation is that one need not choose between being merciful and just. Rather, Christians are called to work for justice—but in a spirit of love and mercy.

Christian conciliation includes the goal of just resolutions, because God desires justice. The Lord wants weights and measures to be honest and every sale to be fair (Prov. 16:11). Christ rebuked the lawyers and Pharisees as hypocrites, because they paid tithes but disregarded "the more important matters of the law—justice, mercy and faithfulness" (Matt. 23:23). The Christian virtues of truth and justice often require disputants to honestly assert their concerns and perspectives. Christians seeking to resolve disputes in a manner pleasing to Christ must wrestle to determine as just a solution as is possible in this fallen world.

Christian conciliation includes the goal of being merciful because of Scripture's (author's paraphrase) call to be "humble, gentle and patient with each other, making allowances for each other's faults because of love" (Eph. 4:2). Parties are reminded to "put on the garments that suit God's chosen people, his beloved: compassion, kindness, humility, gentleness, and patience, forbearing with one another, and forgiving as the Lord has forgiven them, where any of them have cause for complaint" (Col. 3:12, 13). The parties are encouraged to remember Christ's teachings to "first go and make peace with your brother, and only then come back to the altar and offer your gift"

(Matt. 5:24) and that the Lord will forgive them in the same measure as they forgive others (Matt. 6:12 and 18:21–35).

Christian conciliation includes walking humbly with God, because parties are reminded that all believers are members of the body of Christ. One disputant may be a "hand" and the other disputant a "foot," each viewing the situation from a different perspective. Disagreements between Christians are natural, especially given God's plan for a variety of gifts, talents, experiences, and maturity levels. First Corinthians 12 not only assures us that these differences will exist, but that they are God ordained. One person must walk humbly before God to accept another person's perspective when it conflicts with his own.

Christian conciliation does not necessarily require Christians to reach agreement on the issue over which their dispute arose. Just as a Christian can be loving towards an atheist without adopting his beliefs, similarly two Christians can love each other and be reconciled without agreeing on every factual issue or legal right. Christian conciliation accepts the fact that reconciled Christians can still have differences and when necessary seek just resolutions of those differences through peaceful means within the Christian community.

In summary, Christian conciliation is a means by which people can love their adversaries and at the same time honestly express their concerns about the subject of a conflict. Christian conciliation assists Christians in conflict who are searching for options other than either passively "turning the other cheek" or aggressively seeking justice through the civil courts in "righteous indignation." Christian conciliation simultaneously promotes both God's call for Christian reconciliation and God's call for justice.

The Christian Conciliation Process

The process of Christian conciliation is the three-step process found in Matthew 18:15-17 (NIV):

If your brother sins against you, go and show him his fault, just between the two of you. If he listens to you, you have won your brother over. But if he will not listen, take one or two others along, so that "every matter may be established by the testimony of two or three witnesses." If he refuses to listen to them, tell it to the church; and if he refuses to listen even to the church, treat him as you would a pagan or a tax collector.

As is often the case, Christ's instructions are simple but have profound implications and challenges.

Even the first step of discussing the alleged wrong with the other party alone is more complicated than it appears. The burden is on the injured party to examine and submit his own attitudes and objectives to the Lord. While confrontation arising out of spirits of pride, anger, bitterness, or revenge may satisfy the letter of the law in this passage, it would surely miss its spirit as well as directly disobey numerous other passages (Eph. 4:31, Col. 3:8, and Rom. 12:19).

Thus one deciding to obey this instruction to go and discuss the matter alone must first surrender his attitudes and objectives to the Lord and seek God's purposes in the meeting, to wit: to restore fellowship with the injuring party as brothers in Christ, to help the other person understand the "sin," if any, that manifested itself in the injurious attitude or action, and to help the person be restored to the Lord. Jesus says to go, but the spirit in which we go will determine whether we are there as ambassadors of ourselves or of our Lord.

For example, Joe needs to confess to the Lord that his bitterness, resentment, and slander have been sinful, before he goes to Fred, and then Joe will need to confess these "logs" to Fred before pointing at any "specks" in Fred's eyes. Joe will also need to organize his goals and plan his words so that he encourages cooperation rather than antagonism. This does not mean that Joe cannot confront Fred about his wrongdoing; it means that Joe's confrontation must be designed to benefit Fred by helping Fred to deal honestly with his responsibilities in the situation.

In addition to being complicated, going alone can be unwise. Most lawyers you consult with about a particular problem will advise against such an action. Traditional legal wisdom forbids laypeople from discussing legal controversies outside the presence of their attorneys because litigants may unknowingly compromise their legal rights or inadvertently negate the strength of their case. While the above concerns are real, remember that such a position also conveniently requires the public to involve attorneys in the dispute resolution process.

The presence of insurance coverage for the injury even further complicates matters, because a person could lose coverage for a given incident if he enters into such meetings against the advice of his insurance company. (A party may wish to write the insurer before such an incident occurs. He can request confirmation that he will be able to exercise his convictions regarding Matthew 18:15–17.)

It is no less of a challenge to obey the second phase of the instructions: "But if he will not listen, take one or two others along, so that every matter may be established by the testimony of two or three witnesses" (NIV).

The factor that often leads to an ineffective utilization of this phase of the process is a misunderstanding of the purpose or function of the one or two "witnesses." The text says that every matter may be established by the testimony of two or three witnesses, but of what will they be witnesses? Probably not the original injury, which likely occurred in the absence of others. Rather, they will be witnesses of the parties' efforts and spirits as they seek to resolve their disagreement.

The function of these witnesses is to be a very real reminder to the disputants that the larger Christian community is affected by this situation and that they, as well as unbelievers, see how the parties handle themselves. And a personal spiritual battle begins for people who experience conflict when they permit unforgiveness to find a home in their spirits.

The witnesses are reminders to both parties of God's love and Christian fellowship. They encourage the parties to give and receive forgiveness, and to look at each other in the best light reasonably possible. The witnesses encourage, but do not impose, a resolution that is as fair as possible and that includes a commitment of reconciliation.

Note that these witnesses are not yet permitted to be judges of the parties or situation. Premature judgment is the common mistake which circumvents a powerful opportunity for the parties to reach their own agreement on the issues and to reconcile. The witnesses first act only as mediators between the parties, try to assist the parties in reaching a voluntary agreement, and possibly make suggestions acceptable to both parties.

At this stage both parties need love and understanding from the Christian community, prayerfully given to encourage and equip them to do the right thing about the legal issues and relationship in the dispute. Thus the function of the witnesses as representatives of the Christian community at this stage is much more mediatorial than judicial.

Even when the witnesses' function is clarified, many logistical issues must be resolved. The most important is the identity of the witnesses. Should they be leaders from each of the disputants' fellowship, or should they be people unacquainted with either party but specifically trained in mediation skills and associated with an agency such as the local Christian Conciliation Service?

The representative from each fellowship will probably carry more credibility to give any needed spiritual advice; but an individual or team from a neutral agency may be more objective and may possess better mediation skills and knowledge in areas such as law and/or the subject matter of the dispute that could help the parties reach a mutually agreeable solution. A combination of both approaches is usually available. There are strengths and weaknesses with either approach, so I advocate making prayerful selections on an ad hoc basis, remembering that the people selected should have mediation talents rather than judgmental spirits.

Should the witnesses be selected unilaterally by the injured party, or should both parties agree on who is qualified to serve such a position? Scripture seems to indicate that the injured party can select them unilaterally when necessary, and often the second person's refusal to address the situation voluntarily requires such unilateral decisions. However, whenever possible, it is vastly better for the parties to mutually agree on the identity of the witnesses, a first step in the process to try to break the deadlock.

The parties need to consider whether the discussions before the mediators will be kept confidential from either the civil legal system, the local churches, or both. In many jurisdictions, by mutual agreement the parties can ensure that the mediators will not testify against either side if subsequent legal proceedings become necessary. (For example, see California Evidence Code Section 1152.5.) Such an agreement helps reduce the normal jockeying for position and power and encourages openness and vulnerability. The parties must also agree whether the mediators will be authorized to report on the progress of the meetings to the leaders of their local fellowships.

Having the local church leaders, as well as attorneys and/or factual witnesses, attend any mediation meetings provides other logistical issues to be resolved. Various circumstances will result in a variety of responses, and reasonable people will reach differing conclusions, but the ground rules should be clearly understood by both parties at the outset. A sample mediation agreement used by a Christian Conciliation Service can be found in Appendix C for your reference.

The final phase of the process is to "tell [the matter] to the church; and if he refuses to listen even to them, treat him as you would a pagan or a tax collector." This gives the church the authority to act as judge/arbitrator and to expect the parties to abide by its decision. This authority can be reinforced if the parties execute a binding arbitration agreement, submit the matter to representatives from the church, and thereby cause their written decision to be enforceable through the civil legal system. California's Attorney General Opinion Number 86-701 concludes that such agreements are valid regardless of whether the church representatives are attorneys or laypeople.

Note that Scripture provides for disfellowship as its own method of enforcement. The option of having the decision enforced through the civil courts obviously raises the 1 Corinthians 6:1–8 issue of Christians in courts, but such action may be justifiable at this stage in light of the permission in Matthew 18:17 to treat the other party as an unbeliever [pagan].

There is still a question of who should serve as arbitrator(s). Should it be one person, a small group designated by church leaders, or the entire congregation(s)? More local fellowship involvement may be helpful and necessary, because the weight of the disfellowshipping enforcement will be on that body. Should the same people who have served as mediators act as the arbitrators? (Remember that the mediators have been trying to help the parties reach an agreement and hopefully have not told either party what would be their decisions as arbitrators.)

The latter arrangement would save time and makes a lot of sense if both parties have come to respect and trust the mediators. However, a danger is that one or both parties would have made compromise offers during the mediation process in an effort to settle the dispute of which they prefer the arbitrators to be unaware. The parties must decide whether they can trust the mediators to disregard any generous settlement gestures or whether fresh arbitrators should be assembled.

Another important issue regards the standard to be applied by the arbitrators. The civil law and Scripture will usually coincide, but there are occasions when they can differ. Legal technicalities such as the Statute of Frauds or Limitations can contrast with a Christian's obligation to keep true to his promise. See the California attorney general's opinion referred to above to establish that two parties can empower the arbitrator to determine a resolution consistent with the tenets of their faith rather than the law. A sample clause for that purpose is contained in the arbitration agreement used by a Christian Conciliation Service found in Appendix B.

Finally a word of caution for church leaders involved in cases that require the step of disfellowshipping. Many churches have been sued for the way they "told the matter to the church." Whether your tradition mandates that details of such matters should be shared with the entire congregation or only with the leadership, *be careful*. I refer you to *Church Discipline and the Courts* by Thomas Brandon and Lynn Buzzard (Wheaton, Ill.: Tyndale, 1987) as an excellent resource. In the matter of reconciling disputes, I highly recommend *The Peacemaker* by Ken Sande (Grand Rapids: Baker, 1991) as the most recent and comprehensive book on the subject.

Conclusion

The Christian conciliation challenge presented in Scripture must be prayerfully considered as a viable alternative to the traditional approach to resolving disputes through the civil courts. Christian Conciliation offers many potential rewards and advantages but it is not without risks and challenges. If you find yourself embroiled in a dispute with another Christian, I would encourage you to consult the Association of Christian Conciliation Services, Inc. (Appendix D), to which the Christian Legal Society (4208 Evergreen Lane, Suite 222, Annadale, VA 22003, 703-642-1070) has delegated its Christian conciliation responsibilities.

Part 3

Incorporation, Christian Schools, Property, Taxes, and Political Activity

9

Should the Church Incorporate?

What are the advantages of a church incorporating? What are the disadvantages? If a church decides to incorporate, is it necessarily establishing an "unholy alliance" with the state?

This chapter will consider the various options available to a church with regard to organization, focusing on the propriety of incorporation as opposed to other forms of organization.

One of the first issues faced by a newly formed independent local church,[1] and one that established churches may wish to consider or reconsider, is whether to incorporate the church under the laws of the state in which the church is located. The alternative to incorporation is the unincorporated association, which in contrast to the corporation is generally not a creature of state statutory law. Rather, the unincorporated association is guided by principles of the common law, i.e., the body of case law of a given state. Each form has its advantages and disadvantages, and the issue of which to choose should be carefully considered by those in authority in the church.

The purpose of this chapter is to provide a brief analysis of the two forms of organization—the nonprofit corporation and the unincorporated association—and to provide practical guidelines in making the decision of which form to choose. Although both the statutory law of nonprofit corporations and the common law of unincorporated associa-

This chapter was written by Jeffrey A. Aman.

91

tions vary slightly from state to state, they are consistent enough for the kind of general analysis we shall follow here. Most states follow a national model code for the statutory scheme of nonprofit corporations, and most likewise adhere to the same general principles of the common law with regard to unincorporated associations. However, the legal consequences of one form versus another are significant.

Obviously, for the issues raised and treated in this chapter there will be no citations from Scripture. Fortunately (or perhaps unfortunately for our purposes here), the early church was not faced with the ubiquitous "litigio-economic"[2] climate in which we live. Accordingly, although any form of Christian analysis must be informed by the body of Scripture as a whole, there are no definitive verses by which to select one form of legal entity as opposed to another.

The Nonprofit Corporation: An Introduction

The most popular form of legal entity for churches today is the nonprofit corporation. The nonprofit corporation is, by definition, a creature of the statutory law of the state in which the corporation is formed, and includes any corporation whereby no member, officer, or director receives a profit.[3] Most states model their nonprofit corporation statutes after the Model Nonprofit Corporation Act, a nationally recognized statutory scheme developed by legal scholars and practitioners[4] whereby nonprofit organizations of many kinds—religious, charitable, scientific, etc.—may become legally recognized and defined entities under the laws of the state of incorporation.

The first step to be taken by an organization is to incorporate under this act. This usually consists of preparing articles of incorporation and filing them with the secretary of state, along with a filing fee. If the articles meet all the requirements, the secretary of state keeps one copy on file and then sends back to the incorporators a file-stamped copy of the articles, along with a certificate of incorporation, which confirms the existence of the corporation in the state of incorporation.

Before sending the articles to the secretary of state, however, it is wise to check with the secretary's office to see if the proposed name of the corporation is available. If the desired name is already in use, another will have to be selected. For a fee, many states will permit the incorporators to reserve a name in advance of sending the articles to ensure that the desired name will be available.

The act has certain requirements for the articles of incorporation. Most significantly, they must include the name of the corporation, the period of duration, the address of the office of the corporation, the name and address of a registered agent for the corporation in the state,[5] the names and addresses of the original board of directors and incorporator(s),[6] as well as the purposes of the corporation. In addition, the articles must be signed and notarized by the incorporator(s).

There may be other reasons for including certain types of information in the articles of incorporation. For example, if the organization wishes to pursue federal tax exempt status, the articles should include language indicating that upon dissolution of the corporation all of the assets will continue to be used for charitable purposes.[7] Individual states may have similar requirements for obtaining state tax exempt status.

After the incorporation process is completed, the next step for the corporation is to prepare and adopt bylaws. Many churches use the terms *constitution* and *bylaws* interchangeably.[8] The bylaws essentially comprise the governing rules of the corporation and should cover several basic areas.

> At a minimum, church bylaws should cover the following matters: selection of members; time and place of annual business meetings; calling of special business meetings; notice for annual and special meetings; quorums; voting rights; selection, tenure, and removal of officers and directors; filling of vacancies; responsibilities of directors and officers; method of amending bylaws; and purchase and conveyance of property.[9]

It is advisable to place the doctrinal statement and ministry purposes of the church in the articles of incorporation and restrict the bylaws to the procedural aspects of the organization.[10]

After the incorporation process is complete and the bylaws have been adopted, the corporation may then commence its activities as a newly formed corporation. The nonprofit corporation, once it is formed, however, continues to be subject to the statutory framework that was the instrument of its inception. The Model Nonprofit Corporation Act governs many aspects of the corporation. One ongoing requirement is that the corporation file an annual report with the secretary of state, along with a small fee. The report includes completing a form provided by the secretary, and generally reaffirms much of the information contained in the original articles. Any significant change of purpose, for example, would be indicated on the annual report, as would a change in the registered agent, etc. Failure to file the annual report and pay the fee may, in some states, result in an involuntary dissolution of the corporation. Although reinstatement is usually possible after involuntary dissolution, the directors and officers of the corporation should be diligent in following this and all other requirements of the nonprofit corporation act of their state, and seek legal counsel if necessary.

In summary, the nonprofit corporation is the common form of legal entity for religious organizations, including churches, in the United States today. With minimal procedural steps in the process of incorporating and then maintaining the corporate charter, the nonprofit corporation can be an effective means of organization for the local church. The alternative to the nonprofit corporation is the unincorporated association, and there are some significant differences between the two.

The Unincorporated Nonprofit Association

In contrast to the nonprofit corporation, the unincorporated nonprofit association is not a precisely defined creature of statute. Rather, it is a relatively undefined form of legal entity emerging from the common law of the state to the extent that law has established it. *Black's Law Dictionary* defines an unincorporated association as follows: "An organization composed of a body of persons united with a charter for the prosecution of a common enterprise."[11] Although some states have a fragmentary treatment of unincorporated associations in their statutory scheme, it is usually specific to certain types of groups, and in any event does not approach the systematic treatment provided to the nonprofit corporation.[12]

The unincorporated nonprofit association is defined by its name. It is an association of people who have joined together for nonprofit purposes and is not a corporation under the laws of the state in which it operates. It is like a partnership in a sense,[13] but unlike a partnership does not have a profit motive. It is in function perhaps most like its counterpart, the nonprofit corporation, but because it is not governed by statutory law, the rights and duties of the nonprofit association under state law are much less clear, and, in some states, virtually nonexistent.

Forming a nonprofit association may consist of two or more individuals merely agreeing to join themselves toward common purposes. Thus, for example, if a group of four couples decided to begin functioning as a local church in their neighborhood by establishing a name and beginning to hold worship services, their group may have at some point become a nonprofit association. Generally, however, some documents are prepared such as articles of association or a constitution, along with bylaws. In function, then, if not in form, the association operates much like the nonprofit corporation, but without the defining characteristics thereof, and without statutory rights and obligations.

One major problem with the unincorporated association is its lack of legal definition. The extent of definition is strictly a function of the given state's body of case law related to unincorporated associations, which in many cases is almost nonexistent. For example, when an association acquires real estate for the purpose of building a facility, who owns the property? Although historically it was held that an association could not acquire property in its name, most states now have provided, either by case law or by statute, that the property may be held by a trustee of the association for the members of the group. Thus, if the property is later transferred, it would seem that the original members of the group would have to agree to the transfer, since they were beneficiaries when the property was acquired. But what if some of the original beneficiaries are no longer members, and new members have been added? Moreover, what would happen to the property if the church experienced a schism? Issues like these highlight some of the problems with acquiring, holding, and transferring property as an association. As one author has stated, "A clumsier method of holding title to property is hard to imagine."[14]

Another aspect of the unincorporated association that may present problems is that of the liability of its members. Since the legal definition of the association is essentially a group of individuals, when the association enters into a contract each member may be held liable if the contract is breached by the association. Similarly, if, for example, someone is injured on property owned by the association and it is sued for personal injuries, each member is potentially liable. Although historically it was impossible for an association to sue or be sued (because of its lack of recognition as a distinct entity), courts are now permitting such litigation, either in the name of a trustee of the association or, in some states, in the name of the association itself.

In contrast to the nonprofit corporation, the unincorporated nonprofit association is still relatively undefined under the law of most states. Although some progress is being made toward providing some distinguishing characteristics for the association, such as the ability to acquire and transfer property, enter into contracts, and sue and be sued, in many states the association is hampered by its lack of legal recognition. It would seem, then, that the best alternative for the church as a nonprofit organization would be the nonprofit corporation. There remain some factors that should be considered, however, before the decision to incorporate is made.

Should the Church Incorporate?

The primary advantage of the nonprofit corporation in general is that it is defined by statute. Its primary disadvantage, however, especially from a church's point of view, is that it is also *governed* to a large extent by statute. Thus, the benefits that come from being a clearly defined legal entity under the laws of a given state must be weighed against the negative aspects associated with being accountable to the state as a creature of the state's laws. Finally, the relative advantages and disadvantages of incorporating must be weighed against those of operating as an unincorporated association.

As discussed previously, the process of incorporation is a simple one in most states. Once the basic requirements are met, the certificate of incorporation is received and the corporation is then officially recognized. This means that the corporation can confidently acquire, hold, and transfer property; enter into contracts; and sue and be sued in its corporate name. It also means that the liability of the corporation is limited to its assets. The only proviso in regard to limited liability is that the corporation must indeed function as a corporation, i.e., hold all necessary meetings, keep minutes, file its annual report, etc. If these formalities are not observed, third parties may attempt to "pierce the corporate veil" and seek to hold the members of the corporation liable for wrongs done to those dealing with the corporation. This procedure is not a common one, however, and can be avoided by proper attention to the formalities of running the corporation.

One of the primary features of the nonprofit corporation, then, is *limited liability*. So long as the corporate formalities are observed, members can be assured that no litigant will be able to reach their personal assets. The only exception to this rule would be in the case where a member engages in personal conduct which is outside the scope of his normal activities as a member. Thus, as an extreme example, if in the context of discussing a hotly debated topic such as predestination and free will, one class member suddenly got up and punched his fellow class member in the nose, the injured party could sue the other personally and satisfy his judgment from the other's personal assets. Hopefully, the occasion for personal lawsuits will arise rarely in the local church, and then the potential litigants must consider biblical instructions regarding lawsuits among Christians.[15]

Another positive aspect of the nonprofit corporation is that it is able to deal with third parties easily. Virtually all people in the business world understand what a nonprofit corporation is—that it is an authorized legal entity under the laws of the state—and will readily recognize the incorporated church and generally will not hesitate to do business with it.

A final positive feature of the church as a nonprofit corporation is that the directors, officers, and members may generally have a good idea as to the structure of the organization and, from a legal perspective, how the entity is to operate. The rights and obligations of members, directors, and officers, as well as the requirements of the ongoing operation of the church, must be set out in writing in the articles of incorporation and bylaws. Potential and existing members may thus review these documents and get a clear idea of their rights and responsibilities, as well as what to expect of the leadership of the church with regard to procedural items such as annual meetings, voting rights, etc.

The disadvantages of the corporation are really the advantages of the unincorporated association. These negative aspects of incorporation generally relate to the issue of governmental control over the church. One of the first objections to incorporation made by some is that the church, by incorporating, becomes a creature of the state and therefore may be controlled by the state. This may include the ability of a state representative to come in and inspect all of the records of the church that the state's statutes require the church to keep. Another implication of governmental control may be that by voluntarily creating itself under the laws of the state, the church invites more stringent guidelines with regard to discrimination on the basis of religion. In other words, the argument may be made, for example, that because the incorporated church is a creature of state law, it therefore cannot only hire employees who adhere to the church's doctrinal statement. Although no case law has yet developed which would make this potential problem an actual threat, there is a trend in our national jurisprudence toward limiting the freedom of expression of religious belief.[16]

Perhaps less significant are the statutory requirements placed on the incorporated church with regard to keeping records and having those records available for inspection by members and, in some cases, governmental authorities. Unincorporated associations, by contrast, are generally under no state requirement to keep certain records (although the IRS requires that certain records be kept for purposes of substantiating the federal income tax return). Again, this is not a clear threat in the laws of most states at the present time, but the argument can be made that by becoming a creature of statute, the incorporated church runs the risk of subjecting itself to what the legislature deems appropriate for nonprofit corporations. And, unfortunately, there is little lobbying power, especially at the state level, on behalf of churches and other religious organizations.

The primary disadvantage of the unincorporated association is the fact that members may be potentially held personally liable for wrongs done by representatives of the association. And in our increasingly litigious culture, this may be a nearly fatal flaw for this form of organization. A secondary disadvantage, which many states have now taken steps to alleviate, is the general lack of legal definition and recognition of the unincorporated association. The extent to which this latter disadvantage is a problem will depend on the laws of the state in question.

Conclusion

There is clearly a tradeoff in the church's decision to incorporate as opposed to operating as an unincorporated association. Both options are available in virtually all states, and the local church can function in either form as an organized, tax exempt, recognized legal entity. It would seem, however, that the foreboding threat of litigation in our society necessitates a decision in favor of incorporation in most cases. Most churches keep many of the same types of records required by incorporation statutes and generally have nothing to hide. Moreover, although the bastion of religious freedom must be defended vigorously, churches today generally enjoy the same freedoms of religious expression and observance that they have come to expect in our country. Before making the decision to incorporate, though, church leaders are strongly advised to seek informed legal counsel in the state in which they will operate and to weigh the relative advantages and disadvantages of incorporating under the laws of that state.

10

Legal Considerations
for Christian Schools

*What are the major legal issues that must be addressed by a
Christian school? Does a church face new and different problems
if it decides to branch out into this form of ministry? Is an
autonomous Christian school considered a "church" in the eyes
of the law? General guidance in these areas, and more specific
sources for guidance in establishing a Christian school, are presented in this chapter.*

The Nature of a Christian School Ministry

Should the School Be Considered Part of the Local Church?

How should a Christian school relate to the ministry of the local
church that sponsors it? Should the school be called by the same name as
the church? Should the leadership in the church also be the board of the
school? Should standards required of workers at the church be different from those required of teachers, administrators, or other workers at
the school? These are but a few of the questions that arise when discussing the Christian school.

When a local church establishes a Christian school the decision
must be made whether the school is primarily for the benefit of the
members of the congregation, whether it will include other children

not related to the church but for the purpose of evangelistic or social outreach, or whether the church views the school as a service to the broader community.

The answers will largely determine the degree of intimacy between the church and the school. If the school is basically for the spiritual and educational benefit of members of the congregation or also is a ministry of the church to additional children in the community, the likelihood is that the leaders of the church will serve as the governing board of the school. This is the strongest position before the law in a disagreement between government and the Christian school. If the school is seen as a ministry of the church, as are its social services to the community, missionary outreach, church youth groups, etc., the entanglement of the state in church-school affairs will be more obvious but less likely. This position also has the benefit of securing the faithfulness of the school to the doctrine of the local church.

If the church closely relates the school to other ministries of the church, similar standards should be established between other paid workers in the church and those in its educational institution.

School Licensing and Accreditation by State Agencies

Many persons view state licensing and accreditation as very important to maintain standards at a Christian school. Some states require church schools to be licensed or accredited. Certainly if a school is licensed it will more likely have certain minimum standards that may be important to quality education, though there is not necessarily a correlation of these two. Moreover, teachers with certification have met certain minimum education requirements.

To be licensed by the state does not insure quality of education. This may be observed in the spiraling downward trends of public school test scores as contrasted with the largely independent and unlicensed sector, including home schools. Often there may be serious disagreement between religious educators and state educators on what books, curriculum, and facilities are important. That public educators have a necessarily accurate understanding of these concerns can be questionable, and important differences can exist because of the different world views and religious perspectives of the two groups.

Legal Issues of the Christian School

Legal Rights of School Officials Regarding Children and Their Parents

Discipline. Under current law, teachers and school administrators function in some sense in the place of parents (in loco parentis), though certainly not equal with parents. In view of this, they may, if necessary, use physical punishment on students in their care to maintain discipline and guard other children from harm. They must be careful, however, to distinguish this limited corporal punishment from child abuse.

The U.S. Supreme Court has ruled that such corporal punishment does not violate a student's rights. The teacher should be sure to explain to students and parents the types of behavior or actions that are punishable by corporal punishment. This may be done by having the administration explain such actions in a student handbook or by the teacher handing out a page describing discipline to each student at the beginning of the school year.

Even though due process procedures are not needed prior to the administering of corporal punishment, state laws may proscribe certain restrictions. A private school has some advantage over public schools in this area, since attendance is purely voluntary and is a privilege rather than a right. The school should be sure that parents are apprised of disciplinary procedures and types so that they can concur upon enrolling their children.

Even in a private school the punishment should be measured, equitable, and administered in the presence of another authority for the protection of the teacher. Excessive spanking or undue force in spanking could bring legal problems to the teacher and school.

Trespass. It is not uncommon for teachers to confiscate the personal property of students under their care. This may be anything from gum or candy in the classroom to dangerous objects like knives or drugs. There certainly are differences as to how these categories, the rights of the students, and the liabilities of the teachers for the taking of such objects should be treated.

Teachers have a right to confiscate items that prove to be detrimental to the conducting of their classes or are harmful to their students,[1] but they should take care that they do not destroy the property of the students. For example, if a teacher takes away a student's comic book, the teacher may not consider that he can do whatever he desires with the student's property. A policy should be established for the time and circumstances for returning items.

Privileged communication. Students, family members, or other professionals often will confide personal information to Christian school teachers, administrators, and staff. What legal rights and responsibilities come with this information? Does a teacher or administrator have to give others information that could be harmful or defamatory to the student? Does this confidential information have the protection of law as "privileged communication"? And can the courts require the confidant to release the information by a court subpoena?

The basic principle regarding confidential information is the "need to know." School personnel should give this material only to those who have a valid reason for receiving it.[2] Requests for such information should be in writing, and the teacher or administrator should obtain student or parental approval before releasing the information. The transmitted report should contain only factual material, not rumors, hearsay, or undocumented comments.

Prudent guidelines for Christian school staff to follow include (1) limiting negative comments to factually based details, (2) including only first-hand accounts in student and staff files, (3) keeping all files current by removing outdated information, and (4) permitting students and staff to have access to their files, even if this is not specifically required by law.[3] These guidelines conform to the federally established Family Rights and Privacy Act. Some states, however, have set up additional rules regarding student records, and Christian school faculty and administration need to be aware of the specifics of the law in their state.

Physicians, attorneys, and clergymen have a special legal relationship with their clients called privileged information. Courts cannot compel them to reveal what their clients tell them in their professional contacts. The legal status of a teacher or administrator as a counselor is not clearly established. Certainly such an individual does not have the legal status of these other professions regarding privileged information. However, the trend of legal decisions supports the concept that information in a counselor-client relationship is privileged.[4] But a wise person will avoid giving absolute guarantees on confidentiality.

Self-defense. Threats and attacks on teachers by students are becoming more commonplace in our schools today, whether public or private. Consequently, Christian school personnel need to be aware of the legal problems involved in self-defense. Self-defense in a school setting refers to three basic types of acts: those a staff member takes to defend himself or herself against a student threatening physical harm, actions to keep a student from harming another student, and efforts to keep a student from damaging school property.

The guiding legal concept for all forms of self-defense is "reasonable force." If the staff member acts reasonably in a situation and a student is injured, then the courts tend to uphold the staff member. Reasonable, however, is defined in terms of each situation. A 150-pound adult lifting a 75-pound grade-school student and throwing him against a wall is an example of unreasonable force, and the courts would probably rule against the teacher. Personnel should apply only such force as is necessary to deal with the problem and cease when the problem ceases.[5] If a teacher becomes aggressive toward an offending student after the initial problem is dealt with, then the teacher is at fault. The severity of force used in defense should directly relate to the severity of the attack.

The law distinguishes between assault and battery. A threat to do harm is assault, while an attack on one person by another is battery. While the gravity of battery is obvious, the seriousness of assault and one's response to it depends upon the ability of the person making the threat to carry it out. A second grader's threat to blow up a teacher's car is technically assault, but a wise teacher would not overreact. A seventh grader, however, is probably capable of slashing the tires on that car, and a threat to do so should be taken seriously and dealt with properly. Immediate response to such assault will go a long way to reducing the risk of harm to school personnel and their property.[6]

Legal Duties of School Officials Regarding Children and Their Parents

First aid and medication. Historically, administering first aid and dispensing medication by school personnel to students has not been a problem. However, in recent years the number of legal problems arising from these acts has increased, so it is important that Christian school staff recognize their legal responsibilities and limitations in this area.

Personnel should respond to medical emergencies with actions that a prudent parent would take in similar circumstances.[7] Treatment of injuries should be limited to whatever is necessary to save life and limb and no more. Excessive treatment of injuries, especially actions that attempt to do things beyond an individual's training, can result in legal problems for the school, not to mention physical harm to the student. The school should have a well-defined policy for dealing with such situations, and personnel should always follow it.

Dispensing medications, including prescription drugs and over-the-counter remedies, can be another problem area. Ideally a medically trained staff person should handle all medications to be administered during the school day. This person would then dispense such medication only with the written permission of the parents. In the absence of such a person the school may opt to officially leave the responsibility for taking medication up to the individual student. Thus the school publicly takes no responsibility for accuracy of dosage, frequency of administration, and any adverse side effects. If, however, the school requires that prescription medication be administered from a central office, then it assumes more responsibility and more liability.[8]

Most states have laws covering the administration of medications, such as insulin, which require injections. Generally these laws require that only medically trained individuals administer injections. If no trained medical staff are available in the school to comply with state law, then the parents must arrange for a nonschool person to carry out the task.

Over-the-counter drugs, such as aspirin, would seem to be free from legal complications, but such is not necessarily the case. A few individuals can have severe medical reactions to the ingredients in over-the-counter medication, and children may not always be the best judges of their physical tolerances. Thus some schools prohibit the dispensing of any over-the-counter medications to any students.[9] Others dispense them in reasonable amounts upon request, while still others require parental permission before giving students over-the-counter medications.[10] Whatever procedure is followed, the school should communicate it to parents and students in writing and stick to it.

Field Trips. Field trips usually are a delight to students, a welcome change for teachers, and a potential source of legal problems for the school. Intelligent foresight and preparation can reduce the risks faced by a Christian school when sponsoring field trips. Such problems come from four areas: instructions given students and parents, transportation arrangements, supervision while on the excursion, and preparation for emergencies.

The instructions should be included on the parental permission form as well as given in writing to the students. They should describe the nature of the trip, objectives, items to bring, and specific information about unusual or potentially dangerous situations that might be encountered. If the school does not notify parents of potential problems, then it may well be liable for injuries.[11] No student should be permitted to attend without a signed permission form on file with the school. While a parent's signature on a permission form, especially one containing detailed information, may protect the school against some lawsuits, it is no defense against negligence. Consequently, the school must carefully evaluate how it conducts the trip, beginning with transportation.

Transportation should be in school vehicles, owned or rented, if at all possible. The use of private vehicles may make the school liable for the acts of such drivers, who are legally agents of the school. Adequate supervision includes supervising students during transportation. Written instructions should be given before the trip, and the rules strictly enforced.

Supervision at the site is usually the responsibility of the school. If the class has been invited to tour a facility, then it is an "invitee," and the major responsibility for supervision and safety is that of the host. If, however, the class has asked permission to visit, then it is a "licensee" and is responsible for supervision of the students.[12] The number of accompanying adults depends on the nature of the site and the abilities of the students. Enough adults should be present to provide reasonable supervision for all situations the class may encounter.

Emergencies arise, and the legal problems they pose usually focus on the nature of the school's preparation. The most common emergency is the unusually disruptive student who will not respond to normal discipline. Under no circumstances should a student be put off a bus or out of a car because of discipline problems. If he or she must be removed from the group, then an adult must accompany the student. Field trip personnel should plan for other emergencies as well. This would include first aid kits, safety equipment, and trained professionals as needed. Reasonable precautions will do much to eliminate liability in emergency situations.

Supervision and liability. Teachers are responsible for supervising students as well as educating them. When teachers serve as hall monitors, lunchroom supervisors, or playground supervisors, they are carrying out a vital part of their legal responsibilities as teachers.[13] Students must be given adequate supervision at all times, and failure to provide such supervision can result in serious legal problems for the school. This includes students who are not under a teacher's direct authority, such as students whom the teacher observes acting improperly in a hallway or restroom. If a student is injured in such circumstances, and if the teacher knew about the situation but made no effort to interfere with the dangerous behavior, then the teacher may be liable for an act of omission.

Reasonable supervision does not mean that a teacher cannot leave the classroom for any reason. Courts evaluate the reasonableness of a given situation in light of several factors, including the teacher's reason for leaving, the length of the absence, the maturity of the students, and the nature of the class activity. Obviously, more direct supervision is required in a laboratory or shop class than in a history class.[14]

Teachers or other staff should be adequately trained to supervise the activities to which they are assigned. A substitute with no training in gymnastics could be liable for injuries to a student if the substitute were to continue the regular activities of an advanced tumbling class to which he or she had been assigned.

The details of supervision may be summarized in one concept: The teacher must provide the type of care that a reasonable and prudent parent would provide in similar circumstances.

Can there be a duty to accomplish education? Can a person sue a Christian school for failure to educate? In other words, is there such a thing as educational malpractice? Courts appear unwilling to allow this type of suit against both public and private schools.[15] Obviously, a private school that simply took a student's tuition dollars and made no attempt to provide instruction would be guilty of a breach of contract. But the school has no legal duty to ensure that the student learns.

If, however, the school's promotional literature or other documents promise specific items, such as a certain number of hours in a given subject, or a specified level of proficiency, then the courts tend to construe such statements as a contract.[16] Failure to provide the stated items can be grounds for a breach of contract suit. Christian schools would do well to evaluate their promotional literature in light of this concept.

Questions of child abuse. What legal responsibilities do Christian schools face in the area of child abuse? Aside from their obvious responsibility to ensure that students are safe on their campuses, Christian schools have two other responsibilities: reporting suspected abuse and restricting corporal punishment so that it does not become abusive.

Most states have laws that require, not merely recommend, that teachers report all suspected cases of child abuse to designated government authorities.[17] Each school should know the required steps and inform all personnel of their responsibility in this area. Usually the state laws provide immunity from libel or slander suits for the person reporting the suspected abuse. The key word in these laws is *suspected*. The teacher does not have to have absolute proof that abuse is happening to file a report. Child abuse is not limited to bodily or sexual mistreatment. It includes malnutrition, lack of proper clothing, and inattention to medical and dental needs, among others. If a school official suspects child abuse and does not report, then he or she may well be breaking the law.

The second problem is corporal punishment. Generally the courts have recognized the practice of corporal punishment within schools as a proper means of discipline. This acceptance is guided by the concept of "reasonable force," and that is usually evaluated by the presence of marks on the person so disciplined. If a Christian school decides to include corporal punishment in its discipline practices, then it should (1) notify parents and obtain their written consent to such punishment, (2) provide parents and students with a written list of offenses which merit such discipline, (3) choose only one school official to administer the punishment, and (4) administer a limited number of swats in the presence of a witness.[18]

Legal Issues for Teachers in the Christian School

What rights do Christian school faculty members have in matters of discipline and dismissal? The courts have traditionally granted private schools extensive freedom over their internal standards and discipline procedures for both faculty and students.[19]

This is especially true for religious institutions, where the standards are usually an expression of religious convictions and practices. The relationship between the institution and faculty members is defined by a contract. However, the specific standards of conduct expressed in the contract, their definition, and application are left up to the individual school. Courts do not evaluate the reasonableness of a school's rules unless they go against some pervasive public policy.

The courts do require that contractual law be followed, which means that documents such as faculty handbooks, school catalogs, and application forms be kept up to date with current school practices. This material is the legal basis for the contractual relationship, so any conflict between what is said and what is done can be grounds for legal problems.[20]

Faculty should expect the school to provide written statements regarding expected conduct, especially those offenses for which an individual will be terminated. They should expect the school to be impartial in its application of these standards and not favor one class or individual over another. But when a teacher signs a contract, he or she accepts the standards and practices of an institution as defined by that institution.

The federal government has taken a hard stand against discrimination through specific legislation. Titles VI, VII, and IX of the Civil Rights Act are the most familiar parts of this legislation. Title VI prohibits discrimination on the grounds of race, color, or national origin in any program or activity receiving federal financial assistance. This prohibition impacts hiring and firing practices. Few Christian primary and secondary schools receive federal financial assistance, but veterans' benefits through the V.A. program, which many college students receive, are considered a form of government financial assistance.

Title IX prohibits discrimination based on sex, but provides that exemptions may be made for institutions where its application would go against the established religious convictions of the organization. Title VII prohibits discrimination in hiring, firing, or classification based on race, color, religion, sex, or national origin. This legislation applies to an employer-employee relationship.

What does all this have to do with Christian schools? First of all, each school should carefully examine its stated policies to determine if it discriminates in admitting students on any basis other than religion. If the school wishes to be selective, then the practice should be made public. The practice should also be religiously motivated. Second, each school should evaluate its hiring and firing practices on the same basis. Title VII permits discrimination based on an established religious basis, but does not exempt Christian schools from their responsibility to avoid discrimination on other grounds, such as sex or race.[21] For example, if a school holds that only men should teach religion classes, then a qualified woman candidate may be rejected. If, however, this is not a religious conviction of a school, then the candidate cannot be rejected just because she is a woman. Obviously, each school should specifically define its position on these issues in writing.

Today's news regularly contains reports of courts handing down decisions requiring employers to change their hiring and firing practices to go along with federally mandated affirmative action laws. These decisions may set hiring quotas for employing women and minority groups, or they may force employers to hire people that they do not wish to employ. What impact do these court decisions have on the Christian school in its hiring practices?

Part of Title VII seems to exempt religious institutions, such as schools, from the requirements of the legislation, but there is some disagreement in the courts over the extent of the exemption. Most courts and the Equal Employment Opportunity Commission hold that a Christian school can discriminate on the basis of religion in filling all jobs connected with the institution. Some courts, however, have ruled that the exemption applies only to those jobs which have direct religious significance.[22] Under this interpretation a Baptist school, for example, has the right to hire only Baptists as counselors but must hire any qualified person as custodian. No uniform legal opinion exists on this question.

What, then, can a Christian school do to ensure that it will be permitted to hire people who agree with its religious position? First of all, the school should make its religious purpose clear in its founding documents, such as its constitution, charter, mission statement, etc. Second, it should make this practice clear in all literature used to recruit, hire, and train its employees. Third, it should be consistent in its hiring and firing practices. While these steps will not guarantee the school's freedom in this area, they will help the school prove to a court that it is a religious institution in all its functions.

As was stated above, none of this exempts a Christian school from the laws that prohibit discrimination based on sex, race, or national origin. However, it seems only reasonable that Christian institutions would take the lead in providing employment to all qualified members of the body of Christ wherever possible.

Separation of State and School?

Zoning, Safety, and Health Ordinances

Federal and state governments have passed many laws designed to protect the general welfare of their citizens. Our food and water are subject to federal health standards. Cars, bridges, and buildings must conform to government safety requirements. Machinery, equipment, and tools come equipped with mandated safety devices. Christian school personnel may thank government health inspectors when they eat safe food at lunch, but they may have other thoughts when Occupational Safety and Health Administration (OSHA) inspectors stop construction on the school's new gymnasium and fine the Christian contractors for not having proper safety equipment. Where does the government's interest in its citizens' general welfare end and the Christian school's freedom begin?

The law describes the government's right to establish rules to ensure the general welfare as a "compelling interest." Individual states cannot establish laws that conflict with the federal government's compelling interest in a given area, nor can local governments or private organizations establish rules that conflict with the compelling interests of state and federal governments. This includes private religious organizations as well.[23]

The courts consistently support this right of federal, state, and local governments over against the absolute freedom of even religious institutions. No organization, Christian or not, is free from any and all government control. There are significant questions about specific applications of this concept, especially when the issue involves a practice grounded in a religious belief. However, if the government can show that it has a vital interest in a given matter, the courts can and do rule against the private school in such cases. Issues of basic health and safety are examples of areas in which the government's interest would take precedence. Christian schools should cooperate as much as possible with government regulations in these areas. Indeed, it is hard to imagine a Christian belief that would oppose basic standards of health and safety.

Taxation of Christian Schools

Federal and state tax codes distinguish between corporations that are designed to make a profit and those that are not. Corporations whose purpose is to earn profits pay taxes on those profits, while nonprofit corporations do not pay taxes on their income. If a Christian school has incorporated, it has undoubtedly done so as a nonprofit corporation. Income it receives from tuition, gifts, and fund-raising projects is tax-free money. As long as the school operates within the framework of its legal charter as a nonprofit corporation, then it will retain this privilege.

However, if the school engages in profit-making ventures, especially those that compete with other businesses, then the legal situation changes. If the enterprise is small, the customers are primarily constituents of the school, and the profit is returned to the institution, then the courts have generally protected the tax-free status of the school. Large operations have been taxed in some states, so each school should proceed with caution in any venture of this nature.

11

Church Property
and Zoning Ordinances

Zoning restrictions are becoming a major issue as local governments increasingly confront the problems of growth and planning. This factor, combined with a trend toward comparatively harsh treatment of property owned by churches and other religious organizations, has led to important issues of which churches should be aware as they enter into local zoning debates. This chapter provides some guidance for church and other Christian organization leaders to deal more effectively with local governing authorities in matters of property ownership and zoning classifications.

Can a city deny a church's application for a building permit on the grounds that the site plan fails to include adequate off-street parking? Does the city have the right to decide that the proposed use of property is not "religious" and thus does not constitute a "church"? Is it a violation of residential zoning for a group of more than ten people to meet regularly in a home for Bible study and worship? If the zoning classification permits a church to conduct worship services in a residential district, may the church later construct a gymnasium and a child-care facility on the same property based on a belief that these facilities are an integral part of the regular religious activities and ministries of the church?

This chapter was written by Brad N. Gahm.

113

Unfortunately, the answer to these questions could be either yes or no, and there are no concise rules of law to resolve this quandary. The types of property uses that zoning ordinances allow are quite different according to the discretion of each local government. It is impossible to determine if a certain use of church property is permissible without identifying the proposed use and comparing it with the language of the ordinance for the zoning district where the property is located.

Because zoning ordinances vary greatly between communities, this chapter cannot answer specific questions regarding church property and zoning. However, it presents some general principles of law as a planning guide to uses of church property that will not run afoul of common zoning ordinances, and to suggest challenges that may be raised if a use of church property is ruled to be in violation of a zoning ordinance. To understand these general principles, we must begin with the legitimate constitutional interests associated with the free exercise of religion granted by the First Amendment that conflict with the enforcement of zoning ordinances through the exercise of the state's police power.

"Free" Exercise and the Police Power

The authority of, and limitation upon, a municipality to regulate church property is a reflection of the qualified grant of religious freedom under the First Amendment. The free exercise clause guarantees an unrestrained freedom to believe, but not freedom to act.[1] The freedom to hold religious beliefs and opinions is absolute, but the freedom to act, even when the action is in accord with one's religious belief, is not totally free from legislative restriction.[2] Every use of church property, whether it is construction of a church building, using a home as a meeting place for worship, or operating church recreational facilities, is a form of religious conduct rather than religious belief. Therefore, the conduct is not free from regulation.

Even though religious conduct may be regulated, there must be a strong justification for infringement on this First Amendment right. The Supreme Court has held that the free exercise of religion is a fundamental right that must be protected, often at the expense of other interests that may be of high social importance.[3] The free exercise of religion may be restricted only to prevent an immediate danger to other interests that the state may lawfully protect.[4] One of these substantial interests is the preservation of residential tranquility in the orderly development and management of land.

The state's interest in promoting the orderly development of land is accomplished by zoning. Zoning is the regulation of the use of land, and of the buildings and structures located thereon.[5] The authority from which the state derives its power to zone is the "police power," which is an inherent attribute of state government. When citizens consent to the establishment of government, they empower the government with a natural position of authority known as the sovereignty of the state. The police power is an exercise of sovereignty rather than a right that is expressly granted by constitution.[6]

The police power is best defined as the exercise of the sovereign right of a state to promote order, safety, health, morals, and the general welfare.[7] Zoning ordinances are a specific exercise of the police power used by local governments to regulate the development of land. The Supreme Court has granted broad discretion to local governments to use zoning to protect the public interest, even when the city may have concluded nothing more than that a certain use of land would be harmful to "family values."[8]

Zoning ordinances, generally, are constitutional unless they are clearly arbitrary and unreasonable, having no substantial relation to the public health, safety, morals, or general welfare.[9] This presumption of constitutionality imposes a significant burden of proof on anyone who challenges a zoning ordinance as an unreasonable or arbitrary restriction on their use of property. When a zoning restriction imposed by an ordinance applies to a use of church property, the zoning operates as a restrictive burden on religious conduct. In that situation, the presumed constitutionality of the zoning ordinance is juxtaposed with the free exercise of religion. The Supreme Court has held that only those interests of the highest order that cannot otherwise be served are sufficient to override the First Amendment right of free exercise of religion.[10]

The due process clauses of the Constitution also protect church property from unfair application of zoning ordinances. The limited scope of this chapter does not permit a detailed analysis of all constitutional issues relating to church property and zoning ordinances. A reasonable summary of the law is that a zoning ordinance that restricts the use of church property is permissible if it is neither arbitrary nor unreasonable, and only to the extent that the state's compelling interest to protect the public health, safety, and general welfare cannot otherwise be served.[11] This proposition serves as the starting point for an examination of the permissible restrictions that zoning ordinances may impose on the use of church property. A brief overview of the procedures and terminology of zoning is necessary as a preface to this examination.

Zoning Procedures

Municipalities, as separate governmental entities, have no inherent authority to enact zoning ordinances; the state must delegate this authority via zoning enabling acts.[12] All fifty states have adopted zoning enabling acts that delegate the police power, in varying degree, to municipalities to enforce zoning.[13] The scope of authority conferred by a zoning enabling act varies from state to state. However, most state enabling acts conform generally to the provisions of the Standard State Zoning Enabling Act.[14]

A typical zoning enabling act authorizes the appointment of a zoning commission that is responsible for establishing zoning districts and the regulations to be enforced within each district. A separate board of adjustment is appointed with authority to determine compliance with zoning regulations and consider applications for a variance from the terms of a zoning ordinance. Every municipality that has enacted zoning ordinances has also created zoning agencies to administer them. The most common titles for these agencies, and the titles used in this chapter, are the commission and the board of adjustment. Church property owners should become familiar with the titles and organizational structure of the zoning agencies in their local community.

Four common zoning issues are the subject of determinations by the zoning commission or the zoning board of adjustment: (1) express exceptions in the ordinance, (2) variances, (3) specific use permits or exemptions, and (4) nonconforming uses.[15] A brief review of these four issues will illustrate common zoning requests.

The text of a zoning ordinance may contain an *express exception* that defines the range of uses permitted within the district. For example, the district may be zoned for residential use (defined as single-family dwellings) with an exception permitting the sublease of a portion of the dwelling to a nonrelative. This exception permits the homeowner to lease his garage apartment to a tenant. A problem could arise if the tenant begins operating an antique shop out of the garage apartment. Although the tenant has maintained a residential use that the exception allows, the leased residence has also taken on a commercial enterprise. The disputes that typically arise in connection with zoning exceptions relate to interpretations of the exception and whether a certain use of property conforms.

A *variance* must be obtained when the property use generally conforms to the zoning classification but fails to meet specific criteria. These deficiencies typically relate to height restrictions, off-street parking availability, setbacks, and use of signs. For example, the zoning for a district may permit construction of a church building. A church begins construction without knowing that the ordinance also includes a maximum height restriction of three stories. The property use itself complies with the zoning, but the steeple atop the building is in violation of the specific requirement for maximum height of buildings. A variance, as the name suggests, could be obtained to permit the noncompliance of one aspect of the property use which otherwise is consistent with the zoning.

Specific use permits are required when the proposed use for the property is not permitted by the ordinance. The most common examples are schools that are required to obtain specific use permits when located in a residential-zoned district. The operation of a school obviously is not a residential use, yet there is good cause to locate a school in a residential district. A change in zoning for the entire district would not be appropriate or practical; thus, a specific use permit is granted for one particular tract of land within the district. A complex and often lengthy process confronts the applicant for a specific use permit, since the zoning commission must be convinced of the reasons why the existing zoning should be disregarded for the proposed use of a particular tract of land.

Nonconforming uses refer to existing property uses that are affected by subsequent zoning changes. For example, rural-zoned districts may be reclassified to commercial and residential areas as a city grows. The property uses existing at the time of reclassification are rendered nonconforming by the new zoning. The new ordinance may include a "grandfather clause" to permit the continuance of existing uses that predate the zoning change. However, the new zoning may have limits for continuing the nonconforming uses. The ordinance may impose a time limit on the grandfather clause, after which the nonconforming use will be prohibited; it may permanently prohibit the nonconforming use if a temporary cessation of the use occurs; or it may strictly prohibit any new construction or enlargement of the nonconforming use.

Advance planning is critical when making a zoning request. Budget planning is an essential component of the business operations of every church and Christian ministry. An analysis of zoning issues should be considered no less important. The appropriate time to consider zoning issues is before a dispute arises.

It is a simple matter to contact local zoning agencies to obtain documents and information detailing the zoning ordinances for the district where the property is located. This information should be evaluated as part of any plan for construction of new buildings or changes in the use of existing facilities. Zoning agency officers are accustomed to working directly with property owners, and these officers are eager to answer questions about zoning procedure. Full advantage should be taken of this free source of information. Neither expertise nor a law degree is necessary for a property owner to acquire a working knowledge of zoning ordinances and procedures. A telephone call or letter to the zoning agency could avoid a zoning dispute and the unnecessary time delays, legal expense, and emotional trauma that inevitably are part of such disputes.

The following two scenarios illustrate how a zoning dispute could arise over church property. First, a church that operates existing facilities might assume that the zoning would not affect construction of a new building to be located on the existing property. Plans are finalized and a building permit is requested to begin the construction. After reviewing the proposed building design, the city inspector denies the building permit, because the structure would violate zoning restrictions for height and parking availability. The church must either change the building plan or make some type of zoning request that would permit the new building as planned. Either course of action involves a costly delay. If the zoning issues had been investigated as part of the initial planning, the need for a variance would have been identified and the zoning request could have been made before the time to begin construction.

The second situation involves the conversion of existing facilities for a new use. A church may have previously obtained a specific use permit to operate in a residential-zoned district. The church thereafter buys houses on lots adjacent to its existing property. When the church begins conducting Bible study classes in these houses, area property owners seek an injunction to prohibit church meetings in these residences. The church's specific use permit probably applies only to the original property boundaries and does not expressly include other residential properties that were subsequently purchased. Even though the church could apply for and obtain a new specific use permit for the additional properties, the resulting delay and poor relations in the neighborhood could have been avoided with a more thorough knowledge of the local zoning ordinances.

If, in spite of preparation and planning, a church or Christian ministry is faced with a dispute about an existing or proposed use of its property, competent legal counsel should be retained immediately. The work previously done to become familiar with the local zoning agencies and procedures will help clarify the points of dispute and the appropriate corrective action to take.

The process for obtaining a variance or specific use permit, or for any other zoning request, will depend on the rules of each local zoning agency. Typically, the property owner must submit a written application including a legal description of the property, an explanation of the existing or proposed use, and the type of zoning requested. A zoning location map, tax plats, and a certified metes and bounds description of the property must accompany the application. In appropriate circumstances, the application may also require flood plain or environmental information, or a transportation impact study if the number of vehicles traveling to the property exceeds an amount specified in the zoning ordinance. The zoning agency provides instructions for preparing the application, including sources from which the property owner can obtain the information and documents that must be submitted.

The application and all attachments must be filed with the zoning commission with an appropriate fee. A hearing may be scheduled for the applicant to make a presentation and obtain an initial recommendation. If approval of the zoning request is recommended, a second hearing is scheduled, and public notices are issued to advise property owners located within a specified distance around the property of the upcoming hearing. This public notice is usually mailed to the adjacent property owners and published in a local newspaper approximately two weeks prior to the hearing. The second hearing gives the applicant and all other interested property owners an opportunity to present their positions on the zoning request, and a final ruling on the application is made by the commission.

Church Property Disputes

The remainder of this chapter covers specific examples of zoning disputes affecting church property. These court opinions and rulings should be viewed as illustrative only and not as formal rules of law applicable in all communities. Every zoning case is unique depending on the specific property use and the precise language of the zoning ordinance. The two most common disputes arising from the zoning of church property are the exclusion of churches from residential districts and the restriction of accessory uses of church property.[16]

Exclusion from Residential Districts

The majority view in the United States traditionally has been that churches are by their very nature clearly in furtherance of public morals and the general welfare, and thus could not be excluded completely from a residential district by a zoning ordinance.[17] Churches have always been required to comply with building codes, fire and safety regulations, and other reasonable regulations irrespective of zoning.[18] These specific regulations have been accepted as a legitimate way to protect public safety in all buildings, including churches. A different question is presented when protecting public safety and the general welfare is sought by a zoning ordinance that makes a blanket exclusion of churches from a residential district.

Although zoning that excludes churches may have a stated purpose to protect against the hazards of additional automobile traffic, congestion, and noise that threaten the legitimate welfare of a residential neighborhood, the traditional attitude of courts has been to reject these ordinances.[19] However, an increasing number of cases have broken from the traditional view and now permit exclusion of churches from residential districts.

In *Lakewood, Ohio Congregation of Jehovah's Witnesses, Inc. v. City of Lakewood*,[20] the Sixth Circuit Court of Appeals upheld a zoning ordinance that restricted the construction of church buildings to areas that comprised only ten percent of the total land area of the city.[21] *City of Lakewood* signals a trend away from the traditional deference accorded to church property. Churches may now be faced with challenges from homeowners in residential-zoned districts that the construction of a church facility increases traffic and noise, changes the character of the neighborhood, or decreases property value in the district.[22] The courts may increasingly be willing to enforce an exclusionary zoning ordinance if additional noise and traffic could adversely affect public safety or change the character or property value of the neighborhood.

If a zoning ordinance is interpreted to exclude a particular church, or all churches, from a residential district, one remedy would be to apply for a specific use permit. But, a church may prefer or feel compelled to directly challenge the ordinance. At least two challenges can be raised to show that a zoning ordinance wrongfully excludes a church from a residential district: first, that the exclusion is based only on the religious nature of the property use; and second, that the ordinance fails to adopt the least restrictive means necessary to protect the public safety or general welfare. Each of these is addressed in the following paragraphs.

A zoning ordinance that makes an exclusion based on the religious nature of the property use usually involves an attempt to define what constitutes a church. This question could occur when a religious organization conducts its activities in a building that does not have the appearance of a traditional cathedral, synagogue, mosque, or other religious structure. Nevertheless, the organization asserts that its practice of religious activity in that building constitutes a church.

This issue was presented in *Synod of Chesapeake, Inc. v. Newark*,[23] where the city ordered the United Presbyterian Church to stop using a building that had previously been a single family residence but had been converted to a combination worship and information center, office, and meeting place for university students. The court overruled the city's order, finding that the activities conducted in the building related to an attempt to make Christianity meaningful to young persons who would not be likely to accept the rigid structure and conventions of traditional Christianity; therefore, the property use constituted a church.[24]

In determining whether a use of property by a religious organization constitutes a church, the focus must be on the activity of the group rather than the beliefs that motivate the activity. In other words, the definition of a church for purposes of zoning is not determined by the nature of the belief but by the nature of the property use. This distinction was recognized by the Supreme Court in *Larkin v. Grendel's Den*[25] where a church was not defined in terms of a commitment to belief in a theistic as opposed to a nontheistic divinity; rather, a church was assumed to be "any building primarily used as a place of assembly by a bona fide religious group."[26] Thus, two key elements that determine what constitutes a "church" for purposes of a zoning ordinance are whether the building (1) has a primary use (2) as a place of religious assembly.

If a Christian ministry is excluded from a residential district on the grounds that the building it uses is not a church, the zoning might be challenged successfully by showing that the building is primarily used as a place of assembly for religious activity, regardless of the appearance of the building or its prior uses. Many contemporary churches no longer limit their activity to formal meetings for worship and prayer. The concept of what constitutes a church has changed from a place of worship alone, used once or twice a week, to a place used day and night throughout the week for various religious and community functions.[27] These various church activities can be accommodated by many different types of buildings, and there should be no attempt to define a church solely in terms of the appearance of the building it occupies. A wide range of property uses have been held to constitute a church where the activities were sufficiently related to a primary use as a place of assembly.[28]

Zoning ordinances typically have not attempted to define a church based on whether the beliefs of the members of the group are deemed to be religious.[29] It is doubtful that any Christian ministry could be excluded by zoning on the grounds that the beliefs of its members do not constitute a legitimate religion. The protection of the First Amendment has been interpreted broadly to include any group that shares a "sincere and meaningful belief" that occupies in their life a place parallel to that of an orthodox belief in God.[30] So long as the members of a group hold a sincere and meaningful belief, according to their own subjective standards, such belief is probably protected under the First Amendment as religious. The Supreme Court has consistently protected the freedom of the individual to define his own religious beliefs rather than substitute a formal legal standard for judging orthodoxy in religion.[31]

Another way to challenge a zoning ordinance that wrongfully excludes a church from a residential district is to demonstrate that the ordinance fails to employ the least restrictive means to protect public safety; it thereby imposes an unconstitutional burden on the practice of religious beliefs.

In the landmark case of *Sherbert v. Verner*,[32] the Supreme Court considered the constitutionality of a workers' compensation statute that denied benefits to a worker who was fired for refusing to work when it violated her religious beliefs.[33] The Court ruled that even if the state could demonstrate a compelling interest for denying benefits in order to avoid fraudulent claims by workers who would feign religious beliefs, there must be a showing that no adequate alternatives exist to protect the state's legitimate interest without infringing First Amendment rights.[34] The Supreme Court concluded that the law violated the free exercise clause by forcing a Seventh-Day Adventist to choose between working on Saturdays, in violation of a religious belief, and refusing to work on Saturdays, which resulted in a loss of unemployment compensation benefits.[35]

The important lesson from *Sherbert* is that First Amendment rights can be violated by a governmental action even when it is far less than a direct order requiring conduct contrary to religious beliefs. If a law merely withholds a benefit because of conduct motivated by religious beliefs, this seemingly benign state action may nevertheless be an unconstitutional burden on the free exercise of religion. This is not to say that every infringement of religious freedom is unconstitutional. The mere fact that an individual's religious practice is burdened by a government action does not mean that an exemption accommodating the practice must be granted. But the state must justify any burden on religious liberty by showing that it is the least restrictive means of achieving some compelling state interest.[36]

A compelling state interest exists to protect and manage land development, and this compelling interest is legitimately served by enforcing zoning ordinances. However, the courts have recognized an important limitation: The specific method adopted in a zoning ordinance to protect land development must be the least restrictive alternative. When churches are uniformly excluded from residential districts, an important question is raised whether the zoning ordinance has used the least restrictive alternative to protect the safety and welfare of a residential neighborhood.

The *City of Lakewood* case, cited earlier in this chapter, prohibited the construction of new church buildings in any residential area. It did not prohibit a church from meeting in existing buildings located in residential districts. The court concluded that the zoning ordinance only prohibited the purely secular act of building anything other than a home in a residential district. The zoning did not prevent the church members from practicing their faith by meeting for worship in existing homes, schools, other churches, or meeting halls throughout the city.[37]

The exclusionary zoning in *City of Lakewood* arguably permitted the alternative that the church could continue to meet in existing buildings. However, the Court did not require proof that this alternative was the least restrictive. The Court shifted the focus away from the restrictive nature of the ordinance and considered only whether a fundamental belief would be unduly burdened by the effect of the exclusionary zoning. This approach wrongly assumes that there should be merely a balancing of competing interests: the free exercise of religion versus the state's interest in protecting the aesthetics of a neighborhood. Courts should require a test which assumes that every zoning ordinance burdens the fundamental right of the free exercise of religion, and then require that the ordinance employ the least restrictive means necessary to protect legitimate safety and welfare interests.[38]

A different type of exclusion was presented in *Grosz v. City of Miami Beach*.[39] An elderly rabbi of an orthodox Jewish sect conducted religious services at his home in a residential-zoned district where churches were excluded. Religious beliefs required the rabbi to conduct the services twice daily with a congregation of at least ten adult males. When neighbors complained about the noise and traffic from these religious services, the city prohibited any service where the number of people attending exceeded ten. The city allowed the services to be held if attendance was limited to not more than ten. The court ruled that there was merely a minimal burden on the free exercise of religion and that the services could be conducted in other nonresidential districts, which constituted approximately 50 percent of the land area of the city.[40]

The problem with the *Grosz* decision is that not only did the zoning ordinance fail to employ the least restrictive alternative, there was no alternative but for a church to locate in restricted areas of the city. Although the city was willing to allow the services when attended by not more than ten people, this conciliatory gesture did not change the fact that the zoning ordinance absolutely prohibited the practice of organized religious worship in large areas of the city.

The court in *Grosz* concluded that because the rabbi and his congregation could relocate their services to nonresidential districts of the city where churches were permitted, the burden on religious freedom was only minimal and was no more than a question of "convenience, dollars, or aesthetics."[41] There was no demonstration by the city that restricting noise and traffic congestion in a residential neighborhood could not have been adequately served by means less restrictive than a blanket exclusion of all churches. Examples of less restrictive means would be to allow churches so long as adequate parking areas were included, or to limit the time of day and number of services which could be conducted.

The religious beliefs of the rabbi in *Grosz* were somewhat unique by requiring him to conduct services twice daily, and his personal circumstances were such that this could be done only at his residence. Admittedly, this is not true for most home Bible study groups and other religious groups that voluntarily meet in the residential homes of their members.

A voluntary meeting in a residence might be considered religious practice that merely expresses a preference to meet in one location as opposed to another. A zoning ordinance that prohibits such voluntary meetings in a residence could be construed as an infringement only on an expression of preference rather than substantive religious beliefs.[42] However, it would be wrong to trivialize the fundamental right of free exercise of religion by characterizing the location of place of worship as merely a matter of convenience, dollars, or aesthetics. Courts should require that the zoning employ the least restrictive means, and reject a standard which only asks whether a nonmandatory practice of a church or religious group will not be too greatly inconvenienced by exclusion from a residential district.

There is no guarantee that every court will adopt the test suggested in this chapter that an ordinance must employ the least restrictive means. For example, the zoning ordinance at issue in *State v. Cameron*[43] prohibited all property uses except single-family dwellings in a residential district. A minister who conducted worship services in his home was prosecuted for violating the ordinance despite his claim that a total exclusion of churches would be "patently excessive" to accomplish the legitimate concerns of noise and traffic regulation.[44] By claiming that the ordinance was excessive, a challenge was clearly presented that the ordinance failed to adopt the least restrictive means. Nevertheless, the court concluded that the ordinance need only be "narrowly drawn to avoid unnecessary intrusion" on the rights of free exercise of religion.[45]

Zoning ordinances that exclude churches from residential neighborhoods could be interpreted to prohibit any religious group that voluntarily meets in a home for Bible study and worship. The mere fact that the meeting is voluntary may, regrettably, lead to the conclusion that prohibiting such a meeting would result in only a minimal inconvenience for religious practices rather than an unconstitutional burden on religious beliefs.

Because there may be increasing hostility towards religious freedom through the use of exclusionary zoning ordinances, Christian ministries should consider a constitutional challenge. First Amendment rights should not be sacrificed to an exclusionary zoning ordinance unless the city has first demonstrated that there are no adequate alternatives that employ the least restrictive means to protect the general welfare interests of a residential neighborhood.

Restriction of Accessory Uses

Accessory uses are types of property uses that are customarily incidental to the primary use of a building or property.[46] The issue of accessory uses may become important as an alternative to making a zoning request for a variance or specific use permit.

The First Amendment does not automatically grant to a church property owner an unrestrained license to construct new buildings or convert existing buildings to a new type of use. The applicable zoning may prohibit any change from the existing property use unless a zoning request is granted. A property owner would certainly find it advantageous if he could add to or alter an existing property use without having to incur the delay and expense of making a formal zoning request for the new use. The significance of a declaration that a certain use is "accessory" to an existing primary use is that there is no further requirement to obtain approval from a zoning agency.[47]

An example of an accessory use for church property is seen in *Corporation of Presiding Bishop v. Ashton*.[48] In *Ashton*, a city zoning ordinance permitted churches to be built in all districts, but there was no definition of what was included in the term *churches*. One church, whose existing facilities included buildings used primarily for religious education and worship, announced plans to use some of its vacant land for recreational facilities and a lighted baseball field. The court refused to grant an injunction sought by neighborhood property owners to prohibit construction of the baseball field. The court concluded that a church is more than merely an edifice affording people the opportunity to worship God, and that a reasonable recreation facility is a permissible accessory use included in the meaning of the term "churches."[49]

In determining whether a particular use is accessory, courts frequently consider whether other religious institutions customarily use their property in a similar manner. If a type of property use is customary for other similar property owners, this may be persuasive that it is an accessory use.[50] Requiring that a use be customary as a precondition for qualifying as an accessory use serves as a limitation on how far a church property owner can vary from an existing primary use. A church cannot assume that it has an unlimited right to declare an accessory use for any activities of its members simply because those activities have some relationship to the church.

For example, in *Marsland v. International Soc'y for Krishna Consciousness*,[51] the court granted an injunction to prohibit a church from establishing a residential facility as an accessory use to its temple. There was no argument that the church itself, as a primary use, was permitted on property located in a residential district. However, a section in the zoning ordinance that prohibited more than five unrelated persons to occupy a residential structure was held to be a valid restriction applying to all residences, and the nature of a residence could not be altered by attempting to declare it an accessory use of the church.[52]

Tents and house trailers used as temporary residences during religious "camp meetings" are not accessory to other existing buildings that are lawfully located on the property.[53] Similarly, because of the compelling interest of a state in providing quality education to children, church schools are not automatically deemed to be an accessory use. A city may enact a zoning ordinance that regulates church schools with restrictions substantially different from those generally applicable to the church itself.[54]

A wide range of property uses have been permitted as accessory to a primary religious use or church. Accessory recreational uses include playground,[55] an activities building,[56] and a kindergarten play area.[57]

Earlier discussions in this chapter considered whether a residential home could be converted for a primary use as a church. A different question is presented when an established church is permitted to operate in a residential-zoned district, and the church wants to use one of its buildings as a residential dwelling which it considers to be accessory to its primary religious property use. Residential uses of buildings located on church property have been permitted as shelters for the homeless.[58] Other property uses that have been permitted as accessory to a church include a day-care center[59] and a drug rehabilitation center.[60]

Zoning disputes relating to accessory uses of church property typically involve an injunction to prohibit the church from conducting a certain type of activity on its property. A challenge can be made by the church property owner showing that it is customary for other churches to engage in similar accessory uses. Also, challenges can be based on the same arguments used in response to zoning ordinances that exclude churches from residential districts. Accessory use cannot be denied on the basis of its religious nature if the primary use of the property is permissible. It may also be possible to show that an accessory use could be allowed subject to certain time, place, and manner restrictions which would be less restrictive than a complete prohibition. An example of appropriate time, place, and manner restrictions was made in the *Ashton* case where the city permitted the lighted baseball field but limited its use to the hours of 7 A.M. to 10 P.M.[61]

Conclusion

The use of church property is protected as a fundamental right under the First Amendment, but not without limitation. Construction of a church building, using a residence as a meeting place for worship, or operating church recreational facilities are forms of religious conduct that can be regulated by zoning. No concise rules of law clearly distinguish between permissible and impermissible uses of church property.

This chapter shows that, as a general rule, a zoning ordinance cannot infringe on any use of church property unless the ordinance is legitimately related to protecting safety, health, and general welfare, and then only to the extent that the ordinance employs the least restrictive means necessary to protect those interests.

Every church and Christian ministry should investigate all facts relating to zoning issues as part of the initial planning and preparation for construction of new buildings or a change in the type of use of existing buildings. Careful planning in the use of church property is the best way to avoid zoning disputes and protect the free exercise of religion.

12

The IRS and Church Finances

This chapter will outline the procedures for tax exemption with the Internal Revenue Service, as well as provide general guidance on such things as depreciating assets, investing funds, and financing building projects. The focus will be on tax issues faced by the church as a financial entity, as opposed to the individual pastor or Christian worker, which will be treated in chapter 13.

Tax exempt status, or the freedom from organizational liability for state imposed tax, is a privilege enjoyed by many American churches and public organizations. This legal protection is perhaps in line with one of the earliest recorded citings of tax exemption, in the Old Testament Book of Ezra: "Also we inform you that it shall not be lawful to impose tax, tribute, or custom on any of the priests, Levites, singers, gatekeepers, Nethinim, or servants of this house of God" (7:24 NKJV)

The command in Ezra is directed toward exempting the individual religious worker from paying a state tax. In our day under the "command" of the Internal Revenue Code it is the religious organization, church, or para-church entity that is freed from the responsibility of paying a tax.[1] Though the biblical exemption refers to the individual rather than the religious entity, the principle remains the same: American law recognizes the value of contributions to society made by the religious organization and encourages those efforts via tax exempt status. Con-

This chapter was written by Michele Bachmann.

gressional grants of tax exempt status are directed at twin goals: first, encouraging private organizations, including religious, along with public corporations to shoulder an effort that must otherwise be fulfilled through direct outlays of taxpayer dollars; second, encouraging an activity that is considered socially desirable.

Consider this excerpt from a congressional committee report: "The exemption from taxation of money or property devoted to charitable or other purposes is based upon the theory that the government is compensated for the loss of revenue by its relief from the financial burden which would otherwise have to be made by appropriations from public funds, and by benefits resulting from the promotion of the general welfare."[2]

Churches and Tax Exemption

Churches enjoy a special status under the statute; they are automatically exempted from the requirement to pay income taxes under the Internal Revenue Code. Churches are under no affirmative duty to formally apply for tax exempt status,[3] nor are they required to file information returns.[4] This exception from notification and information return filing requirements applies to churches, their integrated auxiliaries, conventions or associations of churches, and any organization that is not a private foundation and whose gross receipts in each taxable year are normally not more than $5,000.[5] Although exempt from giving required notices and from filing annual returns, a religious organization is not exempt from IRS examination of its records and books for the purpose of determining the church's tax exempt status. This statement seems to grant a broad right of IRS access to church files. Treasury regulations temper this open-ended grant with the phrase "except to the extent necessary" for IRS to determine whether the organization continues to qualify for tax exempt status under Section 501(c)(3).[6]

If a religious organization is automatically exempt from income tax, why would it bother with the forms, fee, and application procedure to obtain a formal tax exempt status? First, formal exemption assures donors and contributors bona fide deductions for their contributions.[7] This deduction is not limited to income taxes but is also allowed for estate[8] and gift[9] tax purposes. With the formal exemption in place, the organization will be included in the IRS Cumulative List of Exempt Organizations.[10] Second, state and local tax authorities will oftentimes grant an automatic waiver of exemption from income and property taxes based upon a proper presentation of the official IRS tax exempt classification certificate.

Concerning wages and salaries of employees of the religious ministry, social security[11] and unemployment taxes[12] become an option rather than the norm, as is true with for-profit organizations. Also, the entity enjoying tax exempt status is free from paying tax on its earnings.[13] While a church's earnings are often modest, nonetheless freedom from paying taxes is a privilege to be enjoyed. However, some disadvantages do exist for the tax exempt organization. For example, no expenses may be offset from the exempt operation against any unrelated business income.[14] If the church or ministry has unrelated business income, the code will not allow this income to have the benefit of tax exempt status but will tax it under the same rates and in the same manner as taxable income of any corporation.[15] But this also means that the church with unrelated business income is allowed to deduct business expenses, interest losses, and charitable contributions against unrelated business income. In addition, the church is given the ability to carry forward and carry back any unused net capital loss, and the church with unrelated business income is given corporate treatment of capital gains and losses.[16] After passage of the Tax Reform Act of 1986, the capital gains and loss provisions are no longer of significant consequence to the taxpaying entity. However, the religious organization should double check this code section, as many leading tax specialists believe Congress will reactivate lower capital gain rates in the future.

If tax exempt status is denied by the IRS, then disclosure of this result is made to state officials.[17] Also, where the exemption application is withdrawn from the IRS at any time in the application process, note that the application papers along with recorded notes from IRS officials handling the application may be placed in an IRS file for future reference, i.e., for potential future audits of the organization's returns.[18] A taxpayer is well advised to maintain a healthy respect for the power and authority of the IRS to audit, review, or withdraw tax exempt status from an organization. Many a tax protester has asserted his freedom of speech by failing to file, or failing to pay a tax, only to discover himself standing before an unsympathetic tax court. Though meaning to follow the dictates of his conscience, in the end the protester could be financially ruined. Therefore, it is advisable to follow the rules of the tax code and regulations. One does not benefit by skating on the edge of the tax code. Play well within the boundaries of the law, and the religious organization's tax exempt status should remain secure.

What Are the Organizational Requirements for Tax Exempt Status?

Section 501(c)(3) codifies the criteria:

(1) corporations (or unincorporated churches formed under a constitution or bylaws)
(2) organized and operated exclusively for religious, charitable, or educational purposes
(3) no part of the net earnings of which inures to the benefit of any private shareholder or individual,
(4) no substantial part of the activities of which is carrying on propaganda, or otherwise attempting, to influence legislation(s)
(5) and which does not participate in, or intervene in (including the publishing or distributing of statements), any political campaign on behalf of any candidate for public office.

First, the code section itemizes more of a list of "don'ts" for a tax exemption candidate than a list of "do's." For this reason, it is important for the ministry and its attorney to first determine whether the organization complies with the list of criteria enunciated above. An earlier chapter analyzed whether to incorporate the organization and will not be restated here; however, it is important to note a religious organization cannot have as the form of doing business an individual proprietorship or partnership; generally, the group either will form as an unincorporated association or will incorporate.

Second, the religious entity must meet a two-part test. It must be both organized and operated "exclusively" for exempt purposes. Again, the code provides a list of exempt purposes: religious, charitable, scientific, testing for public safety, literary, educational, and prevention of cruelty to children or animals.[19] Interestingly neither the code nor the regulations define the term *religious purposes*. The term *charitable contribution* is defined as a gift to an organization exclusively organized and operated for religious purposes, but again does not define *religious purposes*.[20] Discussion of the definition of religious purposes is beyond the scope of this work; however, an excellent treatment of the subject may be found in the footnote.[21] Looking to the regulations we see that an entity is organized exclusively for exempt purposes only if the organization instrument limits the purposes of the organization to fit within "religious, charitable, scientific, etc.," exempt purposes.[22] Simply, an organization must take care that the purposes written in the organizational instrument are no broader than the 501(c)(3) purposes.

In drafting the articles of incorporation the writer might incorporate the exact code language by stating, "The religious organization is organized exclusively for the purpose of religious and charitable work."[23] Proper wording is crucial for an effective organizational instrument. It must clearly state that the assets must be used for exempt purposes (religious, charitable, educational, etc.). In the event of corporate dissolution, the wording of the organizational instrument must provide that all assets be distributed to another 501(c)(3) organization.[24] Furthermore, if the organization controls a business that contributes all profits back to the ministry, the Internal Revenue Code states, "An organization operated for the primary purpose of carrying on a trade or business for profit shall not be exempt from taxation under section 501 on the ground that all of its profits are payable to one or more organizations exempt from taxation under section 501."[25]

Third, no part of the religious organization's net earnings may inure or accrue for the benefit of a private person. An individual may, of course, receive reasonable payment from the tax exempt entity for services performed for the organization's exempt purposes or for items sold thereto. The IRS denial of exemption is based on a private person funneling tax exempt monies to himself outside of acceptable exempt purposes.[26]

Fourth, an entity is not organized exclusively for exempt purposes if the language of the document provides for more than "an insubstantial part of its activities to attempt to influence legislation, or to directly or indirectly participate in or intervene in any political campaign on behalf of or in opposition to any candidate for office." The admonition from the IRS to the tax exempt candidate seeks to carefully craft the language of the entity's organizational instruments ensuring that the entity's purposes truly conform with the allowable tax exempt purposes of 501(c)(3). Religious entities lose the tax exempt status if a substantial portion of its activities consists of carrying on propaganda or otherwise attempting to influence legislation. Regulations define attempting to influence legislation as urging the public to contact members of legislative bodies concerning support or nonsupport of legislation.[27] The key watchword for religious organizations is "substantial portion." To totally deny churches the right to speak out on legislation is to deny First Amendment protections of freedom of speech and expression. Churches may take a public stand on political issues. The confusion centers on what amount of activities are allowable before they are termed substantial. Congressional policy for limiting tax exempt attempts to influence legislation centers on neutrality concepts. Congress does not believe attempts at influencing legislation should be subsidized through tax exemption. Fifth, a tax exempt organization absolutely may not intervene or participate in political campaigns on behalf of a candidate for public office. Limited voter education activities are allowable, such as preparing a non-partisan voting record.[28]

Tax Exempt Application Process

For information about the application process, telephone the nearest IRS office (800 numbers are available) to obtain Form 1023, the Application for Recognition of Exemption under Section 501(c)(3) of the Internal Revenue Code. This form is used as the organization's first step in formally applying for a ruling or determination letter on exempt status under Section 501(c)(3). Be sure the organization retains a copy of the completed Form 1023 in the permanent records file of the religious organization. After January 31, 1988 Form 1023 applications must have attached a copy of Form 8718: User Fee for Exempt Organization Determination Letter Request. The Revenue Act of 1987 now requires payment of a user fee from each organization applying for tax exempt status. What was formerly a free service from the IRS now requires a payment of several hundred dollars. If the payment is not attached to Forms 1023 and 8718, the IRS will not process the organization's request for exempt status.

Ordinarily, the tax exempt organization provides the IRS with notice within the first fifteen months of life that it is not a private foundation.[29] Happily, churches, interchurch organizations, local units of the church, conventions or associations of churches, or integrated auxiliaries of a church are excepted from this notice requirement.

All requested documents must be physically attached to Form 1023.[30] These may include: current year financial statements, a detailed breakdown of support, revenue, expenses, and proposed budgets for two years detailing the amounts and types of receipts and expenditures anticipated. The last requirement is called for if the organization has been in existence for less than one year.

Other requested items include a conformed copy of the complete organizing instrument, which is a copy of the articles of incorporation first signed by the board of directors and second, accepted by an appropriate government official, or in the alternative, the signed constitution or articles. If the organization is a corporation or an unincorporated organization with bylaws, a copy of the bylaws must also be included with the application. The above listed "conformed copies" must reflect the original documents with all amendments. The organizing instrument, either expressly or by state law, must limit the organization's activities to those allowed under 501(c)(3). The instrument must also provide for proper distribution of net assets upon dissolution.

Each of the above listed attachments should state in writing on the document that it is filed in accordance with Form 1023 and should reflect the date completed and the organization's name, address, and employer identification number. Additionally, the organization should file any collateral information citing court decisions, rulings, or opinions which could expedite the processing of the Form 1023 Recognition of Exemption application.

Once the paperwork is completed, an officer of the organization authorized to sign, or another person authorized by a power of attorney, must sign the application. If power of attorney is exercised, send a copy of the power of attorney along with the application upon filing. At last, file the application and all required attachments with the key IRS office in the district where the organization's principle place of business is located. A list of the IRS key district offices along with respective addresses may be found in the instructions for Form 1023.

Upon receipt of the completed application, the IRS will advise the religious organization of a grant or denial of tax exempt status. Should the IRS deny the status, provisions are made for appeals to higher ranking personnel within the IRS.[31] Should denial of tax exempt status be upheld, appeals to the federal courts are available.[32]

Financial Accounting for Churches

Generally the pastor and church officers plan current fund expenditures to provide a specific program of services for the church with the proposed budget presented to the congregation for a vote. Upon approval the budget becomes the church's operating plan for the fiscal year. Contributions are requested from members to finance church programs, and expenditures are defined within the limits of the written budgetary allowances. Thus, churches are found to operate exclusively by appropriation control, following fund accounting practices. Reporting is made on the cash or modified cash basis with both revenues and expenditures relating to the budget plan, with the common practice relating actual and budgetary amounts to each other on the periodic statements of revenues and expenditures. The operating statement also discloses the relationship of gifts given by the church to help others (benevolent gifts) to the total budgeted expenditures used for ministering to church members. The church current fund balance sheet will commonly disclose only appropriable assets and claims against those assets. Fixed assets, along with long-term debt obligations, are frequently omitted from financial reports, although they may be disclosed in a separate plan fund balance sheet.[33]

Depreciating Assets

Depreciation is a concept dealing with fixed assets. In the church setting, depreciation is usually associated with building programs or the purchase on credit of large tangible assets. Where the church does record fixed assets on the balance sheet, the question arises whether the asset should be depreciated.

Depreciation is oftentimes not taken on a church-owned asset, because the nonprofit organization does not ordinarily determine profit through the direct matching of income and cost. Therefore, depreciation serves a small function. Second, churches often raise the monies needed for major building projects through special fund drives, and similarly hold another such drive when a replacement or addition is needed for the major asset. The depreciation charge then becomes unnecessary, as there is no need to recover the costs of the asset from the church's income. Finally, the last several inflationary decades have proved the market value of a building many times increases faster than the decline in asset value connected with deterioration over time. Logically, it seems silly to measure a loss in value of an asset that has doubled or tripled in value.

Reasons do exist for recording depreciation, including the recent call for churches to fall in line with generally accepted accounting standards. First, depreciation itself is a cost. If the depreciation cost is not a part of the church's financial statement, the statement will not accurately reflect the true costs to the organization. In other words, the church could be misled by thinking the actual costs were less than they were. Second, fixed assets will likely need replacing in the future from the recurring income of the church or religious organization. Without reflecting depreciation on the church's financial statement, the church may be lulled into thinking sufficient funds are available to cover replacement costs. Also, the amount of income available after expenses may vary significantly from year to year in comparison with the timing of replacement cost. Finally, churches are subject to federal income taxes on "unrelated business income." Fortunately, the tax code provides depreciation as a cost allowable to reduce the unrelated business income profits subject to tax. It is wise to record depreciation, as there may be future profits to charge against even if profits do not exist currently.[34]

Investments Through Tax Reform

Much has changed to reduce the favorable tax climate churches once enjoyed. In fact, many financial commentators are stating that the current tax climate is less favorable toward religious entities than at any time in our national history.[35] Several decades ago, churches were allowed to own investment properties while retaining tax-favored status upon disposition of the investment. Properties used by the religious organization or church were exempt from taxation, even though it was held for the purpose of enhancing the church's investment portfolio. State and local governments beset with needs for increased revenues began to sit up and take notice of the church's favored tax position, and today, many states have restricted tax exempt status to only those properties used exclusively for the beneficial purpose of the 501(c)(3) organization. Church-held real estate investments in these states have been liquidated and often converted to investments in securities.

Funding Building Projects

A familiar method of fund raising for the religious organization is the offer and sale of a security. A security is defined in the federal statute as "any share of stock in any corporation, certificate of stock or interest in any corporation, note, bond, debenture, or evidence of indebtedness, or any evidence of an interest in or right to subscribe to or purchase any of the foregoing."[36]

Securities sales is a complex subject beyond the scope of this overview. However, the church contemplating security sales to finance a building project must be mindful that registration requirements for the securities may be required. Registration is a complicated and expensive procedure, and requires assistance of competent legal and accounting advice. The potential problem with securities lies with the determination that an unsophisticated buyer can be harmed. Again, the religious organization must examine whether securities laws are involved before a private or public offering is made. Many churches choose to fund long-range programs through the successful gift annuity plan. Churches view the gift annuity plan as a "win-win" proposition for both the church entity and the parishioner-donor.

Under this plan parishioners invest their funds with the religious organization and increase their income, gaining tax benefits, while the invested funds work to enhance the financial status of a church building project or long-term mission program. Donors in the gift annuity plan present an agreed amount of securities to the church, and in return, the donor receives an annual income of a previously arranged sum for as long as the donor lives. The gift annuity allows the donor to increase his yearly income from the investment without a corresponding increase in taxes due. With actuarial values and the amount of the gift value of the contract applied as a credit for a contribution, the donor may find himself with a full return on his investment inside of three years time, let alone the benefits accrued by the local church.

The charitable remainder annuity trust and the charitable remainder unitrust are deferred-giving programs that could provide previously untapped income sources for the local church. Either trust provides for at least annual payments to a noncharitable beneficiary for an established period of time. At the end of the period, the remainder interest is used for the benefit of the designated charity, in our case, a religious organization. The creator of the trust is entitled to a charitable income[37] and gift[38] tax deduction for the fair market value of the remainder interest.

Such a trust may also be created through a will, entitling the estate to deduct the fair market value of the remainder gift as a charitable bequest.[39] The charitable remainder trust is free from income tax unless there is unrelated business income associated with it. Many rules must be complied with in establishing the trust; therefore, it is advisable to employ qualified legal counsel to draft a trust agreement.

Other methods of donor contributions to the local church include donating life insurance policies with the church as beneficiary. The individual donating the irrevocable policy may deduct both the replacement value of the policy and payment of future premiums. In the alternative, the individual may wish to donate an irrevocable life insurance policy to the church, taking a charitable deduction in return. Many have donated real estate or personal property to the church during life or through their wills at death. Again, the individual or the estate may take a charitable deduction for the fair market value of the donated gift.

(See chapter 14 for more details on contributions.)

Laws concerning the tax exempt organization are rapidly changing, and are becoming increasingly hostile to the once favored tax position of the religious organization. Influenced by the need for greater levels of revenue, governments are eyeing the untapped source of the tax exempt entity to reduce the growing federal deficit. Unfortunately, many proposed changes in the law regarding the tax exempt entity are fueled more by increasing need for state revenue than by substantive policy choices.

13

Tax Planning
for Religious Workers

*What tax advantages does the full-time Christian worker enjoy?
How should such an individual plan his or her financial future in
view of these advantages? This chapter outlines basic financial and
tax principles relevant to the Christian worker.*

Whether a religious worker is considered to be an employee of a religious organization or church or is considered to be self-employed plays a pivotal role in determining how tax laws will be applied. In other words, status is the key concept for religious workers. Employee/self-employed status affects matters such as how social security will be taxed to ministers, how income taxes and deductions are figured, along with numerous other deductions. This chapter explores the ramifications of the religious worker's employment status, social security benefits, income tax, proper filing of tax forms, housing allowance qualifications, qualified retirement plans, along with miscellaneous deductions available to the religious worker.

Employee or Self-Employed?

On what basis is the religious worker classified as either an employee or self-employed? For tax purposes the common law rules are applied by

This chapter was written by Michele Bachmann.

the IRS to determine employment status. A facts-and-circumstances test is used, which means the IRS will look at a particular case with a particular set of factors to make a determination; no hard and fast rule is applied to divergent cases. Treasury regulations state: "Generally, if you perform services subject to the will and control of an employer, both as to what will be done and how it will be done, you are an employee. It does not matter if the employer allows you considerable discretion and freedom of action, as long as the employer has the legal right to control both the method and the result of the services."[1] To receive a definitive word on status, a person may obtain a written ruling from the Internal Revenue Service by filing Form SS-8, Information for Use in Determining Whether a Worker Is an Employee for Federal Employment Taxes and Income Tax Withholding.

Social Security—Who Is Covered?

Both ministers and members of religious orders are covered by social security under the self-employment provisions if they are ordained, commissioned, or licensed by action of a religious body (for the duties performed in the capacity as a religious worker), unless the individual has formally requested and received an exemption from the self-employment tax. The IRS defines "ministers of the gospel" as "individuals who are duly ordained, commissioned, or licensed to the pastoral ministry by action of a religious body constituting a church or church denomination and given the authority to conduct religious worship, to perform sacerdotal functions, and to administer ordinances or sacraments according to the prescribed tenets and principles of that church or church denomination."[2] Similarly, social security coverage also applies to members of religious orders who have not taken a vow of poverty and who have not applied for exemption from social security tax. Note that members of a religious order who have taken a vow of poverty may gain coverage under social security if the religious order or an autonomous subdivision files for coverage for the members through Form SS-16, Certificate of Election of Coverage.

What of the lay employee of the religious organization; must that individual be covered by social security? Yes, automatically all employees are covered under social security unless an exemption is filed using

Form 4361. As an employee, the religious lay worker's salary is subject to social security tax via employer withholding, not through the self-employment tax. However, the religious employer may elect to exclude all employees from social security coverage. If this avenue is chosen, the lay religious worker will not be exempt from paying the social security tax; rather, the employee will be personally responsible for paying the full amount of the tax on his earnings. Although technically following the "self-employed" route, the lay employee should be aware he cannot subtract trade or business expenses in computing the self-employment income. This is to ensure that a like amount of self-employment earnings will be subject to social security tax as compared to the "employee" of the religious organization. Regarding filing, any lay religious worker who receives $100 or more in earnings from an electing church or religious organization is directed to complete Schedule SE in connection with the regular Form 1040 income tax return.[3]

How Is Social Security Paid?

Perhaps nowhere does the employee/self-employed status distinction play a more important role than in the method of paying social security tax, as the tax may be collected in two different ways dependent upon whether the religious worker is considered an employee or is self-employed. If the religious worker is classified as an employee, the Federal Insurance Contributions Act (FICA)[4] requires a portion of the tax burden be paid by the employee, with the remainder paid by the employer. Under the Self-Employment Contributions Act (SECA)[5] the full brunt of the tax is borne by the self-employed individual. Services performed by the religious worker in the course of his employment are subject to social security coverage under SECA. As a result, any monies gained from the performance of these services will also be subject to taxation for social security unless the worker falls under one of the following two categories: (1) The religious worker is a member of a religious order who has taken a vow of poverty, or (2) The religious worker has requested and received from the Internal Revenue Service an exemption from self-employment tax for the services.[6]

To gain exemption from self-employment tax, one must file Form 4361 with the Internal Revenue Service. This form is available to the religious worker who has not previously elected social security coverage and who wishes to be exempt from the self-employment tax for his ministerial services. In filing Form 4361, the religious worker must sign a statement declaring he or she is "conscientiously opposed to, or because of religious principles, the person is opposed to accepting, for services performed as a member of the clergy, public (governmental) insurance that makes payments in the event of death, disability, old age, or retirement. This includes public insurance that makes payments toward the cost of, or provides services for, medical care, including the benefits of any insurance system established by the Social Security Act."[7] The key here lies with the religious worker who must certify that because of his sincerely held religious beliefs he is opposed to accepting public (governmental) benefits of any kind. This formal objection must be founded upon the doctrines, ideals, or principles of the employer-religious denomination or on the specific dictates of the individual conscience of the religious worker. As a caveat, if the religious worker has employment in addition to his religious duties he need not be opposed to accepting social security benefits for services performed in the extra-religious capacity.[8]

Note that a religious worker cannot file an application for exemption if his opposition to the social security tax is based only on economic reasons;[9] this is not considered a valid election by the IRS, and self-employment tax must be paid.

Exemption from Social Security Tax

To begin the process for filing for exemption from self-employment tax by ministers or members of religious orders, the religious worker must first inform his ordaining, commissioning, or licensing body of the church or order that he is personally opposed to accepting public insurance.[10] Next, he must sign a prewritten statement on Form 4361 (available at the local IRS office), which verifies the religious worker is aware of the grounds on which the exemption is allowed and that it is upon these grounds the exemption is sought.[11] The organization with which the religious worker is employed must be a valid tax exempt organization approved under Section 501(c)(3) and must be a church, convention, or association of churches.[12] Form 4361 must be filed with the IRS by the date the religious worker's income tax return is due, no later than the second tax year in which the individual has at least $400 in self-employment earnings, any part of which was a result of employment performed as a minister or member of a religious order.[13]

Revocation of the Tax Exempt Status

A church, religious organization, or religious worker may choose to revoke a previous election to be exempt from social security coverage. In other words, one may opt to get back into the social security system. (Caution must prevail, however, in opting back into the social security system, as once coverage is elected, it is a for-life arrangement, irrevocable; it cannot be changed.[14]) Revocation of the tax exempt status may occur by filing Form 2031, Application for Revocation, and by meeting the following conditions: (1) File before the person becomes entitled to social security old age or disability benefits, and (2) no later than the due date (including extensions) of the federal income tax return.[15] Liability will inevitably result for self-employment taxes and interest for the tax year for which the election back into the social security system is effective. Without an exemption, or if the exemption is revoked, the amounts received for performing services as a religious worker are subject to self-employment tax.

Income Tax and the Pastor

The IRS traditionally regards the minister as self-employed, but it is possible for the pastor to be defined as an employee under the previously discussed common-law test. This status distinction is important as to what can and cannot be deducted from the minister's gross income, especially deductible business expenses. Must a minister file an income tax return? Almost without exception, the answer is yes. The only exceptions are those individuals who fall below the floor of certain income levels. Income levels vary depending upon whether the individual is married, or age 65 or older.[16] The minister will file Form 1040. Assuming they are self-employed for income tax purposes, ministers pay an estimated tax, and as such they cannot use the 1040EZ form or the 1040A short form. A pastor will figure his estimated federal income taxes, along with social security taxes if he is not exempt, on a worksheet attached to Form 1040-ES.[17] The pastor should estimate his adjusted gross income, subtract estimated credits, deductions, and exemptions. From this point, estimated taxable income is multiplied by the applicable tax rate found in the Tax Rate Schedule in Form 1040-ES. The pastor will then file a payment voucher included in Form 1040-ES and send this along with the attached quarterly payment to the IRS. At the end of the pastor's taxable year, he will figure his actual tax liability on Form 1040. If the pastor determines he overpaid tax during the year, he can credit his overpayment against future tax liability. If the pastor has underpaid his tax, he must use Form 2210 to compute any penalty or underpayment.

Pastors who are considered employees of their church or religious organization should receive a W-2 form from their employer to report the salary paid by the church to the pastor.[18] If the pastor is considered self-employed, the employer-church can report the self-employed pastor's earnings on Form 1099, which details nonemployee compensation. What should the pastor include as gross income? Are "love offerings" or seasonal collections a gift, and therefore exempt from income tax, or are they part of the pastor's gross income? Generally, the intention of the transferor (the giver) controls the result of the transaction. If the collection is given with the thought of compensation in mind, it is regarded as income and must be reported as such by the pastor. If the offering is intended as a gift, given with the idea of nothing expected in return, it may be excluded from income.[19] A facts-and-circumstances test is employed by the IRS. If the gift is given by the church entity and is based on years of service with the idea of compensating the pastor for services rendered, the "gift" may be recharacterized by the IRS as taxable income, whereas a freewill offering made up of individual donations given out of a spirit of appreciation and regard for the pastor may be viewed as a true gift, not reportable as taxable income.

Miscellaneous Deductions

The pastor should be aware of several deductions that may be available to him. Among these are job-related expenses, travel expenses, moving expenses, and educational expenses. Job-related expenses include items such as mileage while attending to ministerial duties, supplies needed to perform ministerial tasks, a telephone line specifically for church business. These expenses are deductible by the pastor, but like other available deductions require careful, contemporaneous record keeping of the expenses, i.e., saving canceled checks, credit card reports, receipts. If the pastor has a self-employed status he may deduct job-related expenses from his income using the Professional Expense Schedule C. However, if the pastor has an employee status he must use Employee Business Expense, Form 2106. Travel expenses while allowable as deductions must be carefully substantiated with "adequate records by sufficient evidence corroborating taxpayer's own statements." These expenses must be both ordinary and necessary and come as the result of a pastor performing his professional duties.[20] Moving expenses for a pastor are also deductible, but there is a distance requirement: The new pastorate must be more than thirty-five miles from the pastor's former residence.[21] Educational expenses are deductible for the pastor if they do not qualify him for a new trade or profession, or if they are reasonably necessary to maintain or improve skills in his present profession.[22] Work toward advanced theology degrees would probably be deductible, whereas work toward a law degree would not. Tax laws concerning deductions change rapidly. The above brief overview of potential deductions is a partial list in a rapidly changing tax environment. The pastor should consult his accountant or lawyer for the latest tax changes.

Section 107 Housing Allowance

A pastor must satisfy the following conditions before he can exclude the housing allowance from gross income.

1. A designated housing allowance must be used for a home, that is, "a dwelling place (including furnishings) and the appurtenances thereto, such as a garage."[23] Monies spent by a pastor on a farm or business in addition to the amounts spent on the house will not qualify for the housing allowance exemption.[24]

2. The employing church must state its intent, in writing, that a portion of the pastor's salary is for housing.[25] It is important to the

IRS that the church's intent and the percentage or dollar amount be spelled out in the clearest terms covering what is and what is not included in the pastor's housing allowance, i.e., furnishings, utilities, garage rental, etc.

3. Amounts excluded from taxation are limited to the actual housing expenses the pastor incurs during the particular taxable year. What do "expenses incurred to rent or provide a home" include? The IRS allows rents paid for housing, amounts paid for the purchase of a home, and costs related to providing a home.[26] A church may help the pastor here considerably by agreeing to pay for furnishings, appurtenances, utilities, property taxes, insurance for the home, and repairs to the home.

4. The amount of the housing allowance designated to the pastor is limited to an amount not more than the reasonable value of the pastor's services to the church or religious organization, i.e., his earnings.[27] If the pastor owns his own home, the housing allowance designated by the church or religious organization may not be greater than either the fair rental value of the pastor's home (including furnishings and costs of utilities) or the church-designated allowance.[28] The same limits hold true for the pastor who rents an apartment or other dwelling while serving in the pastorate. The pastor who lives in a parsonage (a residence owned by a church or religious organization), may exclude from his income the fair market rental value of the parsonage. The pastor may also include the cost of utilities and furnishings if the church so allows.

The housing allowance is not reported on the pastor's income tax return. In addition, the W-2 form, issued by the church to the pastor, should not include or list the housing exclusion. For example, if a pastor is paid $35,000 but the church directs that $15,000 should pay for the housing allowance, the W-2 form should list only $20,000 as taxable income. If the pastor is self-employed, the church should report the pastor's salary without including the housing allowance on Form 1099. Any amounts given which exceed the designated housing allowance should be listed as income.

Who qualifies for the housing allowance exemption? Does the "minister of music" or the "minister of education"? IRS revenue rulings have held these individuals are not entitled to the housing allowance exclusion, because these offices do not fit the IRS definition of "an ordained, commissioned, or licensed minister of the gospel."[29] Ministers qualify for the housing allowance only if they are licensed or ordained by their religious denomination or body, and if they perform "substantially all of the religious functions" of an ordained pastor.[30] New court cases have given insight into an expanded definition of "ordained." Before 1978, Rev. Ruling 65-124 was very strict in stating that a minister had to be able to perform "all" the religious functions of the church to be defined as "ordained" for tax purposes. In 1978, Rev. Ruling 78-301 added the word "substantially" to the definition in order to allow Jewish cantors to qualify for parsonage allowance. Until 1989, no case was available to give us a clear definition of the word "substantially." Surviving spouses of deceased pastors do not qualify for the housing exclusion. Also, retired pastors must meet the above listed conditions to remain qualified for the housing exemption.[31]

Qualified Retirement Plans

Qualified retirement plans offer a terrific opportunity for financial planning, and should be taken advantage of as part of a religious worker's compensation package. Both the religious organization and the religious worker will benefit taxwise by implementing a qualified retirement plan.[32] Among the advantages, the employer-church will gain a tax deduction for all contributions to employee retirement plans. Second, the employee will defer payment of tax on his interest income earned on retirement savings. Best of all, the contributions to the retirement fund are excluded from the employee's salary. When retirement funds are paid out to a retired pastor, the IRS views the funds as taxable income and they must be so reported on Form 1040.

Today self-employed pastors may also benefit from a retirement fund, though this was not always the case.[33] The problem was with the term *employee*. Formerly a self-employed person could not by definition become his own employee. Today the term employee may include nearly all self-employed individuals. One exception remains for common law employees, those who are viewed as employed by the church. Even though they may not participate in a Keogh plan for wages received from their services to the employer-church,[34] they may create a Keogh plan for income received directly from parishioners, or for performing marriages, baptisms, funerals, and other personal services.[35] It is a good idea to use an accountant or tax lawyer in evaluating your tax status and making financial decisions. The time you save and the security of making wise decisions that will not cause problems later will be well worth the investment.

14

Charitable Giving: Funding the Christian Challenge

In this chapter, the focus is on the individual church member who wishes to make the best investment of his or her financial resources to further the work of the ministry, while at the same time take advantage of the tax breaks available for such charitable giving.

Charitable Giving in America

In America there is never only one way to do anything. People want a choice for everything, and charitable giving is no exception. This chapter describes more than twenty different ways people can benefit their church or ministry and still receive a tax deduction. Some of the suggestions are remarkably simple, others very complex and require professional help. However, if churches and ministries are going to prosper financially in an age where marketing techniques for charitable dollars are becoming increasingly more persuasive and sophisticated, they will have to rely on building strong relationships with their donors and tailoring financial requests to meet the donors' giving desires and needs. Many of the suggestions contained in this chapter deal with what has commonly been referred to as planned giving. Smaller churches and ministries may feel

This chapter was written by V. William Moritz.

that they are not equipped to handle planned giving prospects, and they are probably right. However, that should not stop the church or ministry from finding reliable help in this area from a qualified professional or consultant. Many donors would love to make these types of gifts to the churches and ministries they care about. However, if the organizations will not give them a chance, they wind up giving to larger ministries or to a denomination that will help them with their planning.

The following information is not presented with the expectation that Christian leaders will become expert in the utilization of the various tools available, but only that they will gain a stark awareness of the possibilities, work harder at helping donors accomplish their giving goals, and know when to get professional help. Fund raising is more an art form than an exact science. It is not so much what is done, but often why, when, how, where, and to whom that is more important. It is possible to use this information resource to procure some substantial gifts for the work of Christ.

Outright Gifts during Life

The federal government actually encourages gifts to churches and ministries by allowing charitable income tax deductions for a variety of different types of gifts. The following eleven types of gifts are in the category of one-time gifts that take place during a person's life.

Gifts of Money

Gifts of money are by far the most common type of charitable contribution received by churches and ministries, and for many ministries it is the only type they know how to receive. The donor can deduct up to 50 percent of his adjusted gross income for a gift of money. If the donor's contribution exceeds 50 percent of his adjusted gross income, he has a five-year carry-over of the excess contributions for use in later tax years.[1] Churches and ministries need to be sensitive to the most convenient methods of giving for their donors. For many on fixed or salaried incomes the monthly pledge is most effective. For others whose income is more sporadic or may be tied to business year-end accountings, the large single gift may be more convenient.

Gifts of Securities and Real Estate Held Long Term

Gifts of securities and real estate that have been held longer than one year receive significant preferential treatment under the tax code. The contributed property is deductible at the full present fair market value. The donor is also not subject to a capital gain on the appreciation of the property. Fair market value is somewhat of an arbitrary standard, defined as the price at which the property would change hands between a willing buyer and a willing seller. When a donor claims an income tax charitable deduction for a gift of capital gain property, the appreciation on the gift is an alternative minimum tax (AMT) preference item. Although most taxpayers are not subject to the AMT, it is important to advise them of this potential problem and have them check it out with their accountants to avoid any unpleasant surprises.

The donor can deduct up to 30 percent of his adjusted gross income in the year of the gift. Again, as with gifts of money, there is a five-year carry-over for excess contributions. Under a special election, a donor may increase his ceiling to 50 percent of adjusted gross income by making the same gift, but electing to reduce the amount of the deduction to the cost basis of the property.[2] If the value of the gift is over $500 the donor must file IRS Form 8283.

Gifts of Securities and Real Estate Held Short Term

Gifts of securities and real estate held for less than twelve months do not receive the same favorable treatment that property held long term receives. The charitable deduction is limited to the donor's cost basis in the contributed property regardless of the amount of appreciation. The donor is, however, allowed to deduct up to 50 percent of his adjusted gross income in the year of the gift, with a five-year carry-over for excess contributions.[3] If the value of the gift is over $500 the donor must file IRS Form 8283.

Gifts of Ordinary Income Property

The gift of inventory, crops, art works created by the donor, or collapsible stock are treated the same as property held short term. The donor will only receive a deduction for the cost basis of the property, not for its fair market value. The donor is allowed to deduct up to 50 percent of his adjusted gross income in the year of the gift with a five-year carry-over for excess contributions.[4] If the value of the gift is over $500 the donor must file IRS Form 8283.

Gifts of Tangible Personal Property Held Long Term

Gifts of tangible personal property held longer than six months, such as art work, books, antiques, etc., come under a related use test for determining the amount of the deduction. A related-use gift is defined as property that is directly related to the exempt function of the organization. Gifts of property that qualify under this related purpose test are allowed a deduction for the full fair market value of the property as of the date of contribution, with no capital gain on the appreciation. The donor will be allowed to deduct up to 30 percent of his adjusted gross income in the year of the contribution, with a five-year carry-over for excess contributions.[5] Gifts of tangible personal property which are unrelated to the organization's function qualify only for a deduction value of the donor's cost basis in the property.[6] The donor may deduct up to 50 percent of his adjusted gross income for this type of gift, with a five-year carry-over for excess contributions. If the value of the gift is over $500 the donor must file IRS Form 8283.

Bargain Sales of Property

A bargain sale is a part sale and part gift that occurs when a person sells a piece of property held long term to a church or ministry for a price below the fair market value. There will be a charitable deduction for the difference between the fair market value of the property and the sale price. There is, however, a slight complication in the capital gains implications. The donor's cost basis in the property must be allocated between the portion of the property "sold" and the portion of the property "given" to the church or ministry based on the fair market value of each portion. Appreciation allocable to the "sale" portion is subject to capital gains taxation while the appreciation allocable to the "gift" portion is not.[7] One additional caution is to watch out for inadvertent bargain sales which result from the transfer of property subject to a mortgage; this will be considered a bargain sale.[8]

Gifts from Corporations

Many individuals find that giving through their closely held corporation or influencing the giving program of a public corporation can be a very attractive way to help a church or ministry at a lower actual cost to them personally. Corporations may give up to 10 percent of their taxable income to a church or ministry. As with an individual there is a five-year carry-over for excess contributions.[9]

Gifts of Life Insurance

Encouraging donors to make a church or ministry the owner and beneficiary of a life insurance policy can create a rather attractive leveraged gift. The gift of a policy on which premiums remain to be paid will produce an income tax deduction for slightly above the cash surrender value of the policy. However, if that amount exceeds the policy's cost basis, the deduction will be only for the cost basis.[10]

Continued payment of premiums will give rise to a charitable deduction for the annual premiums. The gift of a fully paid-up policy will result in an income tax deduction for the replacement value of the policy, unless the amount exceeds the cost basis in the policy, in which case the deduction will be for the cost basis.[11]

Gifts of a Partial Interest in Property

The general rule is that there is no deduction for a gift of less than the donor's entire interest in the property. However, a donor may give a partial interest in a piece of property and receive a deduction for the full fair market value of the interest as long as the gift is an undivided interest in the donor's entire interest in the property. Through the use of this technique a donor could delay the total gift of a piece of property to increase the number of years he would have for the charitable deduction.[12]

Gifts of Remainder Interests in Personal Residence or Farm

The donor can obtain both an income and estate tax benefit by making a gift of his or her personal residence or farm and retaining the right to use the property for life. The life estate may be retained for one or more lives. Generally there is no capital gain to the donor on the appreciation of the property unless the church or ministry assumes the indebtedness. The income tax deduction will be based on the value of the remainder interest transferred to the church or ministry minus any depreciation that has been taken on the property.[13]

Outright Gifts at Death

An outright gift at death, commonly known as a charitable bequest, is any gift included in a person's will or living trust that is triggered by the person's death. A charitable bequest can be a very appropriate way to provide for a family and the church or ministry of choice. Churches and ministries have found that merely providing information on the different options available to people has resulted in many of their members or donors remembering them in their wills or trusts. While this, of course, does not produce current income to the organization, the potential for future funds to the church or ministry can be significant. Given the options listed below, any persons should be able to include the churches and/or ministries of their choice in their estate plans.

A General Bequest

A general bequest may provide a specific sum of money or a designated percentage of the estate to go to a church or ministry. Specific items of property can also be named. A designated percentage is most often the best choice, because it will usually more accurately reflect the donor's priorities if the estate rises or falls in value.

A Residual Clause Bequest

A residual clause may designate the remainder of the estate or a portion of that remainder to go to a church or ministry after the needs of loved ones have been met. Specific bequests are made to family and friends, and then anything left over in the estate goes to the Lord's work.

A Contingent Bequest

A contingent bequest is rarely utilized, but can be one of the most attractive options available to a family who doesn't believe their estate is large enough to make a bequest to a church or ministry. In the will or trust the donor states that should none of the heirs survive him or her at the time of the donor's death, then a portion or all of most of the estate should go to a church or ministry. Many persons who wish to provide for their immediate families would like to see at least part of their estates go to the Lord's work instead of to distant relatives should their spouse and children predecease them or die at the same time. Studies have shown that in as many as 20 percent of the cases where this type of bequest is used, the contingent bequests pay off.

A Bequest Providing an Income

A bequest can be structured to provide an income for a loved one for a term of years or lifetime with the remainder going to a church or ministry. Many times parents who have set up a testamentary trust for their children in their will want to have the full value of the trust assets kept together until the children reach a certain age, to insure that there will be enough money to pay for health or educational needs. But once the children reach that age, the parents would like to see a portion of the trust assets go to a ministry or church at the time they are distributed to the children. Others may wish to make sure that a mother or father is taken care of until death, and then the remaining assets can go on to charity.

Contractual Beneficiary Arrangements

Contractual beneficiary documents, such as insurance policies and retirement benefits, are another important way that individuals can remember churches or ministries. By naming a church or ministry as partial beneficiary or contingent beneficiary, a person can provide for the family and still make a significant gift to the Lord's work. Experts have predicted that the next generation of millionaires will come as a result of insurance proceeds and retirement benefits. A church or ministry could also be named as a residual beneficiary for a fixed-term annuity purchased by the donor with his retirement benefits, so that if the donor failed to survive the term, the balance would go to the Lord's work.

Interest-Free Loans

If a donor has already reached the maximum amount allowable for charitable contributions and would still like to make additional gifts, the interest-free loan may be a legitimate option. The donor can make a loan to the church or ministry of an amount of money or piece of income-producing property using a demand note. The ministry may then use the interest or income earned by the property to further its purposes. The donor then will not have to report the interest or income earned as taxable income. Although uncharged interest is generally imputed to lenders of interest-free loans, the treasury regulations exempt charitable loans up to $250,000 per charity.[14]

Gifts Given in Trust

There are several different types of charitable trusts, as well as gifts given in exchange for an income such as annuities, which call for the church or ministry to assume a fiduciary relationship with the donor. A church or ministry need not be able to administrate these types of trusts and gifts to be able to benefit from them. Many banks, brokerages, and private foundations will set up and administer these types of complicated giving alternatives, usually for a small setup fee and then a commission on the investment return. The accounting and administration for these kinds of gifts can be very cumbersome, so establishing a relationship with an organization or several organizations who can help with these kind of gifts can be very beneficial.

In any of the charitable instruments listed below whereby a beneficiary receives an income, that income may be deferred until a designated later date such as retirement. This allows the principal to increase in size tax free, which provides for larger annual payments and a larger tax deduction at inception.

Charitable Remainder Trusts

Charitable remainder trusts provide that a named beneficiary or beneficiaries shall receive an income from the trust for a period of years or life and then the remaining assets in the trust shall go to a church or ministry. This type of trust is an irrevocable trust and after it is established the donor cannot get the transferred assets back. The donor does, however, receive a charitable deduction in the year that the trust is established for an amount equal to the value of the remainder interest transferred to charity. The amount of the deduction can be computed using actuarial tables in the Internal Revenue Code.[15] There are no restrictions in the Internal Revenue Code about who may serve as trustee, so if the donor has done well with his investments he may serve as co-trustee of the trust.

The amounts paid to the beneficiaries of charitable remainder trusts retain the character they had in the trust. The payments will be treated in the following manner: (1) as ordinary income to the extent of the trust's ordinary income for the year and undistributed ordinary income from prior years, (2) as capital gain to the extent of the trust's capital gain for the year and prior years, (3) as tax exempt income to the extent of the trust's exempt income for the year and previous years, and (4) as a tax-free distribution of principal. There is no capital gain incurred on transfer of appreciated assets to a charitable remainder trust. Nor is there capital gain to donor on a sale by the trust of the appreciated property. However, when the income is received by the donor it will be taxable under the four-tier system. There are two primary types of charitable remainder trusts; the unitrust and the annuity trust.

The charitable remainder unitrust, probably the most common of the two, specifies that the income beneficiary or beneficiaries receive annual payments determined by multiplying a fixed percentage (at least 5 percent and usually no more than 10 percent) by the net fair market value of the trust assets, as determined each year. This type of trust can act as a hedge against inflation, because if the trust earns more than the fixed percentage in interest, the extra is added to the value of the trust, and the payment the following year is based on the new net fair market value. One acceptable variation of this trust allows the trustee to pay only what the trust earns in income, if the income is less than the stated percentage. The deficiency can then be made up in later years when the trust income exceeds the stated percentage.

The charitable remainder annuity trust differs from the unitrust in that it provides for a fixed dollar amount (at least five percent) of the initial fair market value of the property transferred to the trust, to be paid annually to the income beneficiary or beneficiaries. This form of charitable trust provides a fixed payment regardless of the income the trust earns, unless payments from income only are specified.

Gift Annuities

In a charitable gift annuity a donor transfers money or property to a church or ministry in exchange for its promise to pay a fixed amount annually to the donor and a survivor if desired for life. The transfer is really a part gift and part purchase of an annuity. The charitable deduction is based on the value of the remainder interest using the Treasury tables in the Internal Revenue Code.[16] The payment the annuitant receives each year is partially a return of capital that is untaxed and partially an interest payment that is taxable as income. There is a capital gain when the gift annuity is funded with appreciated property. However, the amount of the gain is smaller than it would have been on a sale, and further the gain is reported ratably over the annuitant's life expectancy.[17]

Pooled Income Funds

With a pooled income fund a donor irrevocably transfers money or securities to a church or ministry. The church or ministry then adds the donor's gift to its separately maintained pooled income fund where it is invested together with similar gifts from other donors. Each donor then gets a pro rata share of the fund much like a share in a mutual fund and then receives his share of the fund's earnings each year. The income that the beneficiary receives is taxed as ordinary income. At the beneficiary's death the church or ministry may then remove the principal from the fund and use it for its purposes. A charitable deduction is allowed for the value of the remainder interest as determined by the Internal Revenue Treasury tables. No capital gain is incurred on transferring appreciated assets to a pooled income fund. The fund takes over the donor's basis and holding period.[18]

Charitable Lead Trusts

In larger estates the charitable lead trust can be an excellent vehicle to pass property to other family members without incurring estate, gift, or generation-skipping tax. The trusts are irrevocable and provide that the trust shall make payments to a designated church or ministry for a term of years, with reversion to the donor or to someone else at the end of the term. To avoid income tax to the donor or gift tax to another beneficiary, the donor's reversionary interest or gift must be worth less than five percent of the trust principal. The donor may deduct up to 30 percent of his adjusted gross income with a five-year carry-over for excess contributions.[19]

If the trust is a nongrantor trust, then the donor is entitled to a current income tax deduction in the year of funding. If the trust is a grantor trust, then the donor is entitled to an income tax deduction for the actuarial value of the charitable interest at the time of transfer to the trust, but the trust income is taxable to the donor each year without a deduction for the amount paid to charity. This is valuable only when a donor expects a large amount of income in the year the charitable lead trust is established, with subsequent years at lower levels.

As with the charitable remainder trusts, a charitable lead trust may either be a unitrust or an annuity trust. The unitrust would specify a fixed percentage of the net fair market value of the trust assets for payment to the church or ministry each year, while the annuity trust would specify a fixed amount at the initial funding of the trust and pay that amount each year to the church or ministry.

Charitable Revocable Living Trusts

A donor who is unsure if he or she will need an amount of money or piece of property later in life may set up a charitable revocable living trust. The charitable revocable living trust would pay all of the income or as much of the income as desired each year to the donor for as long as it is in existence. The donor also may invade the principal at any time for any reason. When the donor or donors die, any money left in the trust will then go to the church and/or ministries designated in the trust. The income earned each year is taxable to the donor, because he has retained the right to revoke the trust. However, the estate will receive a charitable estate tax deduction at the donor's death, and the assets will pass to the charities free of probate. If the donor acts as co-trustee with the church or ministry, the trust does not need to file a separate tax return.

Final Pointers on Gifts

Several issues arise routinely regarding gifts to charity. The following is a small list of the most common problems and how to deal with them.

The Price of a Ticket or a Gift Premium

When a church or ministry operates a charitable event or gives away gift premiums for donations, the contribution value is based on the amount given by the donor minus the value of the ticket, meal, or other privilege received. Even if a corporate sponsor paid for the premiums so that it did not cost the church or ministry any money, the value of what was received is what counts. If a gift receipt is given for the contribution, it should reflect the actual contribution value, not the price of the ticket.[20] One caveat: If the church or ministry offers a gift to anyone regardless of whether or not they contribute, then the fair market value of the gift need not be deducted from the contribution.

Enforceability of Pledges

Normally, verbal pledges to give financial support to a church or ministry will not be legally binding on the part of the donor, because the organization has not given up anything for the promise. There are, however, several procedures which can make a pledge legally enforceable. If the pledge was given to entice others to give, then the donor has received some consideration; and if the organization has made it known to the donor that it is relying on the donor's pledge in authorizing expenditures or in seeking other contributions, then there would be "detrimental reliance" by the organization on the donor, creating a legally enforceable promise. The reality of the situation, though, is that it will be extremely bad public relations to try to enforce pledges. However, if there are people who would like to give at a later date and the church would like to use the amount of their pledge as incentive to others or justification for a loan, then the following pledge form may be useful:

In consideration of the pledges of others, I hereby agree to give the (church or ministry), a charitable institution located at _____, _____ dollars by the end of calendar year _____, said amount to be paid at the end of the year. I recognize that the (church or ministry) will rely on my gift in securing the pledges of others and in authorizing expenses of the (church or ministry) to be paid in anticipation of the payment of my pledge.

Substantiation of Charitable Contributions—IRS Form 8283

Strict appraisal, appraisal summary, and information reporting requirements are imposed when property gifts, other than marketable securities, are claimed as income tax charitable deductions. The rules apply to property contributions claimed at over $5,000 per item or group of similar items, whether or not they are donated to the same charity. There is a special exception for closely held stock of $10,000, but if the claimed value is over $5,000, an appraisal summary is required. Easier reporting rules apply for property gifts valued at $500 to $5,000. Gifts below $500 have no special reporting requirements. Any donor making a property gift valued over $500 must complete IRS Form 8283 and submit it with his annual tax return. If the church or ministry sells the item of property within two years of receipt of the gift, it must be reported to the IRS and to the donor on IRS Form 8282. There are penalties imposed for failure to comply with these regulations.[21]

Volunteer Expenses

Actual tangible unreimbursed volunteer expenses are deductible when they are incurred in rendering services for a church or ministry. There is an optional standard mileage rate of twelve cents per mile for unreimbursed automobile expenses. No deduction will be allowed, however, if "there is a significant element of personal pleasure, recreation, or vacation" involved in the travel. Also, unreimbursed baby sitting expenses incurred to render volunteer services are not deductible. It might be wise for churches and ministries to set up special accounts to pay for these kinds of expenses and then allow any interested persons to designate contributions for those purposes.[22]

Services Provided for a Church or Ministry

Services provided to a church or ministry are not deductible by the provider. However, tangible expenses incurred on behalf of the church or ministry, such as materials purchased, are deductible. If the services provided are the same or similar to those you offer to the general public, you may be able to issue a bill to the church or ministry and then forgive it or treat it as a bad debt and obtain a deduction in that manner.[23]

Allowing a Charity to Use a Piece of Property

There is no charitable deduction for allowing a charity to use a piece of property. No deduction will be allowed unless a donor gives away an undivided interest in his or her whole interest (i.e., a percentage interest in the property).

Relying on the Determination Letter of a Church or Ministry

If tax exempt status is sought by a church or ministry, the Internal Revenue Service will determine whether contributions to an organization are eligible for a charitable contribution deduction. It will issue a "determination letter" to this effect to the organization and add the organization's name to its list of qualified organizations.[24]

If the organization is listed in the Cumulative List of Organizations, donors may rely on the fact that gifts made to the organization are deductible for income tax purposes. Even if an organization's determination letter is revoked, a donor may rely on the fact that the organization was listed at the time of the contribution, unless they were aware of the change in the organization's status.[25]

15

Clergy and Political Activity

The IRS's treatment of legislative and political activities by clergymen and organizations exempt from tax under Section 501(c)(3) of the Internal Revenue Code (the Code) is subject to changing IRS interpretations, and it is dangerous to generalize based upon specific cases. Nevertheless, certain general principles may be relied upon with reasonable certainty. These are summarized below, along with the answers to some frequently asked questions. This article should not be interpreted as legal advice respecting any particular fact situation. Clergymen should consult their own tax advisors with respect to their particular circumstances.[1]

An organization is exempt from tax under Section 501(c)(3) if it is:

a corporation, . . . fund, or foundation, organized and operated exclusively for religious, charitable, scientific, testing for public safety, literary, or educational purposes,

. . . no part of the net earnings of which inures to the benefit of any private shareholder or individual, no substantial part of the activities of which is carrying on propaganda, or otherwise attempting to influence legislation (except as otherwise provided in subsection (h)), and which does not participate in, or intervene in (including the publishing and dis-

This chapter was written by Alan P. Dye.

165

tributing of statements), any political campaign on behalf of any candidate for public office.

It is apparent from the language of the statute that an *organization* exempt from tax under Section 501(c)(3) may undertake *no activity whatever* on behalf of or in opposition to any candidate for public office, federal, state, or local. This is an absolute prohibition.

Legislative activities, as contrasted to political activities, are permissible for such an organization. However, the statute specifically prescribes that no *substantial* part of the activities of such an organization may be devoted to activities intended to influence legislation.

The IRS regulations under Section 501(c)(3) elaborate on the general statutory requirements as follows:

(3) *Authorization of legislative or political activities.* An organization is not organized exclusively for one or more exempt purposes if its articles expressly empower it—

(i) To devote more than an insubstantial part of its activities to attempting to influence legislation by propaganda or otherwise; or

(ii) Directly or indirectly to participate in, or intervene in (including the publishing or distributing of statements), any political campaign on behalf of or in opposition to any candidate for public office; or

(iii) To have objectives and to engage in activities which characterize it as an "action" organization as defined in paragraph (c)(3) of this section.

Sections 1/501(c)(3)–1(b)(3)(i) and (ii) of the above regulation merely restate Section 501(c)(3) and its prohibition of political activity and limitations on legislative activity, but subsection (iii) expands the limitations placed upon charitable or educational organizations to preclude Section 501(c)(3) status for so-called action organizations, which are defined to include any organization that contacts or urges the public to contact legislators regarding legislation, or which itself advocates the adoption or rejection of legislation.

The statute does not define the term *substantial* for purposes of determining whether an organization qualifies under Section 501 (c)(3). One court case held that an organization may devote at least 5 percent of its activities to lobbying without losing its tax-favored status, and another court has held that an organization devoting 20 percent of its activity to lobbying does not qualify. Organizations devoting between 5 and 20 percent of their activities to such pursuits are in an area of uncertainty. The IRS has never accepted the applicability of any specific percentage to determine the substantiality of any organization's legislative activity.

In 1976, Code Section 501(h) was enacted to relieve some of this uncertainty. That section sets forth a procedure whereby an organization may elect to expend a specified portion of its budget for legislative activities without any adverse effect upon its tax exempt status. The amount of such activity is computed on a statutorily prescribed sliding scale. As an example, an organization whose total expenditures on all exempt purposes are less than $500,000 per year may devote up to 20 percent of such expenditures to lobbying without paying any tax, and up to 30 percent without losing its tax exempt status. Expenditures exceeding 20 percent, but less than 30 percent, are subject to a special tax, but will not adversely affect tax exempt status.

Under Section 501(h), one-quarter of the allowable expenditure amount may be devoted to so-called grassroots lobbying, defined as attempts to influence the general public regarding legislation. Organizations not electing under Section 501(h) are subject to the old rules. In either case, permissible lobbying must be in the public interest, as determined by the organization.

Section 501(h) may be elected by most organizations qualifying for tax exemption under Section 501(c)(3) of the Internal Revenue Code. However, while the bill was being considered by Congress, there were those in the church community who believed that churches are not subject to the prohibitions against lobbying in any respect. These organizations believed that to include churches and integrated auxiliaries of churches in the relief legislation would imply that the government had the right to revoke their tax exemptions if they engaged in legislative activity. Since they did not believe that this was true, the organizations lobbied for a provision excluding them from the benefits of Section 501(h). The result is that churches, integrated auxiliaries of churches, and members of affiliated groups in which one or more members are churches or integrated auxiliaries of churches are not eligible to elect the provision of Section 501(h). Religious institutions which are not churches or integrated auxiliaries can make this election.

The requirements of the statute may thus be summarized as follow: An organization carrying on public affairs activities may qualify for exemption from tax under Section 501(c)(3) and receive charitable contributions under Section 170(a) if its activities are educational, charitable, or religious; if it does not exceed the limitations imposed on lobbying and propaganda expenditures imposed by Section 501(c)(3) and/or Section 501(h); and if it engages in no activity intended to influence the election or defeat of any political candidate.

Federal elections are governed by Title 2 of the U.S. Code Section 431, *et seq.*, comprising the Federal Election Campaign Act of 1971, as amended. The election laws prohibit contributions or expenditures in connection with any federal campaign by any corporation. Since many churches and charities are incorporated, the prohibition extends to many such organizations. It should be noted that this prohibition extends only to "contributions" and "expenditures." Thus, directly or indirectly, a corporation must *spend money* in support of or opposition to a candidate before a violation can be found. Activity by a minister outside working hours would not constitute a contribution by his church, though political advocacy on church time might. Use of church facilities for a political purpose by a candidate or committee may be the equivalent of a contribution, but merely allowing a visiting politician to deliver a sermon or read Scripture would not.

Discussion

1. Endorsements
   a. Can a clergyman or officer of a nonprofit tax exempt organization publicly endorse a candidate for public office?
   Neither the federal tax statutes nor the federal election law place impediments on individuals expressing their election choices. The fact that a clergyman is employed by a tax exempt organization does not destroy his personal constitutional right to political expression, and such an individual may personally endorse or oppose candidates for office without endangering the tax exempt status of the organization by which he is employed.
   b. Can it be done from the premises or pulpit of the tax exempt organization?
   There is no instance of which we are aware in which the Internal Revenue Service or the Federal Election Commission has sought to take adverse action against a church solely because its minister endorsed a candidate from the pulpit, where it was made clear that the church had no

position on any candidacy. However, a clergyman should not make a regular practice of endorsing candidates from the pulpit, lest his personal position be attributed to his church, and on those occasions when he does do so, he should make it clear to his congregation that the endorsement is a personal one and not that of the institution.

 c. *Can the church or organization endorse a candidate?*

The federal election law prohibits the expenditure of corporate funds in an attempt to influence an election. If the endorsement does not involve such a corporate expenditure, it would be permissible under the election law.

However, Section 501(c)(3) of the Internal Revenue Code prohibits any direct or indirect participation in political campaigns by a charitable or religious organization. This prohibition is broader than that of the election law, and extends to more than the mere expenditure of funds. Therefore, a charitable *organization* (including a church) which endorses a candidate for public office would be participating in a political campaign and would endanger its tax exempt status.

 d. *Can the clergyman or nonprofit organization leader/officer lend his name to political advertisements and have his title listed under his name for identification purposes?*

Just as there is no prohibition against an individual employed by a tax exempt organization engaging in political activity, there is no prohibition against the candidate using the individual's identification with such an organization if it is helpful in his candidacy. Clergy who work on their own time in political campaigns may be identified by their organizational titles.

2. Voter Registration and Education

 a. *Can a Section 501(c)(3) organization encourage or conduct voter registration or voter education activities among church members or on the nonprofit premises?*

Yes. The IRS has ruled that even private foundations may support voter education drives. T.D. Release K-87, May 11, 1969. In this respect, IRS Revenue Ruling 78-248, states as follows:

> Certain "voter education" activities conducted in the nonpartisan manner may not constitute prohibited political activity under section 501(c)(3) of the Code. Other so-called "voter education" activities, however, may be proscribed by the statute.

This revenue ruling contains a number of examples of situations illustrative of the rules as applied by the IRS.

In one example, an organization compiled and generally made available to the public the voting records of all members of Congress. The publication contained no editorial opinion, and its contents did not imply approval or disapproval of the members' voting records. The IRS held that such activity is not prohibited to a Section 501(c)(3) organization.

In another situation an organization was found to qualify as a Section 501(c)(3) organization even though it published a "voter's guide" containing the opinions of various candidates for political office on a wide variety of issues. It is important to note that the issues were selected solely on the basis of their importance and interest to the electorate as a whole. Candidates' positions were ascertained through answers to a questionnaire sent to all candidates.

Important distinctions may be drawn from a third example in which the same sort of questionnaire was sent to candidates in order to prepare a voters' guide, but the questionnaire was structured in such a way that it evidenced bias on certain issues. The organization was held not to qualify for tax exempt status.

> b. *Must voter registration activities be nonpartisan?*
> Yes.
>
> c. *Can the organization spend money for paying registration organizers, or for mailing out registration forms?*
> Yes, if the registration is nonpartisan.

3. Candidate Appearances

> a. *Can candidates speak on the premises of a Section 501(c)(3) organization?*

The Internal Revenue Service has never to our knowledge attempted to revoke the tax exempt status of an organization which allowed political candidates to speak on its premises. It is fairly clear that there is no problem with such practice if all candidates are allowed to speak, rather than merely those endorsed by the leaders of the institution. This is consistent with revenue rulings dealing with broadcasting stations, in which it has been held that providing reasonable air time to all legally qualified candidates for election to public office does not constitute participation in a political campaign. See Revenue Rul. 74-574, 1974-2 C.B. 160.

The question is a closer one if only certain candidates are allowed to address the group with political speeches. It could, of course, be argued that allowing a candidate to speak involves no expenditure or endorsement by the organization or that purely internal communications do not constitute intervention in a political campaign. Further, as we have noted, we know of no instance in which an organization has lost its tax exempt status for such activities. Nevertheless, more care and consideration should be given to such an activity than to an activity where all candidates are provided with the opportunity to speak.

Of course, candidates and public officials retain their rights to religious expression. Ministers should be safe in introducing a candidate present in the congregation at a service, and candidates may be allowed to deliver sermons and read Scripture.

    b. Can public incumbent office holders speak on the premises or from the pulpit?

Yes, though if such officeholders are candidates, the same considerations apply as are discussed above.

    c. Can an organization exempt from tax under Section 501(c)(3) operate forums where all candidates for a particular office come and speak?

Though the Internal Revenue Service has apparently never ruled on this exact question, such an activity is consistent with other IRS rulings. See, for instance, Revenue Ruling 74-574, *supra,* involving appearances by candidates on television stations operated by religious and education groups. See, also, Revenue Ruling 66-256, 1966-2 C.B. 210, in which an organization was held to qualify for Section 501(c)(3) status where it conducted public forums at which elections and debates on social, political, and international matters are presented.

4. Fund Raising

    Can funds be raised at religious services for campaign contributions to candidates, contributions to political parties, or contributions for a legislative battle or moral or educational issue campaign?

An organization may qualify for Section 501(c)(3) status so long as it does not devote a *substantial* portion of its activities to propaganda or legislative activities. Collecting money at a church service does not involve an expenditure of funds which could under most circumstances amount to a substantial expenditure.

In contrast, raising money for a candidate or a political party would constitute indirect participation in a political campaign. Since the prohibition on such activities is absolute, such an activity could result in the loss of tax exempt status.

5. Mailing Lists

Can an organization exempt from tax under Section 501(c)(3) loan or rent its mailing list to an organization carrying on legislative activities or to a candidate or political committee for campaign fund raising?

Both the Federal Election Commission and the Internal Revenue Service would react adversely to a loan of an organization's mailing list for use in a political campaign. Such an activity would constitute a corporate political expenditure to the extent that corporate funds had been used to develop the membership list. It would also constitute participation in a political campaign for purposes of Section 501(c)(3).

The loan of a mailing list to a "legislative" organization must be analyzed using different principles. The election law would not apply, since that statute applies only to political activities rather than legislative ones. The loan could be considered a legislative expenditure to the extent of the cost of providing it, but in any event would be considered such an expenditure only to the extent of any additional cost incurred by the corporation. Presumably, such additional costs would be very slight and would only in a very unusual circumstance result in substantial expenditure.

It is clear that both political candidates and parties and legislative organizations can *buy* mailing lists from charitable organizations. No problem would exist in any of the above cases if the list were rented at its fair market value (the value at which it is rented to other organizations, if at all) to either a political organization or a legislative organization.

We have attempted to deal in general summary form with problems which commonly arise. The reader should recognize, however, that the tax effect of political or legislative activity on a church or charity depends on the precise facts of the particular case. Each church should consult its own counsel with respect to its specific activities.

Part 4

Counseling Church Members Regarding the Law

16

Should Christians Sue?

Does the Bible forbid a Christian from taking another believer to court for any reason? Does this prohibition also apply to suing the unbeliever? Is an organization or business afforded the same protection from a Christian-initiated lawsuit? What if the believer is taken to court? Should he give over everything demanded by the person who sues or may he fight the claims against him? What defenses is the believer permitted? This chapter deals with some of these concerns and more.

"If anyone wants to sue you and take away your tunic, let him have your cloak also." (Matt. 5:40)

Being sued. What does this passage say to those who are being sued? Does it say that a person who is sued must deliver over to the plaintiff everything that he has been sued for? Why does this passage refer to "tunics and cloaks" and not to money? In Old Testament times and in New Testament times there were legal procedures for obtaining money judgments for owed debts. How could the passage refer to *any* man, without distinction as to whether that man may or may not be entitled to a recovery? If the reference is to anyone who wishes to sue, then even those who are not entitled to recover are included, but reason would dictate that the passage refers only to plaintiffs who have a just claim. Why, then, do the words seem to differ from what must be the meaning of this

This chapter was written by Charles R. Chesnutt.

passage? The answer to these questions lies in the historical use and application of the coat and the cloak.

Clothing, in relation to debts, is legally significant in the Old Testament, and also the New Testament. In Old Testament times, a man's coat or cloak was the last thing (before himself or his children) that he would sell or pledge to borrow money to survive. Because the pledge of clothing affected the most basic articles for survival, the law limited what a creditor could do to take it in satisfaction for a debt. For instance, the creditor could not go into the house of the debtor and forcibly seize the article of pledge (Deut. 24:10, 11). The same is basically true today.[1] If the debtor had pledged his clothing, the creditor would have to return it to him each evening so he would have something warm to sleep in (Deut. 24:12, 13; Exod. 22:26, 27).[2] Christ's reference to the coat or cloak does not imply unlimited license to any conceivable legal demand on someone but to the returning of articles that have been pledged to creditors who have not been paid. It is, therefore, not a command to pay money that is not legally owed, but refers to debts from loans that are actually owed. Therefore, the Christian is perfectly free to raise any honest and legal defense in the event that he has been sued.

If the passage refers to the payment of pledges after the release of debt, Deuteronomy 15 then is also a clear statement that a lien should survive a discharge of the debt in bankruptcy, which is basically the case today.

Suing others. Is it righteous for a Christian to sue another Christian when he has been wronged? The apostle Paul speaks directly to this issue: "Now, therefore, it is already an utter failure for you that you go to law against one another. Why do you not rather accept wrong? Why do you not rather let yourselves be defrauded?" (1 Cor. 6:7).

This is a difficult saying, but there are many difficult sayings in the Bible, and their difficulty does not render them unsaid. When this saying is viewed in the light of other doctrine and in the light of present law, however, it becomes more understandable but no less difficult.

Forgiveness is a critical element throughout the Scriptures, and it is God's desire for forgiveness and harmony among believers that forms the basis of this saying by Paul. Paul is clearly concerned here with the inherent contradiction between lawsuits and forgiveness. And Christ made it clear that there is a close relationship between forgiveness of debts and the forgiveness of sin (Matt. 18:22–35).

In the parable of the unjust steward, the kingdom of heaven is like a king who was moved to compassion and forgave his steward the money debt that was owed to him by the steward. The forgiven steward then demanded full payment from another steward. Christ calls the forgiven steward who failed to forgive his debtor a wicked servant: "You wicked servant! I forgave you all that debt because you begged me. Should you not also have had compassion on your fellow servant, just as I had pity on you?" (Matt. 18:32, 33).

Of course, we must remember that this is only a parable, and it does not state directly that a failure to forgive a money debt is sin. As a parable, it simply uses the example of the forgiveness of a money debt as an illustration of the forgiveness of sin.

However, the Greek word which is translated "debt" in this passage is the same word which is likewise translated "debt" or sin in the Lord's prayer. This underscores the close parallel between God's forgiveness of sins and the forgiveness of debts: "And forgive us our debts as we forgive our debtors" (Matt. 6:12).

Although the primary meaning of the Greek word refers to money debts, some translations use the word as "sins" or "trespasses." However, if the meaning of this word were limited to sins and did not include debts also, it would be hard to understand why a different and more precise word for "sins" (and not "debts") is used only two verses later (in Matt. 6:14) in the same Lord's prayer to refer to sins and trespasses and not to money debts. The parallel passage in Luke 11:4 uses a different word that means only "sin." We can conclude that the word in Matthew 6:12 may be read in either way but that it will at least connote the forgiveness of money debts.

Lawsuits that demand money judgments are, therefore, by their nature the antithesis of forgiveness. It seems clear that we cannot forgive and sue at the same time. This results in an apparent theological conflict that must be resolved. It is unrighteous for a man not to pay his debts if he can reasonably do so (Ps. 37:21; Matt. 5:40), but it is likewise unrighteous for a creditor to try to exact payment from someone who *cannot* pay.[3] The resolution of this apparent conflict lies in the fact that not all debt needs to be forgiven. The scriptural ideal is a creditor who has rendered a valid service or made a fair sale and a debtor who is willing and ultimately able to pay in full. This debt need never be forgiven.

The trouble arises when the creditor has not rendered a valid service or made a fair sale but still wishes to be paid in full for it, or when the creditor has rendered a valid service or made a fair sale but the debtor refuses to pay. Situations like these are unjust and have the makings of lawsuits. It is situations like these, however, that Paul addresses when he admonishes with regard to Christians suing Christians: "Why do you not rather accept wrong? Why do you not rather let yourselves be defrauded?" Paul is saying that the harm done by the lawsuit against a fellow Christian may do such harm that it would have been better to be harmed in a lesser way by being cheated or defrauded. Trials usually have no winners. They are arduous tasks that tax the energies and emotions of the persons involved. Even what is won may not be worth the loss of repuation for the individual and Christ's kingdom.

The bitterness and contention generated by Christians attempting to take money from one another do more harm to God's purposes than the enforcement of manmade justice. Nowhere are we told to collect from our enemies, but we are told to forgive them and feed them (1 Cor. 6:6, 7).

Of course, many a lawsuit is fought more for the principle of the matter than for the money. But unfortunately the principle most often so adamantly championed is revenge, and that principle is best left to God.

Sometimes, however, the bone of contention in a lawsuit may not present any issue of forgiveness. The lawsuit may hinge on a totally impersonal legal question that requires a judge vested with the authority of the government to make a decision.

A lawsuit is the result either of one person failing to fulfill a legal obligation or of one person alleging that a nonexistent legal obligation actually exists, or a little of both. A lawsuit is a dispute as to who owes what. Numerous Old Testament laws address the issue of who owes what. These laws are meant to avoid disputes by defining in advance exactly who owes what—under what circumstances. Modern laws are written for the same reason. Old Testament and modern laws are meant not to cause lawsuits and disputes but to prevent them. Just because biblical passages or modern laws provide for the recovery of sums of money for certain reasons does not mean that in all instances that right should be enforced. Very little is said in the Bible about the enforcement of rights of recovery.

The ideal seen in Scripture is not a list of circumstances where the plaintiff is not required to forgive and may sue. The scriptural ideal is for every plaintiff to be ready and willing to forgive every defendant and for every defendant to be ready and willing to make whatever reparation to the plaintiff is righteous and reasonable and scriptural. The scriptural ideal is concord not discord, agreement and reconciliation not lawsuits.

Unfortunately, discord reigns in the courts, not concord. Discord likewise reigns in the business world. If the demands of righteousness require forgiveness in the face of a discordant business world, and if lawsuits, which are standard of the day, are an elemental part of good business practice, how can Christians in business protect themselves if they cannot sue? Can a Christian ever scripturally sue anyone, and if so, whom can he sue and whom can he not sue? Scripture states directly that lawsuits should not take place between or among Christians, even in a clear case of fraud and wrongdoing. If a defendant is not a Christian, however, then Paul's admonition not to sue should not necessarily apply. Thus a lawsuit against a corporation would probably be unaffected by 1 Corinthians 6:7.[4] Also, in the event of proper church discipline, a person may be dealt with as an unbeliever (Matt. 18:17, 18). This may well render such a person outside the scope of 1 Corinthians 6:6, 7. There is no specific scriptural admonition not to sue other persons or entities, such as governments. In determining to sue or not to sue, however, the Christian should keep in mind that just because a defendant is scripturally open to suit doesn't mean that the Christian plaintiff is not at the same time called to forgive the defendant.[5]

For what should a Christian not sue? One of the most common lawsuits is a negligence action. Normally this involves suing someone for injuries. The injury that is the subject of the suit may be the result of a willful and wanton act or a grossly negligent act on the part of a defendant. Exodus 21 provides a biblical basis for recovery for personal injuries that are the direct result of willful or wanton actions, such as intentional injuries and blows to another person or, as specifically mentioned in that passage, injuries caused to a pregnant woman when two men fight each other. Other such willful or wanton actions mentioned in Scripture are situations where an owner of a notoriously dangerous ox permits the ox to have access to people and to injure them, or where a man digs a pit and leaves it open for someone to fall into. These are situations that the law today calls willful or wanton acts of gross negligence, and they can form the basis of recovery today as they did at the time of the law given by Moses. A more contemporary example of grossly neglectful conduct is a drunken driver.

There is, on the other hand, no scriptural basis for recovery against someone for a good-faith mistake. That is, if someone who acts entirely in good faith causes a loss to another person, then the person who suffers loss could not, under biblical law or principle, force the person who causes the loss to repay it. Today, however, most lawsuits are founded upon good-faith mistakes. Such a lawsuit is called a negligence action. The law of negligence says in effect that if one person, who acts in good faith and without any intention to harm anyone, injures another person, then he must pay for that injury. The crux of the difference between a lawsuit to recover for willful or wanton acts and a lawsuit for negligent acts is that where there is a willful or wanton act, the person causing the injury is consciously responsible for the resulting injury; but where there is a negligent act, the person causing the injury may do it without any conscious neglect or intention. Indeed, he may cause the injury while being as careful as he knows how to be. One reason that God has not provided for recovery based on a good-faith mistake is that he knows we are all imperfect. We all make mistakes. Why, therefore, should we hold ourselves to a standard of perfection that none of us can truly meet? However, with the institution of negligence laws our legal system makes each of us, within the scope of the application of those laws, the insurer of everyone with whom we come in contact. The result of these laws is that we insure the world that all of what we do will be without error, which is absurd.

A negligence action is founded on the presupposition that everyone is held to a standard of care of the "reasonable person." The practical application when these lawsuits are tried, is that the reasonable person is one who never makes the mistake. Therefore, all the plaintiff need do is prove that the defendant had a duty to the plaintiff, that duty was broken by an error made by the defendant, and that an injury resulted.

Another common cause of action is a suit for a breach of contract. The Christian plaintiff in this suit should consider whether or not the breach is due to an intentional act or a good-faith mistake.

How can Christians avoid getting into situations that normally can be remedied only through lawsuits? One of the first answers to this is contained in 1 Corinthians 6:5, the passage that outlaws lawsuits among Christians. In this passage Paul asks, "Is it possible that there is nobody among you wise enough to judge a dispute between believers?" Paul indicates here and in the following verse that the proper alternative is to provide for arbitration within the church. Arbitration is a method whereby disputes are settled by the parties agreeing in advance that some third party will make a decision and that they will abide by that decision. It is, in effect, the setting up of a "court" within the church or between people and agreeing in advance what power and authority that "court" will have. Most states have arbitration laws that are just as binding as the courts. A church or group of churches could take advantage of such laws and institute all of the necessary scriptural principles they felt were applicable. Arbitration has another clear advantage: It provides a forum for two parties who are at odds with one another to meet and discuss and come to an agreement. Forgiveness can take place within this context far more easily than when lawyers square off and the plaintiffs and the defendants meet head-on-head in the courtroom. The court system today could hardly be made less conducive to forgiveness and reconciliation than it already is. The parties don't speak to each other, and the lawyers, who are interested only in the legal aspects of the case, battle it out for a fee. There is no reason why litigants could not retain counsel within the context of an arbitration. When honest people with honest lawyers act with the honest intention to achieve forgiveness, justice, and equity among themselves, then God will bless their transaction. The expense and the fees that could be saved with such a resolution could be enormous. Obviously if the parties and actions are not honest, results could be much different, and a trial may ensue.

Another alternative would be for Christians to locate a Christian judge and employ him or her to hear interchurch cases. It may be necessary to pass legislation to permit parties to the litigation to file their suit and agree on a specific judge to hear the case.

Another scriptural admonition which can be used to avoid a situation leading to a lawsuit is Christ's admonition to his disciples in Matthew 10:16: "Be wise as serpents and innocent as doves." Perhaps the first part of this verse, "Be as wise as serpents," is more applicable. Christ suggests that we should be wise in avoiding situations that may result in disastrous consequences. For instance, we should be extremely careful in extending credit. We should get paid in advance or have a third party hold a sum of money to be paid upon completion of a task. We should be aware of all of the facts and aware of the debt structure of persons with whom we deal. We should structure business arrangements so that there is a minimum risk. The old adage that a contract is only as good as the person with whom we contract is true.

This discussion is not intended to offer a final conclusion on every lawsuit or potential lawsuit. It is meant only to be a general discussion on general biblical principles, and not all biblical references to lawsuits have been included. All of Scripture should be applied with care and wisdom to each situation, and each situation should be judged (in light of Scripture) on its own merits.

Monetary concepts in the Old Testament offer further insight into ways to avoid conflicts. For instance, as emphasized in chapter 17 on bankruptcy, Old Testament law systematically discouraged consumer loans and transformed them into gifts every seven years (Deut. 15:2). The scriptural admonition that the borrower is the lender's slave can apply to lenders as well as borrowers.

God's ideal was not vindication but forgiveness, not collection but charity, and not enforcement but wisdom. It is God who is the author of all good things (James 1:17), not lawyers.

17

Is Bankruptcy Ethical for the Christian?

Bankruptcy is often considered by Christians and non-Christians alike as being something sinister or unethical. Some see it as a means to avoid legitimate debt and it is often viewed by Christians as not being an option. The Scriptures, however, provide interesting information on how God views debt and how he provided ways to deal with difficult financial situations into which his people might fall. This chapter tries to dismiss misconceptions about bankruptcy and gives help to those people who are faced with the need to go bankrupt.

In Roman times, when poverty was deadly and rampant, the legal system saw insolvency and debt not as a "circumstance" but as a crime. Creditors in pre-Christian Rome held great power over their debtors. The entire estate of a debtor could be sold to one person who would then pay a certain percentage of the debts to the other creditors.[1] Since the debtor did not obtain a discharge from his debts through this sale, he was still required to pay all his creditors or face other consequences. Since all of his belongings had been sold, he and his family were left with nothing to live on while he attempted to earn enough money to pay the remaining debts. Nothing could release him from these debts short of payment, and if he did not pay them he could be exiled, imprisoned,

This chapter was written by Charles R. Chesnutt.

enslaved, or killed.[2] At one time in Roman history, the hapless debtor could be cut into pieces and divided up among his creditors.[3] At a later time in Roman history the debtor was protected from physical abuse but was never discharged from his debts.[4]

All of these measures had one thing in common: They all placed the value of the debt far above the value of the person who owed it. As in every instance of a balancing and apportioning of rights, where one group is given a major portion, the other group is proportionately limited.

In Rome the rich were given the power of life and death over the poor. It is, of course, easy to decry the poor and fault them for borrowing money that they could not repay. But many of the poor starved. What does one do when one must borrow or starve, or see his children starve? The poor man does exactly what the rich man would do if he had no money. He borrows.

The society in which such laws had sway must have been a society of great cruelty. It is ironic to reflect upon the fact that although such heavy consequences were inflicted for failure to repay, the consequences themselves would seem to render it impossible for a debtor to repay. The situation had not changed by the Middle Ages in Europe, which ushered in such things as the infamous debtors' prison in England, where the debtor would remain until someone else paid his debts for him.[5] The debtor was effectively held hostage until his relatives or friends would pay his debts. If he had no relatives or friends, he would live in prison until the day he died. He would never be free of his debts. If he had left a family outside the prison, the family might be forced to borrow money to eat, and the cycle for the family would begin again, except this time without a father.

What the system of laws like these actually accomplished, aside from providing for useless and corpulent misery on a debtor, was to make it practically impossible for him to ever extricate himself from his debts. The laws were self-defeating. They tended to reduce borrowing to those who were desperate, who were the least likely to pay back their debts. Since the laws often made it effectively impossible for the debt to be repaid, everyone lost: the creditors, the debtors, and the society. Even if he could escape prison, once a man became a debtor he could easily remain one for the rest of his life.

It is apparent from Scripture that God never intended for man to live in this way. God's ideal, set down in the Old Testament, was a society where loans were kept at a minimum by force of law, and gratuity and charity by force of law were kept to a maximum. To accomplish this end God did not outlaw borrowing and lending but instead greatly limited what could be done to a debtor who could not repay. He permitted the loan to take place and the consequent obligation to repay to arise, but he limited the legal obligation to repay to a maximum of seven years only. Every seventh year all lenders were to release their debtors from their debts. The debtors were to be no longer legally obligated to repay the debt. The debtor was free, and by force of law the creditor had made a gift: "At the end of every seven years you shall grant a release of debts. And this is the form of the release: Every creditor who has lent anything to his neighbor shall release it; he shall not require it of his neighbor or his brother, because it is called the LORD's release" (Deut. 15:1, 2).

To underscore God's demands for munificence, the Scripture also says that when the lender loaned, he could not even consider the fact that his debtor might soon be released from an obligation to repay. Indeed, the creditor was chastened if he withheld his bounty, even if he knew that he would never get it back: "Beware lest there be a wicked thought in your heart, saying, 'The seventh year, the year of release, is at hand; and your eye be evil against your poor brother, and you give him nothing, and he cry to the LORD against you, and it become sin among you'" (Deut. 15:9).

The concept is repeated in the New Testament: "Give to him who asks you, and from him who wants to borrow from you do not turn away" (Matt. 5:42 NKJV).

Under God's plan it is the *creditor* who is given the onerous commandment to lend and to give without hope of repayment, *not* the debtor who is punished because he cannot repay. There is a stark contrast between this approach and the laws of the Romans or the laws of the English. The approach in the Bible is precisely the opposite of the prevailing world view. In Scripture it is the debtor who is more important than the debt, rather than the debt being more important than the debtor. In Scripture it is forgiveness of debt and charity that are stressed and *required*, not repayment.

With the introduction of interest and interest upon interest, and penalties for failure to repay, the world at large, in contrast to the principle set forth in Scripture, is effectively regaining repayment without lending. God, on the other hand required lending without repayment: gifts. The exacting of any interest from a poor borrower was against Old Testament law (Lev. 25:37).

It was probably not until 1705 that the British bankruptcy statute of Queen Anne provided for an opportunity for a debtor in Britain to have his debts discharged.[6] The binding nexus between the bankruptcy statutes of Moses in Deuteronomy 15 and that of Queen Anne and the succeeding bankruptcy statutes up to present-day America is this discharge of debts. The discharge of debts means that at one point in time the debtor can become free of his debts even if he cannot pay them. This benign concept forms the core of the belief that a person should, in this life, possess the legal and moral ability to start over. In Deuteronomy 15 and Leviticus 25, God not only permitted the discharge of debt but made it an obligatory and continuously recurring phenomenon. The release of debt found in Deuteronomy and Leviticus carries generally the same result as the release of debt provided for in modern bankruptcy laws, where it is called a "discharge of debt."

There are other similarities between the laws of today and the biblical laws. For instance, under modern United States bankruptcy laws the debtor cannot obtain a release more often than once every six years (11 USC § 727 (a)(8)). Moses provided for seven years (Deut. 15:1). Modern bankruptcy provides for a discharge of certain debts, but not all (11 USC § 523). The biblical bankruptcy has other limitations, but in different areas (Deut. 15:2; Lev. 25). Today, after a bankruptcy has been filed and after a discharge is obtained, the debtor is protected from any legal process to collect his debts (11 USC § 363, 524). The same was true for Old Testament debtors whose creditors could not "exact" their debts (Deut. 15:2; Lev. 25:17).

There are several differences, however, between a scriptural discharge of debts and the modern bankruptcy laws. One of the differences is that the Deuteronomy 15 release of debt did not require the debtor to be destitute or bankrupt before he was discharged. It did not require him to give up any of his assets or to be unable to repay. Not so with the modern bankruptcy. In a modern bankruptcy, the debtor is required to relinquish all that he owns in exchange for the discharge of debts. Under the United States bankruptcy laws, the instant the debtor files bankruptcy, the trustee in bankruptcy effectively owns all of the debtor's possessions and is charged with selling them to pay the creditors.[7] Only certain well-defined assets of the debtor are exempt from this process, those which have been defined as being necessary for the debtor to continue his life.[8] Exactly what assets will survive a bankruptcy and what assets will not varies from state to state.

In the biblical discharge of debts there was no requirement that any assets be sold to pay creditors, as is true under current bankruptcy laws. There were no lawyers, no fees, no judges or trustees; but instead, by pure fiat of law, at a particular time there was simply a blanket discharge of all loans, no matter how much property a debtor had. Within the scope of its application, the bankruptcy process in Deuteronomy and Leviticus was therefore far more liberal and debtor oriented than the one provided for in the United States bankruptcy code. A legal bankruptcy of today can, therefore, be fully in accord with Scripture.

If God saw nothing unrighteous with a very liberal discharge, then it is hard to believe that he would not consider a more conservative or more difficult discharge to be unrighteous under today's laws. God invented the discharge of debts. He is a God of forgiveness and he wants his people to be forgiving people. This includes moral as well as financial forgiveness (Luke 16:1–13). It is righteous to forgive. God's grace and his demand for forgiveness do not apply to the point of reaching the dollar and then stopping. The principle of God's forgiveness includes forgiveness of debt (Deut. 15:1, 2; Luke 16:1–13), the forgiveness of lawsuits (1 Cor. 6:7), and the unlimited forgiveness of all wrongs (Matt. 18:21, 22).

In one area, however, the law in Deuteronomy is more limited than the modern bankruptcy laws. Deuteronomy limited the type of debts which were to be released. It depended upon how the debts arose. Deuteronomy was addressed to "the creditor who lends anything." Thus, the Old Testament bankruptcy laws applied to debts that arose from the lending of something, and not necessarily to debts that arose for other reasons. For example, the Deuteronomy passage makes no provision for a discharge of debts owed for wages. In the Old Testament a wage owed was a nondischargeable debt; the wages of one who was hired was not even to be kept by the employer overnight, and the failure to pay wages was likened to robbery (Lev. 19:13; see also Mal. 3:5; James 5:4). Thus, although today's bankruptcy laws may permit the discharge of debts owed for wages, Scripture would probably see the discharge of those debts as unrighteous. Another example is the obligation to specifically perform in a contract, or a debt incurred by fraud, even if it was a loan (see Ps. 37:16, 21).

Of course, the bankruptcy, or more accurately the discharge, of the Old Testament was written for the agrarian society of those times and not for the modern world system of commerce. To approximate the provisions of the Bible in today's world, issues that did not exist in Old Testament times must be addressed in the form of statutory law, but that statutory law should follow the underlying principles of honor and righteousness and truth and charity which we find throughout Scripture.

Bankruptcy Is a Calculated Risk

The Old Testament lenders were certainly well aware of the law which limited their right to recover. This is clearly indicated in Deuteronomy 15:9. The same is true today. One has only to read a security device (a mortgage or a lien) used by any bank or professional lender to understand this. The risk of bankruptcies being filed by borrowers is clearly anticipated by lenders and understood as a calculated expense of business. Banks lend money and creditors extend credit with the express purpose of making more money. Investors borrow that money for the same purpose. The success of the borrower's enterprise is a calculated risk that the bank takes when it advances a business loan. The bank will make money if the enterprise succeeds, and it may lose if the enterprise doesn't succeed. To ensure that it does not lose its investment, the bank may take a larger ownership in the enterprise (in the form of a lien or a mortgage) than the borrower himself has.

The loan that the bank makes is an investment for the bank as well as for the borrower, and both the bank and the borrower are, or should be, well aware of the intrinsic risks. The bank and the borrower are, therefore, in a sense united in a joint effort to make a profit for both. The bank almost becomes the unofficial "partner" of the borrower.

The same is true for the bank or credit card company that lends money or extends credit for consumer purchases rather than business purposes. They lend money and extend credit for the purpose of making as much money as possible, with the understanding that some of the people who borrow from them will go bankrupt. They take the calculated risk that the borrower will be able to pay back what he has borrowed. In one sense they are "partners" with the borrower, hoping for the borrower to make more money and repay the lender much more money than he was loaned.

These "partnerships" rise and fall together. If one such partnership falls, there is no biblical reason for the borrower in that partnership to isolate all the loss to himself and to fail to apportion the lender's loss to the lender in accordance with applicable bankruptcy law. Therefore, unless there is a specific biblical provision to the contrary, utilization of today's bankruptcy statutes is neither unexpected, unscriptural, nor unwise. Except where there is a biblical provision to the contrary, the bankruptcy laws provide a breadth of application which may well permit a bankruptcy in accordance with scriptural principles.

Money Management

The Old Testament lending laws show us not only God's principles that should underlie debtor-creditor relations, but they also demonstrate righteous principles that should govern money management.

It is certainly obvious that a society that discharged all loans every seven years was probably a society where few loans were made, and then only under the most compelling of circumstances or to borrowers who were very trustworthy and able to pay back the loan.

Deuteronomy 15:7–9 required the lender not to consider the upcoming year of release; therefore he must lend even though he knew that the debt would soon be discharged. But this applied only to borrowers who were poor and in true need of help. It did not apply to borrowers who were not really in need. And Leviticus 25:35–37 required loans without interest to those in need. Therefore, we can surmise that the lenders of the Old Testament were probably very careful to determine if a prospective borrower was really in need before lending to him prior to the year of release. Not only did the year of release provide an opportunity for debtors to begin anew, but it also had the effect of limiting lending only to those in real need. Lending was more an aspect of charity than of commerce. By the utilization of the year of release and the command against exacting interest, God structured the law of Israel in such a way that living on credit was practically impossible for those who did not need it to survive. God's provision for the protection of the creditors whose debts were released was not to permanently hold the debtor to the debt. God desired to make the risk of lending abundantly clear to the lenders so the lenders would be fully aware of the risks. Precisely the same is true today. Every commercial and consumer lender knows of the risk of bankruptcy. The major difference between the Old Testament lending and today's methods is that today the release from debt is not automatic and there are no laws to prevent the charging of interest. The result is that massive profits can be generated by the use of the 17 to18 percent interest rates, or more, in consumer credit transactions. These profits override the risk of bankruptcy and those who pay back their loans are in effect not only paying back their own loans but also the loans of the bankrupt borrowers as well.

Since Scripture is clear that God's original idea was to severely curtail lending, and especially consumer lending, it follows that his original idea was also to severely curtail borrowing. This fact speaks volumes to today's commercial credit lifestyles. It is clear that God never meant us to live on other people's money, but to live on our own. Consumer borrowing as a way of life and consumer lending as a business have no basis in Scripture. Living on credit cards and time payment plans or long easy terms or the like are devices that never existed for God's people in biblical times. And these devices are a snare today. They are the means of producing an illusion of wealth, a fiction, a belief that we can own or do own those things which, in reality, we do not truly own or cannot obtain. These are the sparkling instruments of pride and vanity. They are the ultimate temptation: wealth without money and appearance without reality—demons in the garb of angels.

A Purpose for Borrowing

Although interest and commercial lending were not permitted in Israel, it was permitted to extend commercial credit at interest to the gentiles and heathen (Deut. 23:20). It is foundational in Old Testament Scripture that Israel should prevail over the gentiles and the heathen nations (Deut. 28:1). One of the ways this was to be accomplished was through commercial and consumer lending at interest by Israel to the gentile people and nations. In Deuteronomy 28, God set before the people of Israel blessings and curses. One of the blessings was that God would bless the fruits of their labor so that they should lend to the gentiles and not borrow from them. Israel should, therefore, be the "head and not the tail" and "above only and not beneath." On the other hand, if they did not obey the commandments of God, they should suffer severe curses, one of which was to be in the opposite position: The stranger in the land would lend and the Israelites would borrow; the stranger would become "very high" and the Israelites "very low"; the stranger would become the "head" and the Israelites the "tail" (Deut. 28:12, 13, 15, 43, 44). It is through lending at interest that one can gain domination over another: The borrower becomes a "slave" of the lender. In Scripture, a result of borrowing, therefore, was a curse.

A bankruptcy is an effective means to deliver a debtor from an impossible debt and to break the cycle of borrowing. It will not, however, cure the debtor of the habits of an unscriptural lifestyle. Bankruptcy, if it occurs because of consumer borrowing, is something that should happen no more than once in a lifetime, if then. It should be a means to change and to adjust to a way of life based on the reality of ownership rather than the fiction of borrowing. It should be used in conjunction with a decision to live without incurring debt, and this decision should be the primary focus of the pastor who counsels those of his congregation who find themselves enmeshed in the snares of consumer debt. A bankruptcy should be the end of something and the beginning of something. It should be the end of an overwhelming debt burden and the beginning of a new way of life. If it does not signal the beginning of something, then it may well signal the end of something, because once a bankruptcy is filed, it may not be available for quite some time in the future.[9]

18

The Christian Leader's Guide to Criminal Law

Criminal law is that system of laws and courts that exists for the purpose of punishing people who break the criminal laws. This system should be clearly distinguished from the civil law system, where the purpose is to balance rights and equities between private parties. In the United States today, the civil system and the criminal system are completely separate. They consist of separate laws, separate legal procedures, and offer separate courts. With only rare exceptions, no legal proceeding is both criminal and civil.

In the arena of criminal law, the "plaintiff," that is the prosecutor, always represents a governmental entity. Each different governmental entity prosecutes in its own court, from cities that prosecute their traffic tickets in municipal courts to the United States government that prosecutes federal crimes in federal courts. It is always a governmental entity that prosecutes; an individual cannot prosecute in a private capacity. Instead, the victim of the crime, who is the counterpart of a plaintiff in a civil case, becomes a witness for the prosecution, the governmental entity. This system provides a lawyer for the victim of the crime by funding the prosecution without requiring the victim to pay anything for the service. Thus, effective criminal prosecution does not depend on

This chapter was written by Charles R. Chesnutt.

victims having the money and initiative to hire their own attorneys to prosecute.

It is a different matter for the person who has been accused of a crime, the defendant. The defendant is required to hire his own attorney if he is able to do so. If he is not able to hire a lawyer, the court will appoint one to defend him at the government's expense. It is the constitutional right of defendants to have their own legal counsel if charged with a serious crime, even if they cannot pay for it. Anyone charged with a crime should request an attorney as soon as possible.

The criminal system is constructed for the purpose of subjecting a person convicted of a crime to the most physically distasteful experience that the law allows: prison. Because of this purpose of the criminal system it normally produces the most extreme and desperate attempts on the part of defendants to avoid its consequences. Because criminals will vociferously protest their innocence and do absolutely anything within their power to establish it, it follows that protestation of innocence, even when coupled with prior cooperation with police, will probably be of little avail when the actual prosecution begins. The result of this is that if an innocent man is prosecuted by mistake, he is nonetheless prosecuted just as vigorously as a guilty man, no matter how much he protests.

If a pastor becomes aware of the prosecution of someone and his advice and counsel are sought, his best advice to the person charged with or arrested for a felony is that a competent attorney be hired as soon as possible. A felony prosecution, even if won, can be a disastrous and life-changing experience and a good attorney hired in time may be able to avoid prosecution. Such an attorney is well worth the fee, even a high one. Sometimes Christians who have been wrongly accused of committing a crime will delay the hiring of an attorney because they view the prosecution as something that they can "work out." This is a trap for the unwary. Therefore, the pastor is well advised to obtain a list of good criminal lawyers for referral, possibly from a friendly prosecutor or a judge.

Generally, criminal prosecution consists of four parts:

1. A prior existing law
2. A violation of that law

3. A fact-finding procedure (trial) to determine if the violation has occurred, and if so,
4. Punishment for the breach of that law

The prosecution of a guilty man often resolves itself into a question of how much punishment will be given, rather than whether or not the defendant is innocent. The reason is that prosecutions do not normally begin unless there is fairly convincing evidence that the defendant is guilty, and where there is convincing evidence, the defendant will often be willing to come to some agreement with the prosecution with regard to a sentence and agree to a guilty plea. This is called a plea bargain. If the defendant is actually guilty he deserves to be prosecuted and punished, and the only real issue to be decided or agreed upon is the amount of punishment that he will receive. (It is the experience of many attorneys that the majority of those accused of crimes are actually guilty.)

The punishment of crimes has, from the very birth of humanity, been a foundational aspect of God's dealings with man. Indeed, the nation that fails to punish crimes is under a curse of God (Num. 35:33).

The Word of God is intimately wedded with concepts of criminal law. In the Garden of Eden we see the first example of a criminal proceeding. All the elements of a criminal prosecution were there: a prior existing law, a violation of that law, a fact-finding procedure by a judge, and a resulting punishment.

The prior existence of the law is basic, because without the law there is no transgression of the law (Rom. 4:15). The prior existing law that was violated in the Garden of Eden was God's command not to eat of the fruit of the tree of the knowledge of good and evil; the judge was God, who conducted a fact-finding proceeding (an interrogation of Adam); and the resulting punishment was the expulsion of Adam and Eve from the garden. We see the same process repeated throughout the Bible, and in various forms and degrees in probably every criminal court in the world. Ultimately all of mankind will be defendants in a criminal proceeding known as the judgment. At the judgment, however, many of us will have an attorney to represent us: Jesus Christ (1 John 2:1). Many will not.

A principal right in America is that a defendant in a criminal prosecution must be proven to be guilty before the law can punish him. Put it another way, a man is innocent until he is proven to be guilty. This foundational principle is normally accepted and understood as being a wise and valid cornerstone for criminal law. The alternative, which exists in some other countries of the world, is that the accused is guilty until he can prove himself to be innocent. If he happens to be in prison, this can be a rather difficult task. In the United States, it is the prosecutor who must prove him to be guilty before he can be punished. The prosecutor bears the burden of proof because the defendant is presumed to be innocent until the prosecutor can prove him guilty. It is this technicality that requires that the defendant not be imprisoned (punished) until he has been proven guilty. The defendant is proven guilty at a trial. Until his trial he is presumed innocent and therefore should be free. Unfortunately, setting a man free who has just been arrested for a crime that he has indeed committed could defeat the purpose of the system. He may be dangerous and commit another crime before being convicted of the first one. Further, because the law requires proof of guilt, most persons charged with crimes are not charged until the prosecution has substantial evidence of guilt. This means that most of the defendants who are released because they are presumed to be innocent but are in fact guilty and may well be dangerous.

There are two opposing rights here: the right of the general population to be protected from criminals and the right of all citizens to remain innocent until proven guilty. The compromise between these two opposing rights is the bail bond system. Although the accused is presumed to be innocent, the state still has a right to take him to trial and try to prove him guilty. If the facts indicate that the defendant will not attend his trial, then the court can hold the defendant in jail without bond until he is tried. If it appears that the defendant will attend his trial, then the court can let him go until his trial is set. But usually, however, to ensure this does occur, the court may require the defendant to put up a certain sum of money or property to guarantee that he will return. This is his bail. The theory is that he will be sure to return to his trial so that he does not lose his bail that he has placed with the court. Of course, if it appears to the court that the defendant is dangerous, then the court has the option to set the bail very high, or to set no bail at all. In this way some defendants are released before trial and some are not. Normally, a bonding company will be necessary to secure the release of a defendant. The fee for the bonding company ranges from 10 percent to 15 percent of the amount of the bond and this fee is nonrefundable. Shopping around for a low-priced bond is a wise idea. Bonding companies are normally open twenty-four hours. Be very careful when dealing with bonding companies.

If the defendant or his parents have cash or property, then a cash or property bond may be posted to avoid the bonding company and its fee. Instructions as to how the cash or property bond is posted can often be obtained from the authorities in charge of the jail or the Clerk of Court.

The pastor is usually called on after the defendant has been arrested and a bail has been or will be set. The primary concern at that time is to get the defendant out of jail. This is accomplished in one of three ways.

First, a judge or magistrate sets the amount of the bail, and the defendant then pays the bail—the amount of money that must be put up to get the defendant out. Usually, when someone is charged with a felony, a judge or magistrate has to set the bail and the defendant has to stay in jail until it has been set. Sometimes lawyers can get a bail set early.

Second, if there is a "menu" or list of the bail amounts for particular misdemeanor offenses, and the defendant is charged with one of those offenses, it is not necessary for the bail to be formally set by a judge or magistrate. After the defendant pays the appropriate bail, he is released.

Third, the case fits into a category which permits the defendant to be released without putting up a cash or property bond. With this method, the defendant or some other party who acts as surety for the defendant gives his written promise to pay a certain amount of money to the court in the event that the defendant does not show up as scheduled. In many jurisdictions this is called "a release on his own recognizance." Often there are governmental organizations which screen defendants to determine if they fit the criteria for release without putting up a cash bond. A pastor should not sign a bond or sign any written contract with a bonding company; it is unscriptural because he would be signing as a surety (Prov. 22:26).

If a defendant cannot be released on his own recognizance, he may pay his bail by either placing money or property with the court or other proper authority; this is called a cash bail bond or a cash bond. Or, the defendant may obtain a guarantee (a bond) from an insurance company to pay the bail in the event he does not appear; this is called a bail bond. The first method is the better method because it costs nothing but the interest that would have been earned on the money that is placed with the court. As soon as the case has been completed the money is returned to the person whose name is on the receipt, no matter whether the defendant wins or loses. A word of caution here: If the money is given to the defendant to pay the bail and the defendant's name is on the receipt, and if the defendant later loses his case and receives a fine, the cash bond may be forfeited to pay for the fine. In some jurisdictions the court may permit the bond to be used to pay the fine no matter whose name is on the bond receipt. Anyone intending to place a bond for someone should investigate and determine the procedure in advance.

If the cash or property is not available, then a bonding company should be consulted. Its fee will usually be a percentage of the amount of the bond. If a bonding company is hired, the fee paid to the bonding company is not refundable. If the defendant does not appear in court when he is supposed to, the judge will declare the bond to be forfeited and whoever has placed the bond with the court will lose the entire amount of the bond. A bonding company will go after the defendant and may sue everyone who signed for him, if the defendant does not appear.

In summary, if someone in the pastor's ministry should be under criminal proceedings, the pastor should be aware that usually the criminal charges have been filed for a good reason and that protestation of innocence by guilty persons is expected. But guilty or not, the defendant still is in need of a criminal attorney and should not attempt to be his own lawyer. This is the first advice a pastor should give someone accused of a crime.

19

Benefits of Preventive Lawyering

The first thing we do, let's kill all the lawyers.
William Shakespeare, *Henry VI, Part II, Act 4, Scene 2.*

Negative experiences with lawyers have led many people to believe that adopting Shakespeare's suggestion would be a benefit to society. Many lawsuits conclude with both parties wondering who really won.

The frustration of losing a lawsuit may cause the client to question why his lawyer was unable to persuade the judge or jury. This is because the expense of pursuing litigation probably would not have been acceptable unless the client believed that his case was just. On the other side, the party who wins the lawsuit likely is equally dissatisfied. He has believed from the beginning that he has done nothing wrong, and now he has an official court document that confirms it. He also owes a lot of money to his lawyer for proving what he already believed to be true.

Why has experience caused many people to expect that any professional involvement with a lawyer will be unpleasant? The answer is that the services of a lawyer are sought too often only as a last resort. In our legal system, which uses the adversarial process, the first appearance of the lawyer typically comes after all efforts have failed to resolve a dispute by agreement. Lawyers would naturally be unpopular if viewed only as "hired guns" to sue people.

This chapter was written by Brad N. Gahm.

It is unimportant whether lawyers are popular; they are well paid and deserve no extra measure of sympathy. However, it is important to the client that the services of a lawyer be used effectively. Litigation requires the unique skills and expertise of a lawyer. Yet, for many legal matters the client may only need a counselor and not an advocate. The purpose of this chapter is to highlight types of legal services that can be used to avoid lawsuits. Knowing how to use a lawyer to avoid disputes is the basic concept of preventive law.

Preventive law is a systematic method of conflict avoidance. Conflict avoidance is simple in theory and yet obviously difficult to achieve as evidenced by the proliferation of lawsuits.

The concepts of preventive law permit the client and the lawyer to develop a systematic approach to anticipate and analyze problems and to structure agreements and business practices before an actual conflict occurs. Three preventive law techniques or methods can help avoid conflict: the legal audit, the litigation audit, and continuing legal education. Each of these techniques uses the services of a lawyer in different ways to avoid legal disputes.

Legal Audits

A legal audit is a comprehensive, periodic review of business operations. It does not focus on a particular business transaction or legal dispute; rather, it is a general review of all business procedures to ensure compliance with applicable laws. A distinguishing feature of the legal audit is its comprehensive scope.

Every business recognizes the need for a regular financial audit to reconcile the books with accepted accounting procedures. Likewise, a legal audit is necessary to review business practices in terms of legal standards. For example, a legal audit of a Christian ministry might include a review of tax records and tax exempt status, a review of insurance policies to determine adequacy of coverage and limits of liability, and a review of local zoning ordinances that affect the use of buildings and property.

A lawyer is used for two primary purposes in a legal audit: first, to identify legal issues relating to every business operation, and second, to give advice on how to comply with the law. After receiving this legal advice, the client can perform the legal audit by applying the guidelines and instructions provided by the lawyer. If the client discovers a particular business practice, method of record keeping, or other matter that does not comply with the legal requirements that the lawyer identified, corrective action can be taken before a legal dispute occurs. A legal audit should be conducted at least once every year, and should include every aspect of the Christian ministry's operations.

Litigation Audits

A different preventive law technique is the litigation audit. Its purpose is to understand why a lawsuit occurred and how similar problems could be avoided in the future. The distinguishing feature of a litigation audit is its narrow focus on a particular legal dispute or lawsuit. If a Christian ministry is involved in a lawsuit, the services of a lawyer might be used simply to prosecute or defend the specific allegations in that case. A litigation audit looks further to analyze all of the facts and circumstances that led to the filing of the lawsuit.

An example of effective use of a litigation audit is in a personal injury lawsuit. Assume that a church is sued because a child was injured when he fell into a ditch that was created during construction of a building. The normal duties of a trial lawyer in defending the church might require only that the lawyer prove that the construction company, rather than the church, had a duty to maintain adequate protective barriers around the ditch. The church would probably win the lawsuit or reach a favorable settlement, then pay its lawyer, and the matter would be finished.

A litigation audit would seek additional services from the lawyer to advise how future construction contracts should be written to specify the type of warnings to be erected around hazardous conditions, or to expressly state the type of supervision which the construction company should provide to guard these hazards. This example shows how a litigation audit produces specific recommendations to be implemented that will avoid future legal disputes arising out of similar situations.

Continuing Legal Education

A third technique for conflict avoidance is continuing legal education (CLE). As the name implies, a CLE program is structured like an educational seminar to provide information about recent legal developments. Lawyers in most states are required to attend CLE programs. Clients who are concerned about preventive law can benefit from this same information presented in less technical terms.

A CLE program does not necessarily relate to the specific business operations or current legal disputes that are subjects of legal audits and litigation audits. A CLE program is more broadly structured to review legal issues of general interest. For example, the decisions of the United States Supreme Court regarding the free exercise of religion under the First Amendment affect the practice of religious beliefs. Every Christian ministry should be aware of current trends in First Amendment law even if that ministry is not specifically involved in the religious practice or belief which was at issue in the sample case. A lawyer can explain recent judicial decisions and give an opinion on whether courts could be expected to expand the law to different fact situations. In this way a Christian ministry can use CLE as a way to practice preventive law.

An additional benefit of CLE is that the members of a church or Christian ministry have access to information that will assist them in acting as responsible Christian citizens. Many Christians have become more involved in government because of concern over wide ranging issues such as school prayer, home school education, abortion, and pornography. The belief that Christian values should be considered as part of all public policy may lead some people to organize groups that work for the election of certain candidates to public office.

During the past decade Christians have dramatically increased their visibility and influence at all levels of government. But this has not happened without close scrutiny from the news media and criticism from many people. What are the limits, if any, for using Christian values as the basis for laws? Does the Constitution require an absolute "separation of church and state" that would prohibit a certain active Christian from serving as president? A CLE program is an excellent means for Christians to educate themselves about these important issues. Numerous periodicals and books contain legal information relevant to Christian ministries. A lawyer can help identify the most useful publications and schedule speakers and seminars that cover pertinent topics.

The preventive law techniques of a legal audit, litigation audit, and a CLE program offer different methods to anticipate and avoid legal disputes. Each technique uses the services of a lawyer in different ways as counselor and adviser to identify potential problems and to take action before a dispute occurs. The benefits of avoiding legal disputes are obvious. Nevertheless, preventive law is too often ignored, especially by Christian organizations.

The most common reason, or excuse, for not practicing preventive law is cost. Paying for legal advice may seem to be an expensive luxury before a lawsuit is filed. However, preventive law should be considered a fundamental part of business planning, and thus the cost must be treated as a normal operating expense. The value of quality legal advice is realized in the prevention of legal disputes. Clients too often fail to appreciate that the cost to resolve a future legal dispute will usually exceed the current cost to carefully plan and implement methods to avoid that dispute.

Selecting the Right Lawyer

To establish a preventive law program, it is important to select the lawyer who is best prepared to provide the type of legal service that you need. At least two basic questions arise in selecting a lawyer. First, what are the lawyer's individual qualifications, expertise, and experience to meet your particular needs? Second, how do you find the lawyer; where do you look?

Deciding which lawyer you should hire requires matching your legal needs with the lawyer's personal qualifications. For example, common legal needs for Christian ministries may deal with tax exempt status as a charitable organization, operations as a not-for-profit corporation, or the purchase and development of real estate. A lawyer engaged in general business practice may have sufficient skills to represent each of these needs. A lawyer who specializes in public or administrative law may be needed if the ministry is involved in a complicated zoning dispute. Likewise, representing a ministry's First Amendment right to the free exercise of religious beliefs may require the expertise of a constitutional lawyer.

Just as many doctors specialize in particular fields of medicine, most lawyers tend to develop their areas of expertise. State bar associations offer certification by a Board of Legal Specialization for lawyers who pass a test demonstrating exceptional knowledge of a particular area of law. The skills of a board certified lawyer may be needed only in unusual situations. Even without formal board certification, many lawyers develop special skills in a particular area of law simply through years of experience. When choosing a lawyer, do not hesitate to ask about the lawyer's certification or expertise for the type of service that you need.

Additional considerations in selecting a lawyer are how much money to pay for the service, and the amount of individual attention you expect to receive from the lawyer. A simple illustration of this is the difference between a lawyer who is part of a large firm and a lawyer who operates a solo practice. A large firm may be able to respond to the needs of its clients by offering the services of a senior partner, several associate lawyers, legal assistants, and information systems that provide access to meticulous research. A call from you, regardless of how complex the problem or how quickly the answer is needed, can be met by a cadre of lawyers and their support staff—all for a commensurate price.

On the other hand, if you want one person to call "my lawyer," a solo practitioner is usually better able to provide that personal attention. A solo practitioner may also charge a lower hourly fee. One tradeoff may be that the personal attention a solo practitioner provides must be divided among all of that lawyer's clients, thereby sacrificing the lawyer's ability to give an immediate response in some situations. Choosing the right lawyer is not merely a question of selecting either a large law firm or a solo practitioner; you should compare your needs with the advantages that each offer.

A final consideration in selecting a lawyer is the lawyer's ability to give objective advice regardless of what you would prefer to be told. Objective legal advice must give equal attention to facts and legal issues that help the case, as well as those which undermine it. For this reason, it may be better to use a lawyer with whom you have no close social relationship. In some cases, a friend might be the worst choice as your lawyer if the relationship interferes with the ability of either of you to be objective. You must have confidence that the lawyer will provide objective advice, and then be willing to accept the advice, which may include establishing a preventive law program whose costs could be offset by the benefit of avoiding future legal disputes.

Even if you know the type of lawyer who best meets your needs, you may still face the question of how to make a selection. Where do you look to find the lawyer? The two most immediate sources are by referral from other people and from a listing in the telephone directory. In either case, you should question the lawyer extensively to determine whether he or she possesses the qualifications that you need.

Lawyers may also be located through lawyer referral services, prepaid legal service plans, and legal clinics. A lawyer referral service is available through many local bar associations. This service is typically provided by telephone at no charge, and is used only to match a lawyer with a person who needs a particular type of legal service. The referral service is responsible only for putting the lawyer and prospective client in contact with each other, and then they may negotiate an agreement for services and fees.

Prepaid legal service plans have become increasingly popular as a low-cost means of providing routine legal services. A prepaid legal service plan resembles a form of insurance in which the lawyer's fees are paid by the plan rather than by the client. People who join the plan (known as subscribers) pay an annual fee or premium. Many employers, unions, and similar organizations sponsor prepaid legal service plans. In addition, private companies may offer such plans to any person who wants to join as a subscriber.

The benefits available from prepaid legal service plans can vary significantly, and thus a careful review of benefits should be made before enrolling in the plan. The two most important distinctions in plan benefits are, first, access service plans versus comprehensive service plans, and second, open panel plans versus closed panel plans.

Access plans provide basic legal services such as telephone consultations, document review, letter writing, and preparation of wills. These basic services are the only benefits which are fully paid by the plan. Other legal services may be available for a discounted additional fee. By contrast, a comprehensive plan would pay the fees for all types of services requested by the subscriber. Of course, the yearly fee may be higher for the comprehensive plan as compared with the access plan. An open panel plan permits the subscriber to choose his own lawyer, while a closed panel plan requires the subscriber to use only lawyers who have been selected by the company that administers the plan.

Prepaid legal service plans have been an important and positive development in providing low cost basic legal services for people who choose not to hire a private lawyer. It must be understood, however, that because these plans charge lower fees they will maintain their profit margin through efficient delivery of legal services. Lawyers who work for a prepaid legal service plan may have incentive to do their work in the shortest amount of time possible. This does not mean that the quality of legal services is diminished, but it may limit the amount of individual attention and time available for consultations with clients. Prepaid legal service plans offer an important alternative for people who may need only basic routine legal services.

A final means of locating a lawyer is through legal clinics operated by private foundations or law schools. These clinics are customarily staffed by lawyers who volunteer their time, known as "pro bono" services, or by law students who are supervised by their professors. Most legal clinics require the client to demonstrate financial need and typically are intended to assist only those people who cannot afford a lawyer. However, a legal clinic may be willing to take a case which involves a unique question of law. This may be of particular benefit to a Christian ministry having a case involving a constitutional question arising under the First Amendment right of free exercise of religion.

Conclusion

The preventive law techniques of a legal audit, litigation audit, and CLE program require the cooperative effort of both the lawyer and the client. The subjects addressed in this book are useful as a general guideline for identifying the issues most commonly confronting Christian ministries. Using this book as a starting point for discussions with a lawyer is an example of practicing preventive law. This will help you evaluate the potential problems confronting your Christian ministry and obtain the legal advice to try to avoid a possible lawsuit.

Appendixes

Appendix A

Glossary of Legal Terms

Affidavit A written or printed document of fact made voluntarily and affirmed by oath before an appropriate person.

Affirmed Ratified; made firm.

Agent One who acts for another.

Allegation The statement of a party to an action, setting out what he intends to prove.

Amicus curae A friend of the court; one who volunteers help.

Appellant The party who takes an appeal from one court to another.

Appellee The party in a cause against whom an appeal is taken.

Arbitrary Without adequate determining principle; capricious or at pleasure; despotic.

At bar Before the court.

Bona fide In good faith; genuine.

Capricious Unfounded; at pleasure.

Case law The aggregate of reported cases as forming a body of jurisprudence.

Cause of action The right which a party has to institute and carry through a proceeding; a matter for which an action can be brought; the entire state of facts that give rise to an enforceable claim; the act on the part of the defendant which gives the plaintiff his cause of complaint. A cause of action arises when that is done which should not have been done, or that is not done which ought to have been done.

Corporate function Used synonymously with proprietary function.

Curia A court of justice.

Declaratory Explanatory; designed to fix what before was uncertain.

Demurrer An admission of fact with reservations as to the truth *or* application of the facts to the case; a type of objection.

Dictum A statement; a remark or observation.

Dissent Contrariety of opinion; refusal to agree.

Domain The complete and absolute ownership of land.

Due process Law in its regular course of administration through courts of justice.

Easement The right which one person has to use the land of another for a special purpose.

Encroach To enter by stealth into the rights of another; to intrude.

Enjoin To require; command; positively direct.

Error A mistaken judgment or incorrect belief.

Ex post facto After the fact; by subsequent matter.

Feasance A doing of an act; a performing or performance.

Flagrant Wanton; nefarious; glaring; notorious.

Fraud An intentional perversion of the truth; a false representation of fact.

Governmental function A governmental function of a city is of that kind which arises, or is implied, from the use of political rights under general law, in the exercise of which the city is as a sovereign, and such power is held by the municipality as a political subdivision of the state, to be used for public purposes; governmental functions are those conferred or imposed on a municipality as a local agency of limited and prescribed jurisdiction, to be employed in administering affairs of the state, and promoting public welfare generally.

Inception Commencement; opening, initiation; the beginning of a cause or suit or court.

Injunction A prohibitive suit issued by a court of equity forbidding the committing of an act which is being threatened to be done, or the stopping of the commitment of an act already begun.

Legal defense A defense which defeats recovery, such as an act of God, the assumption of risk by participant, or contributory negligence on the part of the plaintiff.

Liability The state of being bound or obligated in law or justice.

Litigation Contest in a court of justice for the purpose of enforcing a right.

In loco parentis In place of the parent; instead of a parent; charged factitiously with a parent's rights, duties, and responsibilities.

Mandamus We command; this is the name of a writ which issues from a court of superior jurisdiction, and is directed to a private or municipal corporation, or any of its officers commanding the performance of the particular act therein specified.

Malfeasance The doing of an act which is wholly wrong or unlawful.

Mandate A command, order, or direction, written or oral, which a court is authorized to issue and a person is bound to obey.

Misfeasance Performance of an act which might lawfully be done but which was done in an improper manner.

Negligence The failure to observe, for the protection of the interests of others, that degree of care, precaution, and vigilance which the circumstances justly demand, whereby such other person suffers injury.

Nonfeasance The omission to perform a required duty; some act which should have been performed.

Nuisance In creating or the maintenance of a nuisance, the wrongfulness must be in the acts themselves rather than in the failure to use the requisite degree of care in doing them. It is the violation of an absolute duty. A nuisance is a condition which is (a) offensive to the senses of a person of ordinary sensibilities, (b) inherently dangerous or defective, (c) obstructing the reasonable and comfortable use of one's property, or (d) in violation of the laws of decency.

Obligation Legal duty.

Omission The neglect to perform what the law requires.

Ordinance Rule or law passed by the legislative body of a city.

Per curiam By the court; a phrase used in the reports to distinguish an opinion of the whole court from an opinion written by any judge.

Permissive Allowed; that which may be done.

Per se In itself.

Precedent Authority followed in courts of justice; a previous decision in a similar case.

Prima facie At first sight; presumable, a fact presumed to be true unless disproved by some evidence to the contrary.

Promulgated To publish; to announce officially.

Proprietary function A proprietary function of a city is of that kind which is ordinarily of a business or private nature in which the provision of service is a convenience to the people, and in which a direct charge or assessment is usually made by the city for such use.

Proximate Immediate; nearest; direct, next in order; in its legal sense, the closest in a causal connection.

Pursuant A following after or following out; live in accordance with or by reason of something; conformable; in accordance with.

Quasi As if; almost as it were; analogous to; indicates that one subject resembles another in certain characteristics, but that there are material and intrinsic differences.

Quid pro quo Something for something; an equivalent or consideration.

Remand To send back.

Res ipsa laquitor A general way of saying that the circumstances attendant upon an accident are of themselves of such a character as to justify a jury in referring negligence as to the cause of that accident.

Respondeat superior Let the master answer; this maxim means that a master is liable in certain cases for the wrongful acts of his servant, and a principal for those of his agent.

Respondent One who makes or files an answer in a cause; a defendant.

Right An enforceable claim or title to any subject matter whatever; either to possess and enjoy a tangible thing or to do some act; pursue a course, enjoy a means of happiness, or to be exempt from any cause of annoyance; also, one's claim to something out of possession; and also, a power, prerogative, or privilege.

Seriatim Severally; separately; individually; one by one.

Sine quo non Without which not; that which the thing cannot be; an indispensable requisite or condition.

Solecism Supreme or highest in power; possession, or entitled to; original and independent authority or jurisdiction.

Stare decisis Let the decision stand; to abide by, or adhere to, decided cases.

Statute The written will of the legislature which is expressed in the form necessary to constitute its part of the law.

Succinct Brief; precise; exact.

Supposition A conjecture based upon possibility; a probability that a thing could or may have occurred without proof that it did occur.

Supra Above; upon. This word occurring by itself in a book refers to a previous part of the book.

Tort A legal wrong other than a crime or breach of contract.

Ultra vires Acts committed beyond the authority of a corporation or body to act.

Waiver Voluntary surrender of a right of privilege.

I am unsure of the original source of this glossary. I picked it up in law school and am indebted to whoever prepared it.

Legally Binding Arbitration Agreement (Sample)

Believing that God desires Christians to submit their disputes to other Christians rather than the civil courts, the parties hereby agree that the provisions for *binding arbitration* set forth in this agreement shall be the sole and exclusive remedy for resolving any controversy or claim between the parties arising out of or involving:

It is further agreed that each of the parties waives whatever right he/she might have to initiate or maintain a civil lawsuit or seek any other remedy against the other party in a federal or state court of law in connection with this claim, except to enforce this agreement and any agreement reached or award granted through this process.

The parties agree to submit the above issues to a three-person arbitration panel consisting of _____ (name) _____, _____ (name) _____, and _____ (name) _____, for a legally binding arbitration decision. Each of the above arbitrators has accepted Jesus Christ as his personal Savior and Lord and believes the Bible to be the inspired Word of God. All issues submitted to arbitration decision rendered by the panel may be entered as a judgment in any court having jurisdiction.

Believing that Christ desired to reconcile the parties, the parties agree to discuss the dispute with each other and the panel in an attempt to come to an agreement on an appropriate resolution of the dispute. If the parties are unable to reach an agreement, they agree that the arbitration award shall be issued and they shall be legally bound by it.

Because each party is committed to the resolution of this dispute in a manner that is pleasing to Christ, he/she understands and acknowledges that any agreements or arbitration awards resulting from this process may differ greatly from, and could be of litigation or other approaches to the resolution of the dispute. For example, CCS arbitrators will take into consideration both scriptural principles and civil law and thus are not required to decide that dispute in strict accordance with civil cases, statutes, and regulations. Each party agrees to release the CCS arbitrators and conciliators, CCS, and related parties from liability in relation to claims arising out of these, similar, or equally advantageous outcomes, which he or she could have obtained from a judge or jury.

Each party understands and acknowledges that under CCS policy:

(I) all mediators or arbitrators and other persons associated with CCS are strictly prohibited from giving any legal advice to either party, whether or not such mediator or arbitrator or other person is an attorney, and in that regard each party agrees and acknowledges that no attorney-client relationship is created between the party and CCS or any of the mediators or arbitrators, or any other person associated with CCS;

(II) each party is encouraged to consult with the party's attorney and other advisors concerning the party's legal and financial rights and obligations in this dispute before signing this agreement and commencing the arbitration process as well as during the proceedings (attorneys may be present), and before any agreement is entered; and

(III) Christian conciliation attempts to achieve a change in future conduct through a reconciliation of the parties, not through retribution or punishment; therefore, CCS arbitrators will not award punitive damages.

Each party represents that to the best of his/her knowledge no aspect of this dispute is or might be covered by any insurance policy. Each party understands and acknowledges that if any aspect of the dispute is covered by any insurance policy, a decision to submit the dispute to mediation or arbitration pursuant to this agreement without the express written consent of the insurance carrier could result in the loss of insurance coverage with respect to such dispute.

CCS charges fees to help meet its expenses. The administrative fee for these proceedings is $250 per party for the first ten hours of conciliation panel meetings and $25 per hour per party after ten hours. The mediators or arbitrators are volunteers and are not paid by CCS for their mediation or arbitration services, except that _____ (name) _____ receives a salary as the CCS director.

Each party agrees that if a dispute arises between that party and CCS or any of its mediators, arbitrators, directors, officers, employees, or agents, that party hereby agrees to give up his/her right to have any such dispute decided in a court of law and their right to a jury. Instead that party agrees that such dis-

pute shall be resolved by legally binding arbitration as provided by
_____(state)_____ law. In case of such dispute the parties to the dispute
shall jointly appoint a neutral arbitrator, or if they are unable to agree on a neutral arbitrator, a panel of three arbitrators—one selected by CCS, one by the
other disputant(s), and a neutral arbitrator selected by the arbitrators selected by
the parties.

No party is required to accept as a neutral arbitrator a person who is unable
to affirm agreement with the Christian Legal Society Statement of Faith.

_____
Date

_____
Date

_____
Date

                                          Christian Conciliation Service of

                                          _____(city)_____

                                          By:_____

Mediation Agreement (Sample)

The undersigned parties agree to enter discussions and negotiations in an attempt to resolve their dispute regarding:

under the supervision of the Christian Conciliation Service of _____(city)_____ (CCS). The parties agree to the involvement of CCS because they desire to resolve the dispute in a manner that is pleasing to Christ.

Because each party is committed to the resolution of this dispute in a manner that is pleasing to Christ, he/she understands and acknowledges that any agreement reached in the mediation process concerning the dispute may differ greatly from, and could be substantially more disadvantageous to him/her than, the outcome of litigation or other approaches to the resolution of the dispute.

Each party agrees to release the CCS mediators, CCS and related parties from liability in relation to claims that any of these people or entities failed to provide any party with the same, similar, or equally advantageous outcome which he or she could have obtained from a judge or jury.

The parties agree to submit the above issues to a panel of mediators consisting of _____(name)_____, _____(name)_____, _____(name)_____, and _____(name)_____, each of whom has accepted Jesus Christ as his personal Savior and Lord and believes the Bible to be the inspired Word of God.

Each party understands and acknowledges that under CCS policy:
(I) all mediators and other persons associated with CCS are strictly prohibited from giving any legal advice to either party, whether or not such mediator or other person is an attorney, and in that regard each party agrees and acknowledges that no attorney-client relationship is created between the party and CCS or any of the mediators or any other person associated with CCS: and

(II) each party is encouraged to consult with the party's attorney and other advisors concerning the party's legal and financial rights and obligations in this dispute before signing this agreement and commencing the mediation process, during the mediation process (each party's attorney may be present), and before any agreements are reached concerning the dispute.

The parties agree that evidences of statements made in the course of the mediation shall be inadmissible for any purpose in any proceeding in a court of law, as provided in _____ (state) _____ Evidence Code Section _(number)_ (a copy of which is attached and incorporated by reference). However, each party further understands and acknowledges that statements made by him/her during the mediation process could be verified outside of the CSS process and used to the party's disadvantage in subsequent legal proceedings if the dispute is not resolved through the mediation.

Each party represents that to the best of his/her knowledge no aspect of this dispute is or might be covered by any insurance policy. Each party understands and acknowledges that if any aspect of the dispute is covered by any insurance policy, a decision to submit the dispute to mediation without the express written consent of the insurance carrier could result in the loss of insurance coverage with respect to such dispute.

CCS charges fees to help meet its expenses. The initial administrative fee for this mediation is $250.00 for the first 10 hours of the mediation panel's time, and $25 per hour for every hour thereafter. The mediators are volunteers and are not paid by CCS for their mediation services, except that _____ (name) _____ receives a salary as the CCS director.

Each party agrees that if a dispute arises between that party and CCS or any of its mediators, directors, officers, employees, or agents, that party hereby agrees to give up his/her right to have any such dispute decided in a court of law and their right to a jury. Instead that party agrees that such dispute shall be resolved by legally binding arbitration as provided by _____ (state) _____ law. In case of such dispute the parties to the dispute shall jointly appoint a neutral arbitrator, or if they are unable to agree on a neutral arbitrator, a panel of three arbitrators—one selected by CCS, one of the other disputant(s), and a neutral arbitrator selected by the arbitrators selected by the parties.

No party is required to accept as a neutral arbitrator a person who is unable to affirm agreement with the Christian Legal Society Statement of Faith.

_____

Date

_____   _____

Date

_____   Christian Conciliation Service of

Date

_____(city)_____

By: _____   _____

(number) Communications during mediation proceedings

(a) Subject to the conditions and exceptions provided in this section, when persons agree to conduct and participate in a mediation for the purpose of compromising, settling, or resolving a dispute:

(1) Evidence of anything said or of any admission made in the course of the mediation is not admissible in evidence, and disclosure of any such evidence shall not be compelled, in any civil action in which, pursuant to law, testimony can be compelled to be given.

(2) Unless the document otherwise provides, no document prepared for the purpose of, or in the course of, or pursuant to, the mediation, or copy thereof, is admissible in evidence, and disclosure of any such document shall not be compelled, in any civil action in which, pursuant to law, testimony can be compelled to be given.

(b) Subdivision (a) does not limit the admissibility of evidence if all persons who conducted or otherwise participated in the mediation consent to its disclosure.

(c) This section does not apply unless, before the mediation begins, the persons who agree to conduct and participate in the mediation execute an agreement in writing that sets out the test of subdivisions (a) and (b) and states that the persons agree that this section shall apply to the mediation.

(d) This section does not apply where the admissibility of the evidence is governed by Section _(number)_ or _(number)_ of the Civil Code or by Section _(number)_ of the Code of Civil Procedure.

(e) Nothing in this section makes admissible evidence that is inadmissible under Section _(number)_ or any other statutory provision, including, but not limited to, the sections listed in subdivision.

(d) Nothing in this section limits the confidentiality provided pursuant to Section ___(number)___ of the Labor Code. Paragraph (2) of subdivision (a) does not limit either of the following:

(1) The admissibility of the agreement referred to in subdivision (c).

(2) The effect of an agreement not to take a default in a pending civil action.

Christian Conciliation Ministries of North America

The Association of Christian Conciliation Services has members through-out the United States. This list includes regional contacts who can provide you with conciliation assistance or refer you to other members in their regions. To be included on this list, an individual must be involved in the ACCS Conciliator Training Program.

CALIFORNIA
> **Hollywood** • CCS of Los Angeles • Bryan Hance • 1800 N. Highland #507 • 90028 • (213) 467-3331
> **Malibu** • Peter Robinson • I.D.R. • Pepperdine School of Law • 90263 • (213) 456-4655
> **Novato** • Bay Area CCS • Tim Arensmeier • PO Box 617 • 94948 • (415) 382-9162

COLORADO
> **Lakewood** • CCS of Denver • Richard Wise • 1545 S. Kline Ct. • 80232 • (303) 988-3230

FLORIDA
> **Melbourne** • Francis Bradley • CCS of Brevard • 427 Timberlake Dr. • 32940 • (407) 242-1421

ILLINOIS
> **Elmhurst** • John Steven Cole • CCS of N. Illinois • P.O. Box 54 • 60126 • (708) 834-4740

KANSAS
> **Overland Park** • CCS of Kansas City • Blaine Robison • 6405 Metcalf #307 • 66202 • (913) 362-2102

MICHIGAN
> **Lansing** • CCS of Central Michigan • Anne Bachle • 1710 E. Michigan • 48912 • (517) 485-2270
> **Redford** • CCS of SE Michigan • Donald Remillard • 26847 Grand River #19 • 48240 • (313) 533-9140

MONTANA
    Billings • CCS of Montana • Ken Sande • 1537 Ave D., #352 • 59102 •
    (406) 256-1583
    Bozeman • Mark Bryan • PO Box 1371 • 59715 • (406) 586-8565
    Helena • Michael Becker • 428 N. Benton • 59601 • (406) 442-7450
    Lewistown • James Stogsdill • 314 Bank Electric • 59457 • (406) 538-2623
    Kalispell • Harold Kellam • 28 Dale Dr. • 59901 • (406) 752-2400
NORTH CAROLINA
    Trinity • Trinity CCS • Forrest Horn, Sr. • 415 Creekview Dr. • 27370 •
    (919) 434-5449
    Blowing Rock • Lynn Pace • Rt. 1, Box 273 • 28605 • (704) 295-9404
OHIO
    Circleville • John Bowen • 208 N. Scioto • 43113 • (614) 477-1688
OREGON
    Portland • Will Wright • CCS of Portland/Vancouver • PO Box 9070 •
    97207 • (503) 231-1624
PENNSYLVANIA
    Allentown • Everett Forner • 2460 Lisa Lane • 18104 – (215) 394-7887
TENNESSEE
    Memphis • J. Maxwell Williams • 100 N. Main St., 17 Fl. • 38103 •
    (901) 522-2083
TEXAS
    Austin • Christian Reconciliation Center • Barbara Horan • PO Box
    202133 • 78720 • (512) 328-3662
    San Antonio • CCS of San Antonio • Jobeth McLeod • PO Box 15717 •
    78212 • (512) 227-0638
VIRGINIA
    Annandale • Christian Legal Society • Brad Jacobs, Exec. Dir. • 4208
    Evergreen Ln. #222 • 22003 • (703) 642-1070
    Fairfax • F. Mather Archer • PO Box 396 • 22030 • (703) 642-1070
WASHINGTON
    Seattle • CCS of Puget Sound • Mark Albertson • 424 N. 130th • 98133 •
    (206) 367-2245
WYOMING
    Gillette • Frank Stevens • P.O. Box 1148 • 82717 • (307) 682-1444

Endnotes

Chapter 1
A Biblical View of Law and Government

1. Sir William Blackstone recognized one more category, the natural law, which he distinguished from the law of nature. The natural law is man's distorted interpretation and application of the law of nature. (See further discussion in next chapter.)
2. Rousas J. Rushdoony, *Institutes of Biblical Law* (Philadelphia: The Presbyterian and Reformed Publishing Company, 1973),. 4.
3. Hadley Arkes, "Morality and the Law," *The Wilson Quarterly* (Spring, 1981), 102.
4. Ibid., 101.

Chapter 2
The Origins of Anglo-American Law

1. Gary Amos, *Defending the Declaration* (Brentwood, Tenn.: Wolgemuth & Hyatt, Publishers, Inc., 1989).
2 Ibid., 5.
3. Ibid., 7.

Chapter 3
An Introduction to the American Legal System

1. For a superb, eminently readable introduction to the United States Constitution and the ideas reflected in it, see Mortimer J. Adler, *We Hold These Truths* (New York: Macmillan, 1988).
2. 304 U.S. 64 (1938).

Chapter 4
Church and State in America

1. See the selected bibliography at the end of the book.
2. For example, John Whitehead, *The Second American Revolution* (Elgin, Ill.: David C. Cook, 1982).
3. See Mark A. Noll, et al., *A Search for Christian America* (Westchester, Ill.: Crossway Books, 1983). NA
4. For an analysis and critique of the theonomic view, see H. Wayne House and Thomas Ice, *Dominion Theology: Blessing or Curse?* (Portland, Oreg.: Multnomah, 1988).
5. It is assumed that Christians, as good citizens, will be involved in the political processes of their nation.
6. Randall Terry, *Operation Rescue* (Springdale, Penn.: Whitaker House, 1988).

221

7. Franky Schaeffer, *A Time for Anger* (Westchester, Ill.: Crossway Books, 1982).

Chapter 5
A Look at the First Amendment

1. The Ninth Amendment states: "The enumeration in the Constitution of certain rights shall not be construed to deny or disparage others retained by the people."
2. The Tenth Amendment states: "The powers not delegated to the United States by the Constitution, nor prohibited by it to the States, are reserved to the States respectively, or to the people."
3. U.S. Constitution, First Amendment

    For Incorporation:
    Justice Black, dissenting in *Adams v. California* 332 U.S. 46, 47 (1947).
    Curtis, *The Bill of Rights as a Limitation on State Authority: A Reply to Prof. Berger*, 16 Wake Forest Law Review 45 (1980).

    Against Incorporation:
    Fairman, *Does the 14th Amendment Incorporate the Bill of Rights?* 2 Stanford Law Review 5 (1949).
    Alexander M. Bickel, *The Least Dangerous Branch: The Supreme Court at the Bar of Politics* (Indianapolis: Bobbs-Merrill, 1962), 102.
    Raoul Berger, *Government by Judiciary: The Transformation of the 14th Amendment* (Cambridge, Mass.: Harvard University Press, 1977), 137, note 11.

4. "Nor shall any State deprive any person of life, liberty, or property, without due process of law. . . ."
5. Free Exercise: *Cantwell v. Conn.* 310 U.S. 296 (1940). Establishment: *Everson v. Bd. of Ed.* 330 U.S. 1 (1947).
6. Speech: *Gitlow v. N.Y.* 268 U.S. 652, 666 (1925).
7. Press: *Near v. Minnesota* 283 U.S. 697, 701 (1931).
8. Assembly: *DeJonoe v. Oregon* 299 U.S. 353 (1937).
9. Petition: *DeJonoe, supra: Hague v. CIO 307 U.S. 496 (1939); Bridges v. California* 314 U.S. 252 (1941).
10. See Nowak, Rotunda, and Young, *Constitutional Law*, 2d ed., (St. Paul: West Publishing, 1983), 418-19.
11. *Sherbert v. Verner* 374 U.S. 398 (1963). Since the writing of this chapter the Supreme Court ruled that the state only had to use a rational basis test to proscribe the use of peyote in the religious practices of some Oregon Indians. Some have argued that this case opens the door for substituting the rational basis test in place of compelling test. At this point the court has followed the rational basis test only in a situation where the full exercise activity is in violation of a statute of general applicability, here a criminal activity. To safeguard against this some constitutional scholars have advocated pain-free exercise with another Constitutional right, such as free speech. See *Employment Division, Department of Human Resources of the State of Oregon v. Smith*, 108 S.Ct. 1444, 485 U.S. 660, 99 L.Ed. 2d 753, *rehearing denied* 110 S.Ct. 2605, 110 L.Ed. 2d 285

(1990). It is anticipated that Congress will soon restore the requirement for a compelling state interest before a free exercise practice can be abridged.

12. For a proper interpretation of the establishment clause rejecting and refuting the absolute separation formula see: *Jaffree v. Board of School Commissioners of Mobile County* 554 F.S. 1104 (U.S. Dist. Ct. S.D. Alabama, Jan. 1983). Unfortunately reversed in ____F2d____. But the decision is still on appeal to U.S. Supreme Court. This is the famous Alabama Prayer Case. The work predominately relied on by the court is *Separation of Church and State: Historical Fact and Current Fiction* by Robert L. Cord (Grand Rapids: Baker, 1988). In this author's opinion, Cord's book is one of the best historical renditions of the founding fathers' intent regarding the establishment clause. See also John Eidsmoe, *The Christian Legal Advisor* (Grand Rapids: Baker, 1984), 118-203.

13. *Lemon v. Kurtzman* 403 U.S. 602 (1971).

14. 397 U.S. 664 (1970).

15. *Lemon v. Kurtzman* 403 U.S. 602 (1971).

16. 451 U.S. 772 (1981).

17. *Grace Brethren Church v. California*, 50 U.S.L.W. 4703, 4705 (1982).

18. 440 U.S. 490 (1979).

19. *Sherbert v. Verner* 374 U.S. 398 (1963). (See endnote 11 on the compelling interest test.)

20. 406 U.S. 205 (1972).

21. See *Ohio v. Whisner* 351 N.W. 2d 750 and the ordeal of these Christians in *Ohio's Trojan Horse: A Warning to Christian Schools Everywhere* by Allan Grover (Greenville, S.C.: Bob Jones University Press, 1977). See also *The Messianic Character of American Education* by R. J. Rushdoony for religious objections to the public schools.

22. 450 U.S. 707 (1981).

23. First held in *U.S. v. Ballard* 322 U.S. 78 (1944).

24. *Thomas* 450 U.S. 715-16.
For a more in-depth presentation of the free exercise clause see Eidsmoe, *The Christian Legal Advisor*, 161-203 (further cited as CLA).

25. See discussion of *Widmar v. Vincent* and *Bender v. Williamsport School District* in the free speech section.

26. For a full discussion of free speech see Pritchett, *The American Constitution*, 3d ed., (1977), 313-33; for an excellent book on free speech from a Christian perspective see Cal Thomas, *Book Burning* (Wheaton, Ill.: Crossway Books, 1983).

27. *Niemoko v. Maryland* 340 U.S. 268 (1951); see also *Kunzk v. New York* 340 U.S. 290 (1951), which involved a city ordinance that prohibited public worship meetings on the street without a permit from the police commissioner. The ordinance was unconstitutional because it gave the commissioner too much discretionary power.

28. Eidsmoe, CLA, 203-22. Professor Eidsmoe is presently teaching at O.W. Coburn School of Law, Oral Roberts University.

29. Eidsmoe, CLA, 205.

30. *Lehman v. Shakee Heights* 418 U.S. 298 (1974).
31. 454 U.S. 263 (1981).
32. *Bender v. Williamsport Area School District* 563 F.S. 697 (1983).
33. *Lubbock Civil Liberties Union v. Lubbock Independent School District* 669 F2d. 1038 (5th Cir. 1982).
34. *NAACP v. Alabama* εx rel. Patterson 357 U.S. 449, 460-61 (1958). For an excellent discussion of the church's role in politics and public policy see Buzzard and Ericsson, *The Battle for Religious Liberty* (Elgin, Ill.: David C. Cook Publishing Co., 1982), 223-31. This book is an excellent handbook of religious freedoms and should be read.
35. *Constitutional Law* 1004–1008 at note #10 of this chapter.
36. Ibid. at 1006 citing *Thomas v. Collins* 323 U.S. 516 (1945).
37. Blackstone, *Commentaries on the Laws of England*, IV, 151, 152.
38. See Pritchett's discussion of Free Press (see endnote 26) at 298-312, 333-50.
39. *Lovell v. Griffin* 303 U.S. 444 (1938).
40. *Palko v. Conn.* 302 U.S. 319 (1937).
41. *Pierce v. Society of Sisters* 268 U.S. 510 (1925); *Meyers v. Nebraska* 262 U.S. 390 (1923).
42. *Constitutional Law*, 3d Ed. 735 (1983).
43. 406 U.S. 205 (1972).
44. 435 U.S. 618 (1978).
45. Civil Rights Act of 1871, 42 U.S.C. 1980.
46. Eidsmoe, CLA, 219.

Chapter 6
The Minister as Counselor

1. 47 Cal. 3d 278, 253 Cal.Rptr. 97, 763 P. 2d 948 (1988), *cert. denied*, 104 S. Ct. 1644.
2. A *complaint* is the name for the original document the plaintiff(s) files in order to begin a lawsuit against the defendant(s).
3. A "wrongful death" action is one in which the survivors of the deceased seek damages for loss of life from those who have allegedly caused it due to their negligence. For example, medical malpractice claims seeking damages from the doctor or hospital for the patient's death are "wrongful death" actions.
4. 47 Cal. 3d at 307, 308-09 (emphasis supplied). The court did not rule on the dismissal of the counts for negligence, since the entire case was remanded for trial on the merits. 204 Cal.Rptr. at 309.
5. 240 Cal.Rptr. 215 (Cal. App. 2 Dist. 1987).
6. 322 U.S. 78 (1944).
7. Samuel E. Ericsson, *Clergyman Malpractice: Ramifications of a New Theory*, 16 Valparaiso Univ. Law Review 1 (Fall 1981), 177-78 (citations omitted).
8. 763 P.2d 948, 949–950.
9. 763 P.2d at 955–956
10. Ibid. at 960, quoting Ericsson, *Clergyman Malpractice*: 163, 176.

11. Ibid. at 960–961, 964.
12. See, for example, H. Newton Maloney, et el., *Clergy Malpractice* (Philadelphia: Westminster Press, 1986); Lynn R. Buzzard and Thomas S. Brandon, Jr., *Church Discipline and the Courts* (Wheaton: Tyndale House, 1987); William Harold Tiemann and John C. Bush, *The Right to Silence* (Nashville: Abingdon, 1983); J. Carl Laney, *A Guide to Church Discipline* (Minneapolis: Bethany House, 1985).

Chapter 7
Church Discipline and the Right of Privacy

1. *Everson v. Board of Education of Ewing Township*, 330 U.S. 1, at 18, 67 S.Ct. 504, 513 (1947).
2. U.S. Constitution, Amendment Article I.
3. *McCollum v. Board of Education*, 333 U.S. 203 (1947).
4. 310 U.S. 296 (1940).
5. 330 U.S. 1 (1947).
6. *Glover v. Baker*, 76 N.H. 393 (1942).
7. *Lemon v. Kurtzman*, 403 U.S. 602, at 614 (1971).
8. Ibid., 614.
9. *Presbyterian Church in the U.S. v. Mary Elizabeth Blue Hull Memorial Presbyterian Church*, 393 U.S. 440 (1969); *Ganzales v. Roman Catholic Archbishop of Manila*, 280 U.S. 1 (1929); *Walz v. Tax Commission*, 397 U.S. 664 (1970).
10. *Engle v. Vitale*, 370 U.S. 421 (1962).
11. *School District of Avington Township Pa. v. Schempp*, 374 U.S. 203 (1963); *Widmar v. Vincent*, 102 S.Ct. 269 (1981).
12. *Walz v. Tax Commission*, 397 U.S. 664 (1970).
13. *McGowan v. Maryland*, 366 U.S. 420, 81 S. Ct. 1409 (1961).
14. *Committee for Public Education v. Nyquist*, 413 U.S. 756, 93 S.Ct. 2955 (1973).
15. *West Virginia State Board of Education v. Barnette*, 319 U.S. 624 at 642 (1943).
16. The term *nova* as defined by Webster's: "A star that suddenly increases greatly in brilliance and then gradually grows fainter." *Webster's Twentieth Century Dictionary*, 2d ed. 1978.
17. Oklahoma Bar Journal, vol. 60, No. 3 (January 1989).
18. Ibid.
19. Ibid.
20. Ibid., 144.
21. Ibid., 148.
22. Prosser, William, *Law of Torts* (1941).
23. *Cason v. Baskin*, 30 So.2d 635 (1947).
24. *Continental Optical Co. v. Reed*, 86 N.E. 2d 506, 119 Ind.App. 643 (1948), rehring den, 88 N.E. 2d 55.
25. Ibid.
26. Ibid.

27. *Trustees Pencader Presbyterian Church in Pencader Hundred v. Gibson*, 22 A.2d 782 (1941).
28. *Canovaro v. Brothers of Order of Hermits of St. Augustine*, 191 A. 140 (1937).
29. *Linke v. Church of Christ of Latter Day Saints*, 71 Cal.App.2d 667 (1967).
30. *Kubilius v. Hawes Unitarian Congregational Church*, 79 N.E.2d 5 (1948).
31. Ibid.
32. Ibid.
33. 80 U.S. 679 at 728-729 (1871).
34. The Scriptures could not reasonably be used to support informing those outside the church body of such church actions.
35. Oklahoma Bar Journal, at 149.
36. Ibid. at 150.
37. For further study, see Jay A. Quine, "Court Involvement in Church Discipline," Part 1, *Bibliotheca Sacra,* Vol. 149, No. 593 (Jan.–Mar., 1992): 60–73; and Jay A. Quine, "Court Involvement in Church Discipline," Part 2, *Bibliotheca Sacra,* Vol. 149, No. 594 (Apr.–June, 1992): 223–36.

Chapter 9
Should the Church Incorporate?

1. We say independent because most local bodies that are denominationally affiliated will follow the legal guidelines of the denomination. Most major denominations today are incorporated.
2. "Litigio-economic" is a term coined by the author to denote the increasing influence of litigation on economics in our society. Witness, for example, the increased cost of insurance and medical services due to extremely large verdicts in personal injury cases.
3. This obviously does not mean, however, that a member, officer, or director may not perform services for the corporation and receive compensation for those services.
4. Since a majority of states follow the Model Nonprofit Corporation Act in their statutory framework, it will be used in the balance of the analysis here.
5. There are several purposes for the registered agent. One significant policy reason for requiring that there be a registered agent with an address for the corporation is so that third persons dealing with the corporation will have an avenue of "official" communication with the corporation. Similarly, in most states service of process (of litigation proceedings) may be obtained over the corporation by serving the process on the registered agent.
6. Some states only require that there be one incorporator, which in some cases is the attorney representing the organization.
7. See IRS Publication 557 for the precise language suggested by the IRS to be used in the articles of incorporation.
8. Although there may be a technical distinction between a constitution and bylaws, in practice they serve the same purposes. For a comment on the distinction

between the two, see Richard R. Hammer, *Pastor, Church & Law* (Springfield: Gospel Publishing House, 1983), 136.

9. Hammer, ibid. at 136–37.
10. See Hammer, ibid. at 136.
11. Henry Campbell Black, *Black's Law Dictionary*, 5th ed. (St. Paul, Minn.: West Publishing Co., 1979), 1373.
12. See Howard L. Oleck, *Nonprofit Corporations, Organizations, and Associations*, 4th ed. (Englewood Cliffs, N.J.: Prentice-Hall, Inc., 1980), 98-100.
13. However, many states now have statutes governing the law of partnership.
14. H. Oleck, *supra* note 12, at 111.
15. See chapter 8, "Reconciling Disputes among Christians."
16. See, for example, Richard John Neuhaus, *The Naked Public Square* (Grand Rapids, Mich.: William B. Eerdmans Publishing Company, 1984); John W. Whitehead, *The Freedom of Religious Expression in the Public High Schools* (Westchester, Ill.: Crossway Books, 1983); and John W. Whitehead, *The Second American Revolution* (Elgin, Ill.: David C. Cook Publishing Co., 1982).

Chapter 10
Legal Considerations for Christian Schools

1. Laurence Kallen, *Teachers' Rights and Liabilities Under the Law* (New York: Arco Pub. Co., 1971).
2. Robert L. Monks and Ernest I. Proulx, *Legal Basics for Teachers* (Bloomington, Ind.: Phi Delta Kappa Educational Foundation, 1986), 17.
3. Ralph D. Mawdsley and Steven P. Permuth, *Legal Problems of Religious and Private Schools* (Topeka, Kans.: National Organization on Legal Problems of Education, 1983), 25.
4. Monks and Proulx, *Legal Basics*, 18.
5. Ibid., 13.
6. Ibid., 14.
7. Ibid., 19, Mawdsley and Permuth, *Legal Problems*, 18.
8. Mawdsley and Permuth, *Legal Problems*, 19–20.
9. This is the position recommended by Monks and Proulx, *Legal Basics*, 21.
10. Others claim that this more moderate approach is acceptable. See, for example, Mawdsley and Permuth, *Legal Problems*, 20.
11. Mawdsley and Permuth, *Legal Problems*, 14.
12. Monks and Proulx, *Legal Basics*, 23.
13. Ibid., 32.
14. Mawdsley and Permuth, *Legal Problems*, 39.
15. Ibid., 52.
16. Ibid., 52–53.
17. Monks and Proulx, *Legal Basics*, 11.
18. Mawdsley and Permuth, *Legal Problems*, 27.
19. Ibid., 41.
20. Ibid., 51.

21. Ibid., 86–87.
22. Ibid., 87–89.
23. Ibid., 69, 73–75.

Chapter 11
Church Property and Zoning Ordinances

1. "Freedom to adhere to such religious organization or form of worship as the individual may choose cannot be restricted by law . . . the [First] Amendment embraces two concepts—freedom to believe and freedom to act. The first is absolute but, in the nature of things, the second cannot be." *Cantwell v. Connecticut*, 310 U.S. 296, 303-04 (1940).
2. *Braunfeld v. Brown*, 366 U.S. 599, 603 (1961).
3. *Wisconsin v. Yoder*, 406 U.S. 205, 214 (1972).
4. *Board of Education v. Barnette*, 319 U.S. 624, 639 (1943).
5. 1 A. Rathkopf, *The Law of Zoning and Planning*, §1.01[3][a] (4th ed. 1977).
6. Ibid., §1.02.
7. 1 P. Rohan, *Zoning and Land Use Controls*, §1.02[4] (1978).
8. "A quiet place where yards are wide, people few, and motor vehicles restricted are legitimate guidelines in a land-use project addressed to family needs . . . the police power is not confined to elimination of filth, stench, and unhealthy places. It is ample to lay out zones where family values, youth values, and the blessings of quiet seclusion and clean air make the area a sanctuary for people." *Village of Belle Terre v. Boraas*, 416 U.S. 1, 9 (1974).
9. *Euclid v. Ambler Realty Co.*, 272 U.S. 365, 395 (1926).
10. *Yoder*, 406 U.S. at 215.
11. *Belle Terre*, 416 U.S. at 8; *McDaniel v. Paty*, 435 U.S. 618, 625 (1978); *Thomas v. Review Board*, 450 U.S. 707, 718 (1981).
12. 1 Rathkopf, §1.02[2]; [2]; 5 Rohan, §35.03[1].
13. 1 R. Anderson, *American Law of Zoning*, §2.19 (3d ed. 1986).
14. Recommended by the U.S. Dept. of Commerce, 1926, reprinted in 5 Rathkopf, supra note 5, Appendix A at 765-70.
15. 1 Rohan, supra note 7, §1.02[5].
16. Note, *Land Use Regulation and the Free Exercise Clause*, 84 COLUM. L. REV. 1562, 1568 (1984).
17. 2 Rathkopf, §20.01[2](a); 2 Anderson, §12.21.
18. See e.g. *City of Sherman v. Simms*, 143 Tex. 115, 183 S.W.2d 415 (1944).
19. See e.g. *Jewish Reconstructionist Synagogue, Inc. v. Roslyn Harbor*, 38 N.Y. 2d 283, 288, 342 N.E. 2d 534, 538, 579 N.Y.S.2d 747, 753 (1975) *cert. denied* 426 U.S. 950 (1976) "Where an irreconcilable conflict exists between the right to erect a religious structure and the potential hazards of traffic or diminution in value, the latter must yield to the former."
20. 699 F.2d 303 (6th Cir.), *cert. denied* 464 U.S. 815 (1983).
21. Ibid., 699 F.2d at 307.

22. Goldberg, *Gimme Shelter: Religious Provision of Shelter to the Homeless as a Protected Use under Zoning Laws*, 30 WASH. U.J. URBAN & CONTEMP. LAW 75, 88–89 (1986).

23. 254 A.2d 611 (Del. Ch. 1969).

24. Ibid. at 614.

25. 457 U.S. 116 (1982).

26. Ibid. at 121, n.3.

27. *Unitarian Universalist Church v. Shorten*, 63 Misc. 2d 978, 314 N.Y.S.2d 66 (1970).

28. See Annot., 62 A.L.R.3d 197, 206, §5(a)(1975 & Supp. 1990).

29. Reynolds, *Zoning the Church: The Police Power Versus the First Amendment*, 64 B.U.L. REV. 767, 772 (1984).

30. *United States v. Seeger*, 380 U.S. 163, 166 (1965).

31. "The determination of what is a 'religious' belief or practice is more often than not a difficult and delicate task. . . . However, the resolution of that question is not to turn upon a judicial perception of the particular belief or practice in question; religious beliefs need not be acceptable, logical, consistent, or comprehensible to others in order to merit First Amendment protection." *Thomas v. Review Board*, 450 U.S. 707, 714 (1981).

32. 374 U.S. 398 (1963).

33. Mrs. Sherbert, a member of the Seventh-Day Adventist Church, was fired from her job because she refused to work on Saturday, which was the sabbath day of her religion. When she filed a claim for unemployment compensation benefits, an administrative ruling denied her request on the grounds that she was disqualified under the state's unemployment compensation act, which barred benefits to workers who failed, without good cause, to accept available suitable work when offered. Ibid. at 399-401.

34. Ibid. at 407.

35. "Here not only is it apparent that (Mrs. Sherbert's) declared ineligibility for benefits derives solely from the practice of her religion, but the pressure upon her to forego that practice is unmistakable. The ruling forces her to choose between following the precepts of her religion and forfeiting benefits, on the one hand, and abandoning one of the precepts of her religion in order to accept work, on the other hand. Governmental imposition of such a choice puts the same kind of burden upon the free exercise of religion as would a fine imposed against appellant for her Saturday worship." Ibid. at 404.

36. *Thomas*, 450 U.S. at 718.

37. *Lakewood*, 699 F.2d at 307.

38. Comment, *Zoning Ordinances Affecting Churches: A Proposal for Expanded Free Exercise Protection*, 132 U.PA. L. REV. 1131, 1158-61(1984).

39. 721 F.2d 729 (11th Cir. 1983) *cert. denied*, 469 U.S. 827 (1984).

40. Ibid. at 739.

41. Ibid.

42. This is typified by one commentator: "At most, application of the zoning regulation will limit the available sites for building a place of worship and force the church to purchase a more expensive parcel of land in a commercial zone instead of its less expensive counterpart in residential areas. Thus, the exclusion of churches from particular zoning districts places no more than a minimal burden on the free exercise of religion." Reynolds, at 779.
43. 184 N.J. Super. 66, 445 A.2d 75 (1982), rev'd, 100 N.J. 586, 498 A.2d 1217 (1985).
44. The services conducted by Reverend Robert J. Cameron, a minister of the Reformed Episcopal Church, were held from 11 A.M. to noon on Sundays, and included prayers, singing, and preaching. The congregation had previously met in a school, but the services were moved to the minister's home because they could not afford to pay rent in commercial buildings. Ibid., 445 A.2d at 76-77.
45. Ibid., 445 A.2d at 78. The Supreme Court of New Jersey later overturned Cameron's conviction for the reason that the zoning ordinance was vague and lacked sufficient definition of "churches or similar places of worship." However, the Supreme Court never considered whether an ordinance giving a specific definition of "churches" would have been the least restrictive means to protect the legitimate interests of residential neighborhoods.
46. Annot., 11A.L.R. 4th, 1084, 1086, §2(1982 and Supp. 1988).
47. Goldberg, at 97.
48. 92 Idaho 571, 448 P.2d 185 (1968).
49. Ibid., 448 P.2d at 188. "Strictly religious uses and activities are more than prayer and sacrifice and all churches recognize that the area of their responsibility is broader than leading the congregation in prayer. . . . It is a religious activity for the church to provide a place for these social groups to meet, since the church by doing so is developing into a stronger and closer knit religious unit. To limit a church to being merely a house of prayer and sacrifice would, in a large degree, be depriving the church of the opportunity of enlarging, perpetuating and strengthening itself and the congregation."
50. Annot., at 1086.
51. 66 Hawaii 119, 657 P.2d 1035, appeal dismissed, 464 U.S. 805 (1983).
52. Ibid., 657 P.2d at 1037.
53. Portage Township v. Full Salvation Union, 318 Mich. 693, 29 N.W.2d 297 (1947), appeal dismissed, 333 U.S. 851 (1948).
54. Reynolds, at 817-18 n.285.
55. Siegert v. Luney, 111 A.D.2d 854, 491 N.Y.S.2d 15 (1985).
56. Board of Zoning Appeals v. New Testament Bible Church, Inc., 411 N.E.2d 681 (Ind. App. 1980).
57. Diocese of Rochester v. Planning Board, 1 N.Y.2d 508, 136 N.E.2d 827, 154 N.Y.S.2d 849 (1956).
58. St. John's Evangelical Lutheran Church v. Hoboken, 195 N.J. Super, 414, 479 A.2d 935 (1983).
59. Unitarian Universalist Church, supra note 27.

60. *Slevin v. Long Island Jewish Medical Center*, 66 Misc.2d 312, 319 N.Y.2d 937 (1971).
61. *Ashton*, at 192.

Chapter 12
The IRS and Church Finances

1. I.R.C. § 501(c)(3).
2. H.R. REP. No. 1860, 7th Cong., 3d Sess. 1939-1 (PART II) C.B. 742.
3. I.R.C. § 508(a), (b), (c); Reg § 1.508-1 (a) (3).
4. I.R.C. § 6033(aV2).
5. I.R.C. § 508(a); 508(c)(1); 6033(a)(2).
6. Treas. Reg. § 301.7605-1(c)(2).
7. I.R.C. 3 170(a), (c).
8. I.R.C. § 2055.
9. I.R.C. § 2522.
10. IRS Publication 78.
11. I.R.C. § 3121(b)(8)(B).
12. I.R.C. § 3306(c)(8).
13. I.R.C. § 501(c)
14. I.R.C. § 513 defines unrelated business income.
15. I.R.C. § 511.
16. See generally IRS Publication 598.
17. I.R.C. § 6104(c); Treas Reg. §301.6104(c)-1.
18. §11 of Rev. Proc. 72-3, 1972-1 C.B. 698; Treas. Reg. § 601.201(j).
19. I.R.C. 501(c)(3).
20. I.R.C. § 170(c)(2)(B).
21. Richard Hammar, *Pastor, Church & Law* (Springfield, Mo.: Gospel Publishing House, 1983).
22. Treas. Reg. §1.501(c)(3)-1(b)(1)(i).
23. IRS Publication 557.
24. Treas. Reg. §1.501(c)(3)-1(b)(4).
25. I.R.C. § 502.
26. *IRS Exempt Organizations Handbook* § 381.1 (1982).
27. Treas. Reg. § 1.501(c)(3)-1(e)(3)(ii).
28. Rev. Rul. 78-248.
29. Treas. Reg. § 1.508-1(a)(2).
30. See generally IRS Publication 557 for application procedure narrative.
31. Rev. Proc. 80-25, 1980-1 C.B. 667.
32. Rev. Proc. 80-28, 1980-1 C.B. 680.
33. Emerson O. Henke. *Accounting for Nonprofit Organizations* (Boston: Kent Publishing, 1982), 178–79.
34. Malvern J. Gross, Jr., and William Warshauer, Jr. *Financial and Accounting Guide for Not-for-Profit Organizations*, rev. 3d ed. (New York: Ronald Press, 1983), 67–69.

35. Raymond B. Knudsen. *New Models for Financing the Local Church* (Ridgefield, Conn.: Morehouse-Barlow, 1985), 9.
36. I.R.C. § 1236(c).
37. I.R.C. § 170(f)(2)(A).
38. I.R.C. § 2522(c)(2)(A).
39. I.R.C. § 2055(e)(2)(A).

Chapter 13
Tax Planning for Religious Workers

1. Treas. Reg. § 31.3401(c)-1(b).
2. IRS Publication 517, 1; Treas. Reg. § 1.1402(c)-5(b)(2).
3. See generally IRS Publication 517.
4. I.R.C. § 3101 et seq.
5. I.R.C. § 1401 et seq.
6. I.R.C. § 1402 (e), (g).
7. I.R.C. § 1402(e)(1).
8. IRS Publication 517.
9. Rev. Rul. 70-197, 1970-1 C.B. 181.
10. I.R.C. § 1402(e)(1).
11. IRS Publication 517.
12. Rev. Rul. 80-59, 1980-1 C.B. 191.
13. Treas. Reg. § 1.1402(e)(2)-1.
14. Linger v. Com'r, 42 T.C.M. 1068 (1981).
15. IRS Publication 517.
16. I.R.C. § 6012.
17. See generally IRS Publication 505.
18. I.R.C. § 6051.
19. I.R.C. § 102.
20. I.R.C. § 162(a)(2).
21. I.R.C. § 217(c)(1).
22. I.R.C. § 127.
23. Treas. Reg. § 1.107-1(b).
24. Treas. Reg. § 1.107-1(c).
25. Treas. Reg. § 1.107-1(b).
26. Treas. Reg. § 1.107-1(c).
27. Rev. Rul. 78-448, 1978-2 C.B. 105.
28. Rev. Rul. 71-280, 1972-2 C.B. 92.
29. Rev. Rul. 59-270, 1959-2 C.B. 44.
30. Rev. Rul. 78-301, 1978-2 C.B. 103.
31. IRS Publication 517.
32. I.R.C. § 401-409.
33. Self-Employed Individual's Retirement Act of 1962, The H.R. 10 or Keogh Plan, provides retirement equity for the self-employed to enjoy.
34. I.R.C. § 401(c)(2)(A)(ii).

35. IRS Publication 517.

Chapter 14
Charitable Giving: Funding the Christian Challenge

1. IRC Sec. 170(b)(1)(A); Reg. Sec. 1.107A-8(b).
2. IRC Sec. 170(b)(1)(C)(iii); IRC Sec. 170(e)(1); Reg. Sec. 1.170A_8(d)(2).
3. IRC 170(e)(1)(A).
4. IRC 170(e)(1)(A).
5. IRC 170(b)(1)(C)(i). Reg. Sec. 1.170A-4.
6. IRC 170(e)(1)(B)(i), Reg. Sec. 1.170A-4(b)(3).
7. IRC 170(e)(2), IRC 1011(b).
8. Treas. Reg. 1.1011-2(a)(3).
9. IRC 170 (h)(2)
10. Reg. Sec. 25.2512-6(a), IRC 170(e)(1)(A).
11. Reg. Sec. 25.2512-6(a), IRC 170(e)(1)(A).
12. IRC 170(f)(3)(B)(ii).
13. IRC 1011(b), IRC 170 (f)(3)(B)(i).
14. IRC Sec. 170 (f)(3)(A), Reg. Sec. 1.170A-7(a), Temp. Reg. Sec. 1.7872-5T(b)(9).
15. IRS Publication 723A.
16. IRS Publication 123A.
17. Treas. Reg. 1.1011-2(a)(4).
18. IRS Publication 123D, Reg. Sec. 1.642(c)-5(a)(3), IRC 642(c)(3).
19. IRC Sec. 673(a).
20. Rev. Ruling 67-246, 1967-2 CB 104, Rev. Ruling 86-63, 1986-1 CB 69.
21. Reg. Sec. 1.170A-13, Temp. Reg. Sec. 1.170A-13T, IRC Sec. 6050L, IRC Secs. 6652(a)(1)(A)(ix), 6676(a)(1), 6678(a)(1), 6721, 6723.
22. Rev. Ruling 55-4, 1955-1 CB 291, IRC. Sec. 170(k), Rev. Ruling 73-597, 1973-2 CB 69.
23. Reg. Sec. 1.170A-1(g), Rev. Ruling 162, 1953-2 CB 127, Rev. Ruling 67-236, 1967-2 CB 103.
24. Publication No. 78, the Cumulative List of Organizations described in Section 170(c) of the Internal Revenue Code of 1954.
25. Rev. Procedure 82-39, 1982-2 CB 759.

Chapter 15
Clergy and Political Activity

1. Alan P. Dye, "Political Activity by Clergymen" (unpublished manuscript, revised and used by permission).

Chapter 16
Should Christians Sue?

1. Uniform Commercial Code § 9.503.
2. There is no corresponding provision in the Uniform Commercial Code.

3. See the chapter on bankruptcy.
4. A lawsuit against a Christian partnership is a suit against a Christian because each partner in a partnership can be held personally liable for the entire debt.
5. Deuteronomy 32:35; Psalms 94:1; 99:8; Isaiah 34:8; 35:4; 61:2; Jeremiah 51:15; Ezekiel 24; 25.

Chapter 17
Is Bankruptcy Ethical for the Christian?

1. Dalhuisen, J. H., *Compositions in Bankruptcy*, A.W. Sijthoff-Leyden (1968), 6; Alexander L. Paskay, *Trustees and Receivers in Bankruptcy*, Matthew Bender (1968), 3; J. Dalhuisin, *Roman Law of Creditors Remedies*, in ABA Section of International Law, *European Bankruptcy Laws*, 4–5 (1974).
2. Alexander L. Paskay, *Trustees and Receivers in Bankruptcy*, Matthew Bender (1968), 3; J. Dalhuisen, *Roman Law of Creditors Remedies*, in ABA Section of International Law, *European Bankruptcy Laws*, 3 (1974).
3. Ibid.; Nadler, *The Humaneness of the Bankruptcy Law*, 60 Com. L.J. 149 (1955).
4. Ibid.; Code of Justinian, Dig. 2, 4, 25, 48, 19, 1 Nov. 4, 3.
5. Alexander L. Paskay, *Trustees and Receivers in Bankruptcy*, Matthew Bender 1968; 11 Edward 1 (1283).
6. Ibid.; Anne, chapter 17.
7. 11 USC Sec. 541, 363.
8. 11 USC Sec. 522.
9. 11 USC § 727 (a) (8). This section provides that no debt can be discharged if the debtor has previously obtained a discharge under Chapter 7 within six years before the filing of his petition.

Bibliography

Church Finances

Fund Raising:

Berendt, Robert J., and Richard J. Taft. *How to Rate Your Development Office*. Washington, D.C.: Taft Group, 1983.

DeSoto, Carole. *For Fun and Funds*. West Nyack, N.Y.: Prentice Hall, 1983.

Fink, Norman S., and Howard C. Metzler. *The Costs and Benefits of Deferred Giving*. New York: Columbia University Press, 1982.

Fund Raising Management. Published by Hoke Communications, Inc., Garden City, N.Y.

Knudsen, Raymond B. *New Models for Financing the Local Church*. Morehouse-Barlow, 1985.

Schneiter, Paul. *The Art of Asking: Handbook for Successful Fund Raising*. New York: Walker and Company, 1978.

Sharpe, Robert F. *Before You Give Another Dime*. Nashville: Thomas Nelson, 1979.

Sharpe, Robert F., and Phillip R. Converse. *The Planned Giving Idea Book*. Nashville: Thomas Nelson, 1978.

Stern, Sue S., Jon L. Schumacher, and Patrick D. Martin. *Charitable Giving and Solicitation*. Englewood Cliffs, N.J.: Prentice Hall, 1984. (Resource manual with monthly updates)

Non-Profit Concerns:

Gross, Malvern J., Jr., and William Warshauer, Jr. *Financial and Accounting Guide for Nonprofit Organizations*, Rev. 3d ed. New York: Ronald Press, 1983.

Henke, Emerson O. *Accounting for Nonprofit Organizations*. 3d ed. Boston: Kent Publishing, 1983.

Hopkins, Bruce R. *The Law of Tax-Exempt Organizations*. 5th ed. New York: Ronald Press, 1988.

IRS Exempt Organizations Handbook. IRS, Attn: PM:S:DI:P:RR, 1111 Constitution Ave., NW, Washington, D.C. 20224.

IRS Publications 17, 505, 517, 557 ("Tax-Exempt Status for Your Organization"); 598 ("Tax on Unrelated Business Income of Exempt Organizations"); 892 ("Exempt Organization Appeal Procedures").

Lashbrooke, E. C., Jr. *Tax-Exempt Organizations*. Westport, Conn.: Quorum Books, 1985.

Oleck, Howard L. *Nonprofit Corporations, Organizations, and Associations*, 4th ed. Englewood Cliffs, N.J.: Prentice-Hall, Inc., 1980.

Treusch, P. E., and N. A. Sugarman. *Tax-Exempt Charitable Organizations*. Philadelphia: ALI/ABA, 1983.

Clergy Finances

Personal Finances:

Blue, Ronald W. *Master Your Money*. Nashville: Thomas Nelson, 1986.
Fooshee, George, Jr. *You Can Be Financially Free*. Old Tappan, N.J.: Fleming H. Revell Company, 1976.
Hardisty, George. *Plan Your Estate*. Lafayette, Calif.: Carodyn Publishers, 1983.
Skousen, Mark and Jo Ann. *Never Say Budget!* Merrifield, Va.: Mark Skousen Publisher, 1983.
Watts, John G. *Leave Your House in Order*. Wheaton, Ill.: Tyndale House, 1979.

Taxes:

Clergy Income Tax Guide. Nashville: Abingdon Press.
Taxwise Giving. Published by Conrad Teitell. Old Greenwich, Conn.

Religion, Law, and Politics

Adler, Mortimer J. *We Hold These Truths*. New York: Macmillan, 1987.
Amos, Gary T. *Defending the Declaration*. Brentwood, Tenn.: Wolgemuth & Hyatt, Publishers, Inc., 1989.
Berger, Raoul. *Government by Judiciary: The Transformation of the 14th Amendment*. Cambridge, Mass.: Harvard University Press, 1977.
Bickel, Alexander M. *The Least Dangerous Branch: The Supreme Court at the Bar of Politics*. Indianapolis: Bobbs-Merrill, 1962.
Brown, Harold O. J. *The Reconstruction of the Republic*. Rev. ed. Milford, Mich.: Mott Media, 1981.
Buzzard, Lynn, and Samuel Ericsson. *The Battle for Religious Liberty*. Elgin, Ill.: David C. Cook Publishing Co., 1982.
Clouse, Robert G., et al., eds. *Protest and Politics: Christianity and Contemporary Affairs*. Greenwood, S.C.: Attic Press, 1968.
Cotham, Perry C. *Politics, Americanism, and Christianity*. Grand Rapids: Baker Book House, 1976.
Cord, Robert L. *Separation of Church and State: Historical Fact and Current Fiction*. Grand Rapids: Baker Book House, 1988.
Eidsmoe, John. *God and Caesar: Christian Faith and Political Action*. Westchester, Ill.: Crossway Books, 1984.
House, H. Wayne, ed. *Restoring the Constitution*. Dallas: Probe Books, 1987.
House, H. Wayne, and Thomas Ice. *Dominion Theology: Blessing or Curse?* Portland, Oreg.: Multnomah Press, 1988.
Messer, Donald E. *Christian Ethics and Political Action*. Valley Forge, Pa.: Judson Press, 1984.
Montgomery, John W., and Steven W. Webb. *Human Rights and Human Dignity*. Grand Rapids: Zondervan Publishing House, 1986.
Nash, Ronald. *Freedom, Justice and the State*. Lanham, Md.: University Press of America, 1980.

Neuhaus, Richard J. *Christian Faith and Public Policy.* Minneapolis, Minn.: Augsburg Press, 1977.

_____. *The Naked Public Square.* Grand Rapids: Eerdmans Publishing Company, 1986.

Neuhaus, Richard John, and Michael Cromartie, eds. *Piety and Politics.* Lanham, Md.: University Press of America, 1988.

Noll, Mark A., et al. *Religion and American Politics.* New York: Oxford University Press, 1989.

Schaeffer, Francis A. *A Christian Manifesto.* Westchester, Ill.: Crossway Books, 1981.

Smith, Gary Scott, ed. *God and Politics.* Phillipsburg, N.J.: Presbyterian and Reformed, 1989.

Stone, Ronald H., ed. *Reformed Faith and Politics.* Washington, D.C.: University Press of America, 1983.

Webber, Robert E. *The Church in the World.* Grand Rapids: Zondervan Publishing House, 1986.

Whitehead, John. *The Second American Revolution.* Elgin, Ill.: David C. Cook, 1982.

_____. *The Stealing of America.* Westchester, Ill.: Crossway Books, 1983.

Wilson, John F., and Donald L. Drakeman, eds. *Church and State in American History.* 2d ed. Boston: Beacon Press, 1987.

General Books on Christian Concerns and the Law

Richard R. Hammar, *Pastor, Church and Law.* Springfield, Mo.: Gospel Publishing House, 1983.

_____. *Pastor, Church and Law Supplement.* Springfield, Mo.: Gospel Publishing House, 1986.

Eidsmoe, John. *The Christian Legal Advisor.* Grand Rapids: Baker Book House, 1984.

Church Conflicts

Adams, Jay E. *Handbook on Church Discipline.* Grand Rapids: Zondervan Publishing House, 1986.

Baker, Don. *Beyond Forgiveness.* Portland, Oreg.: Multnomah Press, 1984.

Brandon, Thomas, and Lynn Buzzard. *Church Discipline and the Courts.* Wheaton: Tyndale House Publishers, 1987.

Fisher, Roger, and William Ury. *Getting to Yes.* Boston: Houghton Mifflin Company, 1981.

Fenton, Horace L., Jr. *When Christians Clash.* Downers Grove, Ill.: InterVarsity Press, 1987.

Huttenlocker, Keith. *Conflict and Caring.* Grand Rapids: Zondervan Publishing House, 1988.

Sande, Ken. *The Peacemaker.* Grand Rapids: Baker Book House, 1991.

Malony, H. Newton, Thomas L. Needham, and Samuel Southard. *Clergy Malpractice.* Philadelphia, Pa.: The Westminster Press, 1986.

School Issues

Whitehead, John W. *The Freedom of Religious Expression in the Public High Schools.* Westchester, Ill.: Crossway Books, 1983.

Whitehead, John W., and Wendell R. Bird. *Home Education and Constitutional Liberties.* Westchester, Ill.: Crossway Books, 1984.

Monks, Robert L. and Ernest I. Proulx. *Legal Basics for Teachers.* Bloomington, Ind.: Phi Delta Kappa Educational Foundation, 1986.

Mawdsley, Ralph D., and Steven P. Permuth. *Legal Problems of Religious and Private Schools.* National Organization on Legal Problems of Education, 1983.

Zoning

Anderson, R. *American Law of Zoning.* (3d ed. 1986).

Annot., 11 A.L.R. 4th 1084, (1982 & Supp. 1988). Rochester, N.Y.: Lawyers Cooperative Publishing, Inc.

Annot., 62 A.L.R. 3d 197, (1975 & Supp. 1988). Rochester, N.Y.: Lawyers Cooperative Publishing, Inc.

Comment, *Zoning Ordinances Affecting Churches: A Proposal for Expanded Free Exercise Protection,* 132 U. Pa. L. Rev. 1131, (1984).

Comment, *Zoning Ordinances, Private Religious Conduct, and the Free Exercise of Religion,* 76 Nw. U. L. Rev. 786, (1981).

Curry, J. *Public Regulation of the Religious Use of Land.* Charlottesville, Va.: Michie, 1964.

Goldberg, *Gimme Shelter: Religious Provision of Shelter to the Homeless as a Protected Use Under Zoning Laws.* 30 Wash. U.: J. Urban & Contemp. Law 75, (1986).

Note, *Land Use Regulation and the Free Exercise Clause,* 84 Colum L. Rev. 1562, (1984).

Rathkopf, A. *The Law of Zoning and Planning,* (4th ed. 1977). N.Y.: Clarke Boardman.

Reynolds, *Zoning the Church: The Police Power Versus The First Amendment,* 64 B. U. L. Rev. 767, (1984).

Rohan, P. *Zoning and Land Use Controls.* N.Y.: Matthew Bender, 1977.

Walker, *What Constitutes a Religious Use for Zoning Purposes,* 27 Cath. Law. 129 (1982).

Subject Index

239

Cases Cited

247

Scripture Index

Person Index

Chapter Updates for Second Edition
H. Wayne House and John Ketchum

Certain areas of the law have changed since the last printing of *Christian Ministries and the Law* and are deemed to be important to the reader. For a more detailed look at the law for Christian ministries, I recommend Richard Hammar's *The Pastor and the Law* and his bimonthly newsletter, *Church Law and Tax Report*. In addition to those resources, you may want to consult the following for further study:

> *Church & Clergy Tax* (Hammar)
> *Church Guide to Copyright Law* (Hammar)
> *Church Office Planner* (Christian Ministry Resources)
> *Church Treasurer Alert* (monthly newsletter)
> *Pastor, Church, & Law* (Hammar, CD-ROM version only)
> *Reducing the Risk of Child Sexual Abuse in Your Church* (Hammar, et. al.)
> *Risk Management for Churches* (Hammar)

These resources are available from:

> Christian Ministry Resources
> P.O. Box 1098
> Matthews, NC 28106
> (704) 841-8066
> www.iclonline.com

Chapter Five: Church-State Law

Since 1992 some important modifications have been made in church-state law. In 1971, in the case of *Lemon v. Kurtzman*, the Court developed a tripart test (based on *Board of Education v. Allen*) to determine whether a governmental action constituted a violation of the Establishment Clause of the First Amendment. In applying the test, the Court would ask three questions: Is there a secular purpose? Is the action one that neither advances nor inhibits religion? Is there an excessive government entanglement with religion? These are enunciated in *Board of Education v. Allen,* 392 U.S. 236, 243 (1968), and *Lemon v. Kurtzman,* 403 U.S. 602, 612–13 (1971). This test has been used to invalidate activities as establishments of religion (e.g., *Committee for Public Education & Religious Liberty v. Nyquist,* 413 U.S. 756 [1973]; *Wallace v. Jaffree,* 472 U.S. 38 [1985]), affirming a strict separation between religion and the government.

The strict separationist perspective enunciated in *Lemon* and other cases has not been uniformly held. The Court did not feel compelled to an absolute application of the Lemon tests in *Lynch v. Donnelly,* 465 U.S. 668 (1984), when justices held that a nativity scene could be displayed on government property as part of a broader Christmas display. *Bowen v. Kendrick,* 487 U.S. 589 (1988) ruled that charitable and governmental agencies can cooperate without establishment problems. The most significant recent case is *Agostini v. Felton,* 117 S.Ct. 1997 (1997), which holds that governmental aid that assists education of students does not violate the Establishment Clause.

In moving beyond the Lemon tests, the Supreme Court has adopted historical tests (e.g., *Marsh v. Chambers,* 463 U.S. 783 [1983]; *Lynch v. Donnelly,* 465 U.S. 668 [1984]), in which the historical practices in American heritage are favored; an endorsement test (set forth by Justice O'Connor), where there is improper Establishment if persons are made to believe they are excluded from the political community or favored members of that community (e.g., *Allegheny v. ACLU,* 492 U.S. 573 [1989]; *Aguilar v. Felton,* 473 U.S. 402); and the coercion test of Justice Kennedy, in which infringement is minimal unless there is coercion that establishes a religious faith (*Lee v. Weisman,* 505 U.S. 577 [1992]). The Court, then, has moved from a strict separationist approach to one that seeks to accommodate religious expression in society.

Cases regarding free exercise of religion are not so numerous as those concerning establishment of religion. First amendment attorneys often argue religious concerns under the guarantees of free speech. The most important case on free exercise since 1992 is *Church of the Lukumi Babalu Aye v. City of Hialeah,* 508 U.S. 520 (1993). Hialeah, Florida, attempted to restrict the religious sacrificial ritual of the Santeria faith by applying general laws. The city's justification was *Employment Division, Dept. of Human Resources v. Smith,* 494 U.S. 110 (1990). The controversial *Smith* decision ruled that generally applicable criminal statutes can be applied against religious conduct without the need to satisfy the tests established by the Court in *Sherbert,* 374

U.S. 398 (1963), and *Yoder*, 406 U.S. 205 (1972). Only when coupled with another fundamental right does strict scrutiny of state regulation come into play. Under the development of the free exercise of religion jurisprudence in *Sherbert* and *Yoder* the state could only burden a sincerely held belief if it had a compelling state interest. The state was required to achieve its ends through the least restrictive way. *Smith*, however, required no compelling interest of the state if the law was not directed against a religious practice but was generally applicable to the population. In *Lukumi* it was obvious to the court that the law was targeted specifically at the religious practices of the Santeria faith since the killing of animals for food was not forbidden by the government whereas the killing of animals in worship was forbidden.

For a more complete presentation of recent trends in Establishment Clause jurisprudence, see H. Wayne House, *A Tale of Two Kingdoms: Can There Be Peaceful Coexistence of Religion with the Secular State?*, in *Brigham Young University Journal of Public Law*, 203 (1999): 13.

Chapter Six: Clergy Malpractice

It appears that no courts have yet recognized a cause of action for clergy malpractice, although one court in Texas came close in *Sanders v. Casa View Baptist Church*, 898 F. Supp. 1169 (N.D. Tex. 1995). The background of this case is that church employees received marital counseling from, and were encouraged to have sexual relations with, the minister. Sanders brought a cause of action for, among other claims, clergy malpractice. The court recognized that an action for clergy malpractice cannot be maintained because it would require the court to investigate and evaluate religious tenets and doctrines, a violation of the First Amendment. The court did, however, construe the cause of action as one for professional malpractice by a marriage counselor rather than as one for professional clergy malpractice. The court stated: "The Free Exercise Clause does not relieve an individual of the obligation to comply with the neutral laws of general applicability" (898 F. Supp. at 1174). The court found that the complaint stated a viable cause of action in Texas for professional negligence with respect to marital counseling. Thus, at least in Texas, the possibility for a malpractice action exists to the extent that ministerial counseling is construed as marital counseling, as distinguished from spiritual counseling. See John F. Wagner, "Cause of Action for Clergy Malpractice," 75 A.L.R.4th 750 (1990).

Chapter Seven: Church Discipline

Guinn v. The Church of Collingsville, 775 P.2d 766 (Okla. 1989), upholds two propositions: First, a church can discipline its members without fear of judicial intervention only while the person remains a member; second, individuals can terminate their membership without regard to church rules.

Since *Guinn,* the courts have followed the Oklahoma Supreme Court and held that "a church can discipline individuals without fear of judicial intervention" only while "the complaining individual was a member at the time of the disciplinary action" (*Smith v. Calvary Christian Church,* — N.W.2d — , 1998 WL 842259 [Mich. Ct. App. 1998]). As the Michigan Court of Appeals framed the rule: "Where the plaintiff is a member of the church at the time of the defendant church's alleged tortious activity . . . 'the church has authority to prescribe and follow disciplinary ordinances without fear of interference by the state'" (*Smith,* supra, quoting *Guinn,* 775 P.2d at 773–74, and citing *Hadnot v. Shaw,* 826 P.2d 978, 987–88 [Okla. 1992]; see also *Hester v. Barnett,* 723 S.W.2d 544, 559–60 [Mo. 1987]: If plaintiffs were members of the church, "they presumptively consented to religiously motivated discipline practiced in good faith"). But this absolute privilege from judicial intervention applies only if the discipline "does not pose a substantial threat to public safety, peace or order" (*Guinn,* 775 P.2d at 779).

In *Guinn,* the Oklahoma Supreme Court held that once the individual's relationship with the church has been terminated, either by the individual or the church, the Free Exercise Clause no longer shields the church from civil liability (*Guinn,* 775 P.2d at 783–84). While *Guinn* suggests that an individual may voluntarily waive his or her right to withdraw from association with a church, the court in *Guinn* was not presented with that situation. Since *Guinn,* the cases suggest that the courts may uphold an absolute right to unilaterally withdraw from association with a church; see, for example, *Hadnot,* 826 P.2d at 988 ("On the other hand, no citizen of the state may be compelled to remain in a church which his conscience impels him to leave"). If presented squarely with the issue, the courts may very well hold that the right to disassociate from a church cannot be waived.

Even after the member terminates his or her membership, the Oklahoma Supreme Court held that the church can complete the disciplinary process (*Hadnot v. Shaw,* 826 P.2d 978, 989–90 [Okla. 1992]). In this situation, however, the absolute privilege may no longer apply.

In the event of withdrawal or of post-excommunication activity unrelated to the church's efforts at effectuation of valid judicature, the absolute privilege from tort liability no longer attaches. Any action at this point, if it is to be protected, must be justified by other means. Under these circumstances conditional privileges may be applicable. The church may take such steps as are reasonable to protect itself and to complete the process occasioned by the withdrawal or other termination of the consensual relationship with a member (*Guinn,* supra at 775–82; *Hester,* supra at 559–60; cf. *Hadnot,* supra at 987–88).

In such situations, a privilege may apply to activities or communications after termination of membership "if these may be termed as mere implementation of previously pronounced ecclesiastical sanction which was valid when exercised" (*Hadnot,* 826 P.2d at 987). Thus, completing the disciplinary process exposes the church and individuals to civil liability. Any actions after the person leaves the church should be carefully considered, perhaps after consultation with an attorney.

Chapter Twelve and Thirteen: Tax Considerations

Tax laws change each year and have complexities. Beyond the general legal overview presented in this book, it is best to seek specialized, expert explanations of the changing tax codes. I recommend Richard Hammar's newsletter, *Church Law and Tax Report* and the monthly *Church Treasurer Alert,* both mentioned above. In addition, Zondervan Publishing House offers an annual volume on tax issues for clergy.